THE STRATEGY OF
INTERNATIONAL DEVELOPMENT

Also by H. W. Singer

UNEMPLOYMENT AND THE UNEMPLOYED
INTERNATIONAL DEVELOPMENT : GROWTH AND CHANGE
PERSPECTIVES ON ECONOMIC DEVELOPMENT
THIRD WORLD EMPLOYMENT

THE STRATEGY OF INTERNATIONAL DEVELOPMENT

Essays in the Economics of Backwardness

H. W. SINGER

edited by
SIR ALEC CAIRNCROSS AND MOHINDER PURI

 International Arts and Sciences Press, Inc.
White Plains, New York

Published in Great Britain by The Macmillan Press Ltd.

First U.S. edition published in 1975 by
International Arts and Sciences Press, Inc.
901 North Broadway, White Plains, New York 10603

Library of Congress Catalog Card Number : LC 74-21810

International Standard Book Number : 0-87332-068-9

Printed in Great Britain

To the memory of my teachers, Schumpeter and Keynes, and to my friends and colleagues from whom also I was privileged to learn.

Contents

Acknowledgements   viii

Introduction by Sir Alec Cairncross   ix

1   Recent trends in economic thought on underdeveloped countries   1

2   Keynesian models of economic development and their limitations : an analysis in the light of Gunnar Myrdal's 'Asian Drama'   22

3   The distribution of gains between investing and borrowing countries   43

4   The distribution of gains revisited   58

5   Dualism revisited : a new approach to the problems of the dual society in developing countries   67

6   Trade liberalization and economic development   91

7   Some problems of international aid   114

8   Employment problems in developing countries   133

9   International policy and its effect on employment   145

10   Unemployment in an African setting : lessons of the employment strategy mission to Kenya   158

11   Income distribution and population growth   173

12   Science and technology for the development of poorer countries   189

13   Multinational corporations and technology transfer : some problems and suggestions   208

Notes   235

Index   245

Acknowledgements

I am deeply indebted to Sir Alec Cairncross and Mr Mohinder Puri for making it possible for this volume to appear. Alec Cairncross's introduction will be found in this volume. Mohinder Puri carried the burden of the actual work involved in collecting and fitting the various elements together into the present book – he managed to overcome the difficulties and obstacles presented by an author who was too busy and too inefficient to have undertaken this task himself. I also wish to thank Mrs Margot Cameron for all the additional work cheerfully carried out in connection with the preparation of this volume.

Introduction

There can be few more indefatigable contributors to the literature on economic backwardness than Hans Singer. For the past twenty-five years his books, papers, articles, reviews and reports have poured out in an extraordinary variety of publications. Even since he left the United Nations Secretariat in 1969 he has submitted a score of reports, usually in collaboration with others, to international bodies and governments. A full bibliography of his writings would run to hundreds of items.

Most of this has been done in the middle of a busy official life, interrupted by frequent journeys half across the world. There is practically no country that he has not visited, and there are few that he has not advised. He must have addressed a wider variety of audiences in a wider assortment of places about a wider range of subjects than any economist (living or dead). He has moved from continent to continent, expounding, advocating, and devising strategies of economic development. His influence has been felt quite as much by word of mouth in the succession of countries where he has lectured as through the pile of working documents and published papers that survive like a spoor from his travels.

The very facility of his writing has irked some economists, one of whom described him unkindly almost thirty years ago as 'the Edgar Wallace of modern economics'. But the profusion of papers is balanced by an equal fertility of ideas. Hans Singer keeps popping up with some fresh comment or proposal. He is never content to take a negative approach and underline what should *not* be attempted, but is essentially an economic activist, always on the look-out for what might be done and concerned to mobilize support for whatever seems most hopeful. His intellectual energy and versatility are indeed remarkable.

A great deal of what he has written, particularly in recent years, is not easily accessible even to professional economists, much less to the general reader. It is true that two volumes of his essays

have already appeared, one in 1964* and a second in 1970.† But
the first of these has been out of print for some years and the
second does not do justice to his later work or show the development of his views. It seemed to the editors of this volume that it
was high time to gather together the more important of his
scattered contributions over the past few years and issue them in
one volume so as to bring out the span of his ideas and their relationship with one another. It was also suggested to me that I
should provide an introduction taking stock of Hans Singer's
work and of his place in the world of economics and economists.

This suggestion poses some difficulties for me. I do not relish
the idea of writing about an old friend as if he were already dead,
especially when he still gallivants around the world with his usual
vitality and supra-normal productivity. I also hesitate to assess
any economist's work on economic development when I have
hardly so much as set foot in a so-called backward country. I
should be misleading the reader if I led him to believe that my
comments on Hans Singer's work rested on first-hand acquain-
tance with the problems of the less developed countries or on anything more than a casual inspection of the vast literature on
economic development. But this is the smaller difficulty of the
two if, as I am inclined to believe, all countries are backward but
some are more backward than others.

Let me turn first to Hans's career. When he first appeared in
Cambridge in 1933 he had already been trained as an economist
in Bonn under Schumpeter and Spiethoff, had served as assistant
to Spiethoff and taken refuge from Hitler in Istanbul. By 1936
he had completed his (still unpublished) doctorate thesis on
'Urban House Rents' and joined the Pilgrim Trust Enquiry into
long-term unemployment in Britain, working in association with
Walter Oakeshott (later Rector of Lincoln College, Oxford) and
the late Sir David Owen. A year or so before World War II he
joined the staff of the University of Manchester. He worked there
and for various government departments during the war (apart
from a brief spell of internment near Liverpool), entering the
Ministry of Town and Country Planning at the end of the War.

---

* *International Development: Growth and Change* (McGraw-Hill, 1964).
† *Perspectives on Economic Development* (Houghton Mifflin, 1970).
This volume was undertaken jointly with S. Schiavo-Campo.

This was followed by a year at the University of Glasgow before he embarked at the invitation of David Owen on what was to prove the main interest of his life, work for the United Nations in New York.

In the twenty-two years he spent in the Secretariat Hans held a bewildering number of official posts, including Chief of the Development Section and Special Adviser to the Under Secretary for Economic and Social Affairs. Throughout this time he was simultaneously a visiting Professor of Economics at the New School for Social Research. He was also visiting professor during the later sixties at the City University, New York, and at Williams College, Mass. When he finally resigned from the Secretariat in 1969 he came back to Britain as a Fellow of the Institute of Development Studies and Professorial Fellow of the University of Sussex. There he has continued to act as a consultant to the United Nations and other international agencies, to go on missions abroad, and to write, write and write again.

There is a deceptive meekness about Hans Singer, an even-tempered mildness of manner and modesty in debate, that tends to conceal the force of his intelligence and still more of his convictions. He gives the impression of a troubled, uncertain but reasonable man who is used to being contradicted but would not dare himself to contradict. In fact he rarely is contradicted and in fact what he says very often implies a contradiction of somebody else even if he thinks it kinder not to say so. The voice is the voice of sweet reason and the words flow on imperturbably. Just because he expresses himself with such apparent moderation one has to be on one's guard against an uncritical acceptance of his argument.

With the exception of the first and third of the papers included in this volume, all of them date from his move to the Institute of Development Studies in 1969. They provide, therefore, a useful conspectus of his current outlook on development problems after over twenty-five years of continuous study and there is even a postscript to take account of more recent developments which in retrospect may take on the appearance of 'a natural watershed'. Although a wide variety of problems is discussed there are close links between them and the sequence of chapters is intended to bring this out.

First there is the general issue, discussed in the first two papers, of the forces making for and against self-sustained economic growth : the theories and models of development put forward by economists in the industrial countries and their applicability to the less developed countries. Then comes the issue of interaction between the two groups of countries. Is it helpful or unhelpful to borrow capital and technology in order to accelerate development and are the benefits from the transfer fairly distributed? How can dualism in the relations between the richer and poorer countries, and within the latter themselves, be mitigated? These questions form the subject of Chapters 3–5.

The next chapter turns to trade as a factor in economic development and to the contribution that might be made by liberalization of trade on the part of the industrial countries towards solving the problems of unemployment and poverty in the developing countries. This leads on to a discussion of other ways in which aid could be given and to the use of targets for putting pressure on the richer countries to supply a larger flow of financial resources. The problems of unemployment and poverty are then given more extended treatment, with emphasis on the need for a more labour-intensive technology as a means of dealing with the first and on the links with population growth in the second. The role of multinational corporations in bringing about a transfer of technology to the poorer countries is discussed in the concluding chapter.

Broadly speaking there are three major strategic variables in economic growth : capital accumulation, expansion of the market, and technological development. One can conceive of the process as dominated by any one of these or as involving the interaction of all three. One can also put one's money on the power of government to influence one or all of them, or take the view that governments are more successful in impeding than promoting growth. Hans Singer has always taken a hopeful view of governments although he has curiously little to say about the kind of governments that exercise power in the less developed countries and he is a good deal less enthusiastic about development planning than he used to be. Of the trinity of strategic variables he has come to lay increasing stress on technological development. In the first two of the papers in this volume he shows how inappropriate is the use of models of growth that fix on investment as the key variable, especially if these models identify investment with the accumulation of capital equipment, mainly from abroad, and set aside the interconnection between investment and technical progress. He also takes a gloomy view of the possibilities of market expansion (qualified, however, in Chapter 6) because of deteriorating terms of trade and various backwash consequences of increasing dependence on foreign markets. So if one asks what room he finds for hopefulness the answer lies mainly in the possibilities of technology if only aid from the developed countries can be used to exploit them.

The idea which he and others have developed is that of concentrating research and development on devising new labour-intensive methods of production so as to permit of a rise in productivity without detriment to employment. Those who are familiar with the concept of 'intermediate technology' will recognize in this a rather similar idea. But it is no easy matter to devise superior labour-intensive technologies or for that matter to introduce them once devised. If it were, one might suppose that the less developed countries would show more eagerness to make use of second-hand capital equipment and would be encouraged to do so by their governments.

I confess that although I find the idea very appealing I am left unconvinced that its protagonists have fully appreciated the difficulties. It is true that the technology in use in the advanced countries is highly capital-intensive and hence less useful to the less developed countries than a technology more in keeping with their superabundance of labour would be. It is true also that research and development in the advanced countries is enormously greater than in the less developed countries and is not directed towards the needs of those countries for a more labour-intensive technology. But this does not establish the conclusion, most fully expounded in the 'Sussex Manifesto',* that the less developed

* The Sussex Manifesto: Science and Technology to Developing Countries during the Second Development Decade. Institute of Development Studies Communications Series 101 R 1970. Professor Singer was Chairman of the group that prepared the Manifesto.

countries would be materially helped by the diversion of 5 per cent of total research and development in the advanced countries to the special problems of the less developed countries.

Of course, if it were possible to *control* technological development and by a relatively small expenditure of funds, to create superior but very labour-intensive new technology it would be splendid. There is also no need to dispute the critical importance in any country, developed or less developed, of *being able* to generate or adapt new technology.

But like other elements in productive potential, technology responds to market forces: to the enterprise of businessmen at least as much as the activities of scientists. It is not something easily influenced by direct state intervention as distinct from indirect action through the educational system or the system of rewards and penalties to which *business* responds. It is easy, by thinking in terms of science rather than technology, and in terms of research rather than development, to overlook the essentially commercial basis of successful development, technological or otherwise.

Except in a few industries, dominated by so-called 'high technology', progress in technology did not rest in the past, and does not rest even now, on some separable activity called R & D. It was and is far more a matter of engineering design, experimentation in the factory, response to specific pressures either on supply or of demand. Even the activity we call R & D, which hardly existed before 1939, is heavily concentrated on space and atomic research, defence equipment and, in the civil sphere, chemical and electrical applications. It is far from clear how this kind of activity *could* be converted for the evolution of a technology appropriate to the less developed countries and even less clear how advantage *would* be taken of such new discoveries as were made. It is not as if there were no recorded examples of the successful commissioning of just such development work and its subsequent neglect for lack of any machinery for commercial utilization. Without seeking to labour the point (e.g. by citing the efforts at Harwell to convert to non-nuclear applications), I think it reasonable to ask why, if governments can use R & D to such purpose in accelerating development, their efforts in the advanced countries have met with so little success.

The call for more R & D and the emphasis on the need for a new labour-intensive technology is linked with anxiety about employment opportunities. It is of course right to draw attention to the indications of rising unemployment in the less developed countries and to the need to give more priority to finding employment for those who flood into the towns. But is it not equally right to insist that the employment problem is largely a by-product of the population problem? And that the population problem is the unforeseen consequence of technological development in reducing mortality rates? At various points Hans Singer lays stress on the disservices that advanced countries have done or still do to their poorer neighbours. I missed the conclusion that the greatest disservice may prove to have been from the kindest of motives : the prolongation of human life.

Hans Singer's first major contribution to economic thought on development was his analysis in 1949 of the distribution of gains between investing and borrowing countries, reprinted here as Chapter 3. An extensive literature has since come into being, developing arguments along similar lines. In the process, dualism, dependency and deteriorating terms of trade have become political slogans rather than economic concepts. This is perhaps inevitable once discussion turns to the sharing of gains and these can be represented as highly one-sided. No one reading the 1949 article can fail to be impressed by its insight into the dynamic elements in economic development and its emphasis on the need for absorption of the fruits of technical progress through reinvestment of domestic resources. What is less obvious to the reader is why industry should enjoy a monopoly of dynamic influences while primary production is denied them.

This reflection or something like it is the starting-point of a later paper – Chapter 4 – on the same theme of the distribution of gains from trade and investment. In this paper the villain of the piece is not the monopoly of dynamic benefits that industrial countries enjoy because they are industrial, but modern technology and the foreign investment that acts as a carrier and poisons development in backward countries. It is possible to find this a rather extreme view without disagreeing in the least with the conclusion in favour of 'building up . . . indigenous scientific and technological capacities within the developing countries'

(Ch. 4, para 6). Why, one might ask, should a country be worse off by making use of a new technology than by banning its use? This is not the same as asking whether technological change is necessarily to the advantage of the less developed countries. There are obviously many kinds of technical progress that injure them. But to reject a technology on the grounds that it is capital-intensive needs more justification than a passing reference to unemployment. If tractor cultivation allowed two crops to be grown in place of one, who would ban the use of tractors? The simple fact is that modern technology is often more productive both per unit of labour and per unit of capital.

It may be that there is more to be said for a rather different line of argument. A great deal of foreign investment in manufactures (which is now the main target of attack although most foreign investment is not in manufactures) is in consumer goods that may be regarded as luxuries. To bring in foreign capital for this purpose is to commit scarce foreign exchange if the investment is profitable when with higher taxation it might not be necessary at all and when an eventual shortage of foreign exchange may leave no option but to raise taxation.

But it is not the purpose of this introduction to go over each chapter in turn, agreeing here and disagreeing there. It would be grossly unfair to the author if he were to surrender the first word and be denied the last in what is his own book. Moreover he at least holds out some hope to the reader that things can be made to work better, and those who express scepticism of his proposals should be ready, as I am not, with proposals of their own. Let me, therefore, leave off disputing and confine myself to praise.

I am the happier to commend the book because it provoked me to occasional disagreement. It is easy to read, not because it oversimplifies but because Hans Singer has such a complete command of his subject and the power to communicate his ideas simply and vividly. What he has to say is of very great importance and I hope that it will be widely read. It should add to the large number of his admirers all over the world.

ALEC CAIRNCROSS

St Peter's College
Oxford

1 Recent Trends in Economic Thought on Underdeveloped Countries*

BEFORE WORLD WAR II : D-PESSIMISM/U-OPTIMISM

If, in looking at the great sweep of economic thinking from Ricardo to Keynes, we focus on the thinkers' broad attitudes toward the respective future of already developed and underdeveloped countries, we make a rather surprising discovery. In spite of their enormous doctrinal differences and the great diversity of their interests, background, and experiences, they all seem to agree that growth in already developed countries will sooner or later succumb to some kind of obstacle or come up against some kind of ceiling. The reasons which they adduce are as different as one would expect from their diverse general opinions, but they all seem to agree that for one reason or another economic growth will gradually create conditions which will make it grind to a halt. Conversely, in underdeveloped countries, where economic progress has not yet dug its own grave, conditions will be propitious to start the cycle of progress and decay. We may describe this illustrious school of thought which held such long sway as being *D*-pessimistic/*U*-optimistic, where *D* stands for continuation of development in already advanced countries, and *U* stands for starting development in underdeveloped countries.

It will be noted that we do not include Adam Smith in this *D*-pessimism/*U*-optimism school of thought. Adam Smith, writ-

*From *International Development*: *Growth and Change* (McGraw-Hill Book Company, New York, 1960). An earlier version was published in Spanish, under the title 'Tendencias recientes del pensamiento económico sobre los países sub-desarrolados' in *Revista de economía latinoamericana*, vol. 1, no. 1, 1961.

ing as he did at the dawn of the industrial revolution (or the beginning of the 'take-off', to use more fashionable language), did not give much thought to where it might all end – and who can blame him? He was too impressed by the beginnings of the process. He is not easy to classify. Sometimes, because of his flush of enthusiasm about the development of markets, the increased skill that comes with specialization, the economies of scale, one can read into the *Wealth of Nations* a belief that a˙ self-sustaining process has been created here which will feed upon itself. In such passages Adam Smith seems a curiously up-to-date forerunner of the modern 'take-off into self-sustained growth'. At other times, Adam Smith seems dimly to visualize and argue that once the whole nation is a fully developed market, once mechanization has been developed to correspond fully to the degree of specialization in a full market economy, once the economies of scale have been achieved, the movement will lose its momentum and reach some kind of ceiling. It is not easy to say what he argued or would have argued, and it is best not to classify him at all.

But from Ricardo on there can be no quarrel about classification. With impressive unanimity the great economists tended to be *D*-pessimists. It will be instructive to list the divergent reasons for their *D*-pessimism because it results in an interesting conclusion to which we will come a little later.

Ricardo's great worry and gravedigger of progress was, of course, the Law of Diminishing Returns in agriculture. Malthus's great worry and gravedigger was population. Karl Marx's gravedigger was collapse of markets and insufficiency of purchasing power. Schumpeter's chief worry and gravedigger was the undermining of the entrepreneurial spirit, whether from public hostility or from a 'Buddenbrook complex', under which the sons and grandsons of successful entrepreneurs become poets or collectors of art or give their money away. In Keynes's view, the villain of the piece and gravedigger of progress was the 'falling marginal efficiency schedule of capital' : as capital accumulation proceeded, new investment opportunities were gradually used up; and as the rate of interest could not, for various reasons, continue to fall in step with the falling marginal efficiency of capital investment, capital accumulation and progress would come to a stop.

In the more dismal versions of *D*-pessimism, some kind of dramatic *Götterdämmerung* (twilight of the gods) atmosphere surrounded the prediction of the end of progress (especially, of course, with Malthus and Marx if we disregard the Marxian forecast of a new era in which progress would restart itself on a higher plane). In other versions, the petering out of progress is pictured as comparatively painless and accompanied with a great flowering or golden age for civilization, once people's minds are no longer dominated by the desire to expand and acquire more goods.[1]

One could, of course, add to the list of economists and to the reasons which were adduced for the petering out or collapse of progress; thus Jevons thought that the exhaustion of coal or other natural resources would bring things to a halt. It is more important, however, to look at the reasons which make the great economists *D*-pessimists and to realize why this list sounds so familiar now to us who worry about the underdeveloped countries. Worries about lagging productivity in agriculture (Ricardo) – worries about population growth (Malthus) – worries about the lack of markets and purchasing power (Marx) – worries about the failures of, or interference with, entrepreneurship (Schumpeter) – worries about the absence or exhaustion of productive investment opportunities (Keynes) : why has this list such a familiar ring about it? Of course! These are precisely the things that we are worrying about now when we think of the underdeveloped countries! It is an instructive and perhaps chastening thought to realize that all the things that we are worried about in relation to the underdeveloped countries, and that have made so many contemporary economists into *U*-pessimists, were far from unknown to the great economists of earlier days. Quite the contrary : these things were in the forefront of their minds. But they were worried about these things, not in relation to the poor or underdeveloped countries, but rather in relation to the conditions created by economic progress. This is certainly one of the most curious and dramatic reversals of thinking.

Keynes held that there were two barriers to continued economic growth, constituting between them a real trap, in the sense that as one of these barriers was overcome, the community would, *ipso facto*, run into the other. The first barrier was, of course, the inherent tendency of the system toward unemployment, insufficient investment, and a resulting low-level equilibrium of low consumption, low savings, low investment, high unemployment, plenty of idle resources, and slow progress. To this Keynes himself provided the answer by showing that successful investment via the multiplier would create sufficient effective demand. But to the extent that the problem of deficient demand was solved, the community would run into the new problem of falling marginal efficiency of capital. And the more successfully the problem of unemployment was tackled, the faster the marginal efficiency of capital would fall, precisely. Keynes held that in a fully employed community the marginal efficiency of capital would fall 'approximately to zero within a single generation'.[2] According to Keynes, if the postwar era is described as one of full employment and full employment is successfully maintained, the marginal efficiency of capital should be zero by 1980 at the latest. Certainly (writing halfway through the period of this forecast) there is not the slightest evidence for this.

By contrast, the great economists of the Ricardo-to-Keynes era tended to be U-optimists. This followed mainly as a direct consequence of their idea of economic progress being of the self-limiting or grave-digging variety. Since these self-limiting factors would only appear somewhere along the road of economic progress and were created by the force of economic progress itself, it followed logically that they would not operate in the early stages of progress in the underdeveloped countries. If we take Keynes as an example, the marginal efficiency schedule in underdeveloped countries would not have had time to fall very much; splendid investment opportunities would abound since they would not have been used up yet by previous capital accumulation; rates of interest could still in many ways be brought down, by improved financial institutions or otherwise, before they would strike rock bottom.

Apart from being the natural counterpart of their D-pessimism, the U-optimism of the great economists was also a reflection of the historical evidence of their day. They saw other countries joining in the march of progress, one after the other; first Belgium and Holland and France, then the United States and Germany, then Japan, then Russia, then Canada, Australia, New Zealand,

and so forth. Like Adam Smith at the dawn of the industrial revolution, they saw no particular reason to picture any end to this march of progress. No great institutional difficulties were arising in these then 'new' countries even though, as in Japan and Russia, their economic beliefs and policies might differ from those of the pioneers of progress. But it could not escape the economists that the march of progress seemed to be a little selective and seemed, in particular, to be hesitant in the tropical countries and in nonwhite countries. This was generally explained on non-economic grounds : the effect of tropical climate on peoples' willingness or ability to exert themselves, the influence of fatalistic religions and philosophies, etc. The famous theories that the initiative in economic progress could only come through Protestants (Weber), or through Puritans or Calvinists or Jews or religious minorities generally (Sombart) or Prussians (Sombart again) – what were all these theories except an attempt to combine an inborn U-optimism with the facts of life? In economic principle the U-optimism was general, but in sociological application it tended to be limited to the white, or European-style, world.[3]

THE FIFTIES : D-OPTIMISM/U-PESSIMISM

The change-over from what we may perhaps now call the 'classical' view of D-pessimism/U-optimism into its exact opposite has been startling and unmistakable. The prevailing view in the fifties was a combination of D-optimism (a belief in the powers of developed countries to continue self-sustaining growth indefinitely) with U-pessimism (a rather gloomy view of the formidable obstacles and vicious circles standing in the way of the progress of underdeveloped countries).

What are the reasons for this reversal? Take the change from D-pessimism to D-optimism first. In the first place, the Depression of the 1930s was over; war had shown the great power of industrial countries to expand their production even under conditions of great labour and raw-material shortages; the widely predicted postwar slump in the industrial countries had failed to materialize; the effectiveness of Keynesian policies in avoiding inflation (at least of the galloping kind), depression, and stagnation had been impressively demonstrated. A great speeding up of technical progress had occurred, partly under the pressure of war necessities but by no means limited to wartime applications; the development of synthetic materials, in particular, removed part of the Ricardian nightmare of diminishing returns. Perhaps even more important, the immediate postwar period had most impressively demonstrated the capacity of industrial countries to overcome with unexpected ease the effects of even widespread war destruction and war dislocation.

All these developments served to direct attention, in developed countries, away from such factors as physical capital and dependence on natural commodities – in both of which the dangerous traps of falling marginal efficiency and diminishing returns were lurking – and toward the human factor in development: skills, training, attitudes, institutions, research genius, developing machinery for applying new research in production, etc. Once this shift had taken place, the idea of self-sustaining growth became much more plausible. The human mind and its products are not subject to diminishing returns in the sense in which physical capital, labour, or natural materials alone may be assumed to be. Quite on the contrary, there is good reason to assume something like a Law of Increasing Returns in research and human development. As research proceeds, each new discovery has an increasingly widespread and diversified impact on other lines of discovery; with the progress of knowledge unproductive lines of research are increasingly abandoned, and research is concentrated on more productive lines. Investment in education is not only highly productive but also yields increasing returns insofar as cooperating teams of skilled and educated people are worth more than the sums of the individuals of which they are composed. Wherever we look in this area of human investment, we find increasing returns at play.

To us it now seems clear that when Keynes forecast that the marginal efficiency of capital would fall to zero in a fully employed community 'within a single generation', he was seriously in error in assuming simultaneously full employment, a high rate of investment, and a constant technology – almost by definition an inconsistent trio of assumptions. To us it would seem fairly obvious that with full employment and high investment the creation of new investment opportunities by concomitant technical progress would push up the marginal efficiency of capital as fast as, or probably faster than, it is reduced even by rapid capital accumulation. Moreover, such is the complementary character of investment that capital accumulations in sector A will raise the efficiency of capital in sectors B and C. This is true particularly if investment in sector A is part of the accumulation of 'overhead capital' – but in a sense *all* capital is somewhat an overhead.

Finally, it should be noted that the cessation of capital accumulation resulting from a zero rate of marginal efficiency is by no means identical with a cessation of economic progress itself, although to Keynes these two things seem to have appeared as identical. We can have a cessation of capital accumulation – in technical terms zero *net* investment – and still have some amount of *gross* investment, i.e. replacement of older, worn-out capital by new capital. If there has been a sufficient rate of technical progress between the date of the old capital investment and the date of the new investment which replaces it, the superior efficiency of the new capital can produce a tolerable or even high rate of economic progress by itself – even with zero net investment!

On the more purely theoretical plane, the D-optimistic idea of self-sustained growth was impressed by the growth models of the Harrod-Domar type. For such growth models, each increase in output provides the basis for a further increase in output in the next period. The chief mechanism is by reinvestment of part of this increased output through additional savings into additional investment, at capital/output ratios which, in the simple model, are assumed to remain constant (presumably as a result of the human factors mentioned above offsetting any tendency toward diminishing returns). In the Harrod-Domar models, there is no intrinsic reason to assume diminishing returns or self-limiting growth, since additional savings should become progressively easier at rising income levels, and thus the marginal propensity to save may be assumed to rise rather than to fall. If no exhaustion of investment opportunities is presumed, this would make for accelerating or at least self-sustaining growth rather than self-limiting growth. It is, of course, debatable to what extent the intellectual creation of the Harrod-Domar growth models was the cause or merely the expression of the reversal in thinking which took place in the postwar decade – presumably a bit of both.

The watershed from *D*-pessimism to *D*-optimism is well illustrated by the difference in flavour between Domar's earlier and later essays. This is commented upon by Domar himself in the foreword to his collection of essays, *The Theory of Economic Growth*. 'The present-day reader may also be amused (I certainly am) at the timidity with which our growth potential is treated in the four earlier essays. A potential rate of growth of a modest two or three per cent a year is discussed with numerous apologies, reservations and what not . . . And yet compared to prevailing opinion, mine was optimistic.'[4]

In the earlier Harrod formulation, which dates from the *D*-pessimistic period before the war, the emphasis was still on the lack of probability that the economy would in fact follow the straight and narrow path of exponential growth and on the virtual certainty that the diminishing profit rates, chronic unemployment, and idle capital would in fact produce the stationary state forecast in the literature from Ricardo to Keynes. The neutrality – but a neutrality strongly leaning toward a stationary state – of the Harrod-Domar approach in the earlier versions is well formulated by Domar. 'Economic salvation is not impossible; neither is it assured.'[5]

Remarkable as the change-over from *D*-pessimism to *D*-optimism in the postwar era was, those economists whose thinking was shaped in the prewar era still found it difficult to make the turnabout. Thus we often find a gulf between theoretical reasoning still largely determined by an expectation of a stationary condition and descriptive and practical policy reasoning in which the possibility of continued growth is clearly accepted. This gulf remains something of a mystery to perceptive observers, such as Domar. 'Why in spite of remarkable rapid growth, the vision of the stationary state hung so heavily over the thinking of the Great Masters of the last century and still preoccupies many of our contemporaries, is more than I can explain. Even my more broadminded colleagues who love growth, are willing to grant her only a reprieve, but not a pardon . . .'[6]

Yet another reflection, and perhaps also cause, of this change in thought was the notion of the 'take-off into self-sustained growth', most popular in the form put forward by Walt Rostow in his *Stages of Economic Growth.*[7] It is interesting to note that the metaphors of this school of thought are drawn from aeronautics and space research. Once an aeroplane has taken off into the air, it is much easier for it to continue in serene flight than it was to take off and gain altitude; similarly, once a rocket has left the atmosphere of the earth, it is much easier to keep it in a given orbit than it was to fire it off and place it in orbit. The influence of this aeronautical and space element on economic thinking is perhaps more than purely verbal or fashionable. Since, as explained above, the change in view was largely caused by and based upon developments of scientific research and its application to production, it is more than accidental that this should be reflected in the language and approach of economists.

Now let us look at the other side of the coin, namely, the change-over from U-optimism to U-pessimism. In some ways this follows directly from the change from pessimism to optimism in views concerning the more developed countries. This is particularly clear if we look at the take-off theory proposed by Rostow. According to this theory, the underdeveloped countries stand at the beginning of the runway or are not even on it yet, and a terrific concentrated effort will be required to take them down the runway in exactly the right combination of circumstances and at very high speed so that they may become airborne. More directly, according to Professor Rostow, an underdeveloped country must first create a number of diverse preconditions which include changes in institutions and attitudes, the provision of social and economic overhead capital, raising of agricultural productivity and solution of land-tenure problems, etc. Even the successful solution of these tricky problems will only place an underdeveloped country on the runway; then before take-off is achieved, it is necessary for an underdeveloped country to increase its rate of net investment roughly from 5 to 10 per cent within a comparatively short time, to develop a leading manufacturing sector strategically placed so as to have strong linkage effects on the whole economic system, and simultaneously to create the capacity to transfer this impetus to other leading sectors as soon as the first leading sector begins to slacken. It will be seen that these are very formidable requirements indeed. In fact, one begins to wonder how any country has ever managed to achieve a take-off. At any rate, this view of the matter must certainly be classified as an expression of some innate pessimism about the frequency of future take-offs by the present underdeveloped countries.

Similarly, a pessimistic trend of thought concerning the underdeveloped countries can be deduced from the Harrod-Domar growth model. Given the right kind of parameters – particularly a high rate of population growth – lo and behold! the Harrod-Domar equation is converted from a description of cumulative self-sustaining growth into a description of cumulative self-sustaining stagnation. Let the rate of net investment be 6 per cent, the capital/output 3 : 1, and the rate of population growth 2 per cent per annum, and the Harrod-Domar equation describes a state of utter stagnation which will continue indefinitely, until a new element enters the situation to change either the rate of investment or the capital/output ratio or to change the rate of population growth. In fact, many economists have come to assume that the tendency in underdeveloped countries is for the parameters of the Harrod-Domar-type models to bear exactly those relations to each other which will result in cumulative stagnation.

The general picture which has been developed in this postwar decade of pessimism concerning the underdeveloped countries is that of some kind of obstacle or barrier which makes modest initial growth self-sustaining rather than cumulative and which can only be got over by some kind of exceptional 'big push'. The most obvious illustration is that of population. Small advances will simply be eaten up by a fall in the death rate and possibly even an initial rise in the birth rate. To overcome the population hurdle would require a terrific advance in living standards of such a kind as to change fundamentally the attitudes to large families. Yet the achievement of this fundamental improvement is made well-nigh impossible by the self-limiting nature of more modest, slower rates of growth. If only the big push could be achieved, there would then be downhill coasting – but how to get to the top of the hill?[8] The pessimistic turn concerning underdeveloped countries in the postwar decade clearly had a lot to do with the evidence of rapid declines in death rates, associated with simple sanitary precautions (often imported from abroad), and the resulting acceleration in the rate of population increase with its great demands on food, housing, and all forms of social (as opposed to directly productive) capital.

The theory of the big push, or else no progress, had many other implications, quite apart from population. The most important implication relates to the provision of overhead capital – transport and communications, housing, urban utilities, schools and educational systems, hospital and health systems, etc. The provision of this overhead capital is notoriously expensive, i.e. has a high capital/output ratio and a very long gestation period. If the provision of overhead capital is an essential precondition of growth, it is quite plausible that most or all underdeveloped countries may fail to achieve progress because they will never be able to assemble the initially required volume of overhead capital. Let it not be forgotten that the period during which overhead capital is assembled and not much final output appears is also almost inevitably a period of acute inflationary pressures. The impact of these inflationary pressures, as well as insufficiency of total funds required for assembly of the necessary overhead capital, will make it highly probable that underdeveloped countries will not successfully achieve self-sustaining growth, according to this line of thinking.[9]

Another variation of the 'big push' theory is related to the theory of 'balanced growth'. Broadly speaking, this theory (proposed particularly by the late Professor Nurkse) held that while the isolated development of individual lines of production in underdeveloped countries is impossible for lack of a market, the simultaneous development of a number of lines of production will be quite feasible, since the incomes created in producing commodities A, B, and C will return as demand for commodity D. Unless one assumes that an underdeveloped economy has sufficient slack in it and a sufficient volume of unutilized resources to enable it to engage in the simultaneous expansion along a broad front required by the principle of balanced growth – and this is clearly not plausible – this theory is very bad news indeed for the underdeveloped countries. It means that the only road to growth which may be feasible for them is barred. Hence there can be no growth. On the other hand, for the already developed countries the principle of balanced growth is good news. Since expansion is in fact going on along a broad front, the advantages of balanced growth ensure that no market difficulties will be encountered and that growth will continue to sustain itself. It is not accidental that the theory of balanced growth should have been developed and become popular at the same time that pessimism concerning the underdeveloped countries increased.[10]

In reflection of this increasing pessimism, the situation in underdeveloped countries was frequently seen as a system of vicious circles. In the course of time more and more of these were discovered, so much so that someone has recently said, 'The road to economic development is paved with vicious circles'. A vicious circle, in more precise language, is a situation in which various factors are so interlocked that they mutually tend to produce a stagnant or stationary situation from which it is extremely difficult to move away. Perhaps the prototype of all vicious circles is the one which runs around as follows: low incomes – low savings capacity – low investment – low output – back to low incomes. There are many others, such as low production – no surpluses for economic investment – no tools and equipment – low standard of production (a fair description of subsistence farming), and the fact that an underdeveloped country is poor because it has no industry and has no industry because it is poor. This situation can be summed up in the statement, 'One thing leads to another, but nothing leads to nothing'.

Perhaps the clearest connection between the more optimistic view of the prospects for self-sustained growth in the developed countries and the opposite tendency toward pessimism about the underdeveloped countries has been provided by the so-called 'backwash' theory. This theory – with which the name of Gunnar Myrdal is associated – states that the growth of the developed countries, apart from any beneficial, or 'spreading' effects it may have on the underdeveloped countries, also has some harmful, or 'backwash', effects. Examples of such backwash effects are the development of a premature desire for high-level consumption in the underdeveloped countries caused by the demonstration effect of conditions in more developed countries; the spreading of premature ideas in underdeveloped countries about the welfare state, social insurance, minimum-wage legislation, etc., also caused by imitation of conditions in more developed countries; technical progress in the developed countries may have a backwash effect on the underdeveloped countries because modern technology becomes more and more capital-intensive and laboursaving and hence less and less suitable for the underdeveloped countries.

In the classical scheme up to the Second World War, the spreading effects were more emphasized. Thus Alfred Marshall observed that the available stock of technical knowledge at the disposal of newcomers was increasing, and general emphasis was placed by economists on the increasing amount of capital available for newcomers from the wealth of already developed countries. But in the postwar decade the backwash effects received more attention. For instance, in relation to the availability of capital, it became clear that the financing of self-sustaining growth in the developed countries and the utilization of the many new investment opportunities opened up by technical progress would leave very little over for the underdeveloped countries – at least as far as the orthodox mechanism of private foreign investment was concerned.

Another example of a backwash effect is provided by the possibility that the technical progress in the developed countries, which has taken such forms as economizing in the use of raw materials, the development of new synthetic materials, and changes in their industrial structure, might recoil to the disadvantage of the underdeveloped countries in the form of a chronic tendency to weakness in their terms of trade, i.e. the price relationship between primary products and manufactured products. This line of inquiry has been particularly closely explored by Paul Prebisch. Recent years have lent force to his arguments and have justified his concerns, although during the Second World War and the immediate postwar period it seemed temporarily as if there were no cause to worry about primary-commodity prices.

Finally, the emphasis on the human factor in explaining progress in the more developed countries also had pessimistic implications for the underdeveloped countries. The development of human skills, institutions, and change in attitudes is a trickier and more complex affair than the mere injection of physical capital. It may possibly be cheaper, but it is certainly more difficult. Thus, whereas in prewar thinking human difficulties appeared more as exogenous and sociological, they now became endogenous and to that extent more emphasized.

In a way, the change to *D*-optimism can be represented as a return to a yet earlier school, preceding Adam Smith. This is the idea of rectilinear progress or even exponential growth, obviously congenial to the age of reason and enlightenment of the earlier eighteenth century. Thus it is stated that '. . . for William Goodwin, man was the master both of himself and of nature and could wield a cumulative control of the universe. Man, by taking thought about his condition, could progressively improve it subject to no inherent check whatsoever.'[11] There are certainly traces of the possibility of continued progress even in the thinking and writings of the great economists themselves. Such speculations are sometimes inherent when they wonder at the marvels of science and technology, but the surprising thing is still that these wonderings failed to shape their views, as economists, of the future of society more than they did. In Schumpeter's writing, traces can certainly be found of the view that the progress of society may survive the demise of the functions of the capitalist entrepreneur on which it originally depended and that progress itself might be mechanized and acquire an independent existence, being embodied in scientists and teams of trained specialists instead of entrepreneurs.[12]

The growth of science and technology is such that it assumes a life of its own, that it can be depended upon to make available new ideas on a scale sufficient to create investment opportunities to offset any flagging tendencies of the marginal efficiency of capital. In fact, the growth of science and technology, combined with the basis of education and training on which it depends, is such that it may even be said to help to produce the social attitudes and institutions which will make the rapid introduction of new capital not only possible but actual.

THE SIXTIES : THE PENDULUM SWINGS BACK

As the decade of the 1950s rolled on to its close, it became more and more apparent that the facts of life did not really bear out the strong pessimism about the underdeveloped counties which had developed in reaction to the previous optimism. Although there has been much talk of 'an increasing gap between the developed and the underdeveloped countries', the actual facts of the postwar decade are not so clear on this point. The national income of underdeveloped countries as a group increased at about the same rate as the national incomes of more developed countries as a group. If on a per capita basis the rate of progress among the underdeveloped countries was slightly less than that of the developed countries, this was due to differences in population growth and in economic structure rather than to any inherent failure of production to increase in the underdeveloped countries. Industrial output in the underdeveloped countries *taken separately* increased just about as fast as in the developed countries, and the same was true of agricultural output *separately*. If total output rose less in the underdeveloped countries, this could be attributed to the fact that agricultural output, with its slower rate of increase, had a heavier weight in the underdeveloped countries in relation to industrial output than was the case in the developed countries. A number of underdeveloped countries developed quite rapidly during the postwar decade; the growth of the Latin American region as a whole, for instance, compared quite favourably with the more developed countries. Perhaps the impression of 'an increasing gap' was due to the conspicuous failure of some of the underdeveloped countries and regions to join in the march of progress and also attributable to the understandable concern about the continued existence of world mass poverty. It is also a fact that even satisfactory relative increases in the poorer countries look puny compared with the sums represented by the same relative increases in the richer countries. Perhaps one of the most startling facts of life in the contemporary world is that the average income for an inhabitant of the United States *increases* each year by not so very much less than the *total* income of the average inhabitant of India or Pakistan.

The terms of trade of underdeveloped countries also presented a rather mixed picture during the postwar period. The more pessimistic assumptions of a steady long-term deterioration in the terms of trade were not borne out; the terms of trade of underdeveloped countries throughout the postwar period have been more favourable than during the 1930s. On the other hand, the pessimists have been proved right against such people as Colin Clark and also to some extent Arthur Lewis, who both forecast a sharp improvement in the terms of trade primary producers.[13] The fact is that commodity prices did show a weakening tendency from their Korean boom level throughout the 1950s. Thus it was possible for both sides to claim some confirmation of their views, although the balance of the argument seemed to be more with the pessimists.

In brief, then, the facts of the postwar decade did not really lend themselves to any general pessimism or optimism. The picture was mixed. Other elements were present which might make the picture more hopeful. For instance, as the decade went on it became increasingly clear that a far-reaching and probably long-term change had occurred in the attitude of the more developed countries to the question of aiding the underdeveloped countries. The concept of a single world economy began to rise on the horizon. In a remarkable degree, the developed countries recognized a responsibility to assist the underdeveloped countries, and by means which only a few years ago they might have rejected as too heterodox. Even the ill wind of the cold war blew some good for the underdeveloped countries. A great new international movement has arisen under the banner of 'technical assistance' to transfer and adapt mankind's enormous stock of technical knowledge and expertise to the underdeveloped countries.

It was discovered that even though the difficulties of finding productive investment opportunities stressed by the pessimistic school might all be real, they were not unalterable, and that investment opportunities could be created even where they did not naturally exist. It was also discovered that such planning techniques as had guided the war economies of the more developed countries could be applied successfully to the underdeveloped countries and that it was possible to make progress even with limited resources by concentrating them at strategic points where the maximum linkage effect could be obtained. Doubts came to be felt as to whether the complete assembly of economic and social overhead capital was really a necessary precondition in point of time for progress in increasing actual production or whether it would not be possible by judicious strategic use of resources to create limited shortages of such overhead facilities as transport and power, sufficient to cause an increase in their supply but not large enough to disrupt production.[14]

Historical analyses of the development of such countries as England, the United States, France, and even czarist Russia suggest that they did not experience a distinct 'take-off' period, with the tremendous concentrated effort and rapid increase in the investment ratio that this implies. In fact, economic growth seems to have been quite steady, gradual, and organic in those countries, and there now seems to be no compelling reason why this could not also be the case in the underdeveloped countries.

While there was thus enough in the general picture to justify the abandonment of earlier optimism – much evidence of stagnation, weakness of primary commodities, increasingly capital-intensive technology, etc. – yet there also seemed to be a lot to relieve the gloom – evidence of progress, development of international aid and technical assistance, progress in development-planning techniques, etc. In the sixties, the complexity of the real world makes a mockery of any preconceived universal optimism or pessimism. There is a lot of good as well as a lot of bad. The better approach – better than a preconceived optimism or pessimism – seems to be pragmatic, to try to build on the more helpful elements in the picture and strengthen them while reducing the impact of the unfavourable elements.

The change in the climate compared with the pessimistic postwar decade is perhaps best illustrated by a statement made by W. A. B. Iliff, Vice-president of the International Bank, in his opening speech to the 1960 annual meeting of the Bank in Washington. 'The historic transformation which is going on in the underdeveloped world today defies any general "solution"; but it does offer infinite possibilities to the practitioners of economic development.'[15]

In other words, the difficulties in the path of economic development pointed out by the early students of the postwar decade are by no means neglected or considered to be nonexistent. Their spadework has made us much more aware of the problems and difficulties which we have to face. But these difficulties are now felt to be much more in the nature of a challenge which it is not beyond human wisdom and human efforts to cope with. They

B

are not so much felt as immutable and probably insurmountable obstacles. It will be seen that this change is not a return to the general optimism, more implicit than argued, of the earlier economists. In the terms used by Iliff, we may describe the new approach as generally neither optimistic nor pessimistic but as a search for possibilities, whether they be numerous or few.

In general, we may define the new trend in thinking by saying that more emphasis tends to be placed upon the availability of an unutilized potential of labour, human talent (including entrepreneurial abilities), resources of all kinds, savings capacity, fiscal capacity, directions of technological research, etc., and upon the possibilities of activating such unutilized potentials. Whereas the pessimistic postwar decade had emphasized the need for growth by sacrifice and the small (and diminishing) capacity of underdeveloped countries for the big sacrifices required, the new thinking emphasizes the possibilities of growth by a sort of pump-priming process – the creation of a new dynamic setting in which, by good strategy, resource availabilities can be improve, difficulties temporarily bypassed or softened, and a broadening forward movement initiated.

POSTSCRIPT FROM THE POINT OF VIEW OF THE SEVENTIES

Now, ten years later, from the viewpoint of 1974, new attitudes to the development problem and new dimensions and problems have come to the fore. The rise in oil prices, and to some extent the boom in primary commodity prices, look like a natural watershed, as far as effects and prospects are concerned. The concept of a homogeneous 'Third World' has certainly been shattered, with the oil producers clearly having left the ranks of those to whom financial resources are a constraint to their growth and development. Conceivably they will be joined by some other members of the Third World disposing of mineral resources where comparable squeezes can be applied by the producers. On the other hand, the impact on those countries of the Third World which have no strategic commodities to export, but which need to import oil and will also be hit by the oil-induced additional inflation in the rich countries, as well as their certainly reduced ability and their probably reduced will to give aid, looks even gloomier than before. Unfortunately, such countries (which include the Indian subcontinent) contain the bulk of the population of the Third World outside China. Hence the conclusion reached ten years ago in the survey on trends of economic thought, that the picture was 'mixed' without any grounds for preconceived universal optimism or pessimism, is even more dramatically true at the present moment. Economic thought has not yet adjusted itself to this new situation – the time lag may be considerable.

There is however another important direction in which recent thinking has changed and is likely to have a considerable impact on development policies. We have moved decisively towards placing the question of employment and income inequalities within the centre of the picture. The idea that capital-intensive, import-substituting industrialization could absorb the rural surplus labour and create a 'golden age' where rural incomes and rural/urban wages would both rise together, has been shattered against the hard facts of rapid population increase, the increasingly capital-intensive productive technology arising from the concentration of R & D work in the rich countries, the distortion of factor prices and rewards connected with emphasis on import-substituting industrialization, and the education explosion and migration explosion indicating a strong preference for the modern sector jobs. Different authors may attribute different weights to these various elements creating an intolerable imbalance in the process of growth, but the realization of such an imbalance is becoming increasingly common to writers as well as policy advisers. The present path of development may continue to provide aggregate GNP growth – it certainly can for the oil producers and countries in a similarly strong position. But even for those countries the pattern or type of GNP growth, however rapid, will be such as to concentrate its benefits on the foreign investors and multinational corporations which can bring the 'modern' – that is rich-country, capital-intensive, laboursaving – technology to bear upon the modern industrial sector and the small upper-income, local élite groups associated with them. All these patterns of policy objectives, rising income inequality, rising poverty and rising unemployment may go hand in hand with GNP growth and output growth – at least as the latter is recorded by conventional statistics which normally fail to take account of the destruction of informal and traditional sector activities, i.e. most of the employment opportunities. Capital-intensive technology and unequal income distribution create a vicious circle – one of the vicious circles overlooked even in the earlier list. The capital-intensive technology tends to create an unequal income distribution, and the unequal income distribution creates a demand pattern providing a limited market for the products favoured by the carriers of the imported capital-intensive technology. The circle is vicious, partly because it limits markets and assures inefficiency and low degrees of capital utilization, but more importantly because it removes from the limited circle great and increasing masses of the population, particularly the young job-seekers.

It is becoming increasingly clear that new approaches are required to deal with these problems. If any single factor can be pinpointed as crucial, my choice would be the need for the development of a modern labour-intensive technology and range of products suitable for the masses in the developing countries – the majority of mankind, as we may wish to remind ourselves.

The two matters that were listed as giving grounds for optimism ten years ago were the development of international aid and Technical Assistance, and the progress in development planning techniques. As far as the first is concerned, it was reasonable to expect great things ten years ago. But retrospectively aid and Technical Assistance then turned out to be the crest of a wave which has since receded. Although valiant efforts have been made to stabilize the situation through building automatic growth into aid by relating it to rich countries' GNPs, these efforts have withered on the vine in the face of an obvious unwillingness of the most important of the rich countries to continue to give aid the priority which at one time seemed possible. Nor has it been possible to draw the Second World – Russia and her associates – into the aid picture as was once hoped. Now the aid capacity has passed strongly to the oil producers; we do not know what use they will make of this, but it will probably turn out to be spotty and discriminatory within the Third World. Nor has there been much progress to reform the terms, conditions, channels and practices of aid to make it a major pillar of development. The same is also true of the much larger resources going into the developing countries through the operations of the multinational corporations.

The progress in development planning techniques has also turned out to be something of a dead end. It has been largely a technique for increasing GNP, increasing the output of the modern industrial sector and with emphasis on 'modernization'. It may have gained in effectiveness in relation to these specific objectives, but at the same time the objectives themselves have become increasingly questionable. A new emphasis on wider employment, more equal income distribution and reduction of poverty will require new planning techniques, capable of giving expression to a social welfare function rather than a production function. Such new techniques would have to range from a revision of factor prices through wage and income policy to active promotion of redistribution from growth and the ultimate objectives of creating labour-intensive technologies and reducing population growth. While the development of such techniques is still in the future – the first elements are only just beginning to be assembled – it is most encouraging that the need for such new techniques is now widely recognized and that the discussion is so widespread, engulfing such respectable organizations as the World Bank under the leadership of Mr McNamara. The ILO World Employment Programme has played a leading part in developing this new thinking.

Yet another survey ten years further on should be able to indicate whether the promising first beginning towards developing the techniques of poverty-oriented planning has succeeded and whether an effective impact on a more satisfactory type of real development – as distinct from mere GNP growth – has in fact been achieved. But ten years from now is rather an ominous date – 1984! We can only hope and pray that George Orwell was wrong.

2 Keynesian Models of Economic Development and Their Limitations: an Analysis in the Light of Gunnar Myrdal's 'Asian Drama'*

1. AN HISTORICAL PERSPECTIVE

Modern economics and modern economic models originated in the decade of the 1930s when the pressing current problem, namely the world depression and mass unemployment in the industrial countries, became a matter of great concern to everybody including the economists. One man of genius arose among those living at that time, John Maynard Keynes, who managed to see beyond the conventional, traditionally accepted concepts. He developed a new mode of thinking, which he expressed in terms of a model – at least an implicit model, which some of the people working with him made explicit. This model was found extremely helpful in discarding traditional ideas and in finding a solution on the intellectual plane to the problem of mass unemployment in industrial countries: a solution which has quite successfully withstood the test of time, in policy application as well as in theoretical terms.

The guiding principle which Keynes placed in the centre of

* From UN Asian Institute for Economic Development and Planning *Occasional Papers*, Dec 1969 (also published as IDS Communications 54 by the Institute of Developmental Studies).

his model was the principle of maintenance of aggregate demand. Among the many traditional ideas and previously accepted 'sound' views which had to be discarded as a result of the Keynesian model were the current ideas on the propriety of a budget deficit, the monetary policies of governments, the general role of governments in economic life, the function of public works, and so on.

With the help of this new point of view as expressed in the relationships contained in the Keynesian model, this particular problem has been successfully tackled. We can say in the perspective of today that in over twenty years of postwar history the problem of real mass unemployment in industrial countries has not recurred; the adoption of Keynesian policies – now almost universally accepted – presumably had a great deal to do with this. But – and this is relevant for our present subject – in the 1930s it was believed that if we could only solve this one problem of mass unemployment in industrial countries, then no serious problems would remain and an economic paradise would result. This was believed to be the last problem that stood between us and what was called 'economic bliss', the solution of 'the economic problem'.

This last expectation has not been fulfilled. We have not reached the stage of economic paradise or economic bliss. There are many new problems which have taken the place of mass unemployment and in some industrial countries at least the struggle with the new problems seems as hard as it was in the 1930s when we were struggling with unemployment; for instance, problems of balance of payments difficulties which have been largely produced by the successful attempts to achieve full employment, the question of cost-plus inflation which is also strongly associated with full-employment policies, and above all, the problem of the rate of long-term growth. The rate of long-term growth: this is the beginning of my story now, as we turn to development models of underdeveloped countries.

To Keynes himself, for a variety of reasons, the rate of economic growth was not of particular interest. In the first place, Keynes had the mind of an artist, a philosopher, a man whose interests were perhaps more aesthetic than economic, who did not see much sense in any attempt to achieve indefinitely continuing growth once income was already quite reasonable. He even thought there was something rather distasteful and 'not nice' about wanting a lot more growth in such comfortable circumstances. As was clearly expressed in his essay on 'The Economics of Our Grandchildren', he thought it would be much better if countries which had reached a certain income level stopped being too concerned about economic growth; in his opinion any further increase in productivity should be taken out in the form of more leisure, or more equal income distribution such as social services, and more artistic and civilized occupations rather than the pursuit of yet more production.

Secondly, Keynes was not really interested in long-term problems. The problem of the 1930s unemployment was pressing and immediate, and he did not concern himself too much with problems of the distant future. He is, of course, the author of that famous and oft-quoted statement that 'in the long run we are all dead', which illustrates his impatience with long-run economics.

And thirdly, Keynes in many ways was still a faithful follower of classical economics. Although for widely different reasons, the classical economists – Ricardo, Malthus, John Stuart Mills, Jevons, Marshall, Pigou, in a continuing line of classical and neo-classical economic thought – all agreed that long-term, indefinitely continued, economic growth was in any case, unthinkable, in the end they all agreed – and Keynes, too, agreed with them – that the long-run future of the advanced economies would be a state of stagnation : there would be some equilibrium level to which production would tend. Once that equilibrium level was reached, it would be maintained, since the forces of further expansion or further increase in per capita income would cease to operate. In the Keynesian system, this is part of his famous theory of the falling marginal efficiency of capital. As Keynes indicated, after a certain time as capital accumulation continues, the marginal efficiency of capital will fall, not necessarily to zero but towards zero. Before it reaches zero, it will become equal to people's liquidity preference, and once this equality between the falling marginal efficiency of capital and the liquidity preference (which is probably rising as people get richer) is reached, and the two curves intercept, there will be no further accumulation because people will then be more interested in holding any additional wealth in money, offering more convenient liquidity, rather than risk it in additional production.

Thus Keynes had his own reasons for not giving much thought to the rate of growth. The concern with the rate of growth in the industrial countries is a comparatively new phenomenon, more postwar than prewar, post- or neo-Keynesian rather than Keynesian. All this is of great interest and vital to understanding some of the present discussion concerning economic models and their value or limitations.

An admirer, follower and friend of Keynes's, Roy Harrod, appeared on the scene (still set in England). As a faithful disciple of Keynes, he accepted the Keynesian concepts, the Keynesian model designed to deal with the unemployment problems in industrial countries : the concept of national income; the concepts of savings, rates of savings, average and marginal or incremental rates of savings; the concepts of capital investment, physical investment as a percentage of GNP and again average and marginal rates; and so on. By adding the concept of the capital-output ratio, Harrod took the Keynesian concepts and transformed these ingredients into a dynamic model (he called it 'a model of dynamic economics'). Faithful to Keynes, he also stuck to the principle of aggregate demand. That was his guiding concept, just as much as it was Keynes's; but again, in the pursuit of dynamics, he transformed it. He was not interested now in the aggregate demand which produces full employment and how to maintain it, but rather in the aggregate demand which produces a consistent rate of growth, which can be steadily maintained year after year. And this model, known as the Harrod-Domar model (acknowledging important contributions and modifications by Domar) became the basis for the most popular or prevailing development planning models, in spite of important alternatives such as the Cobb-Douglas model and others. This seemed appropriate because when we turn to underdeveloped countries we are interested in the rate of growth of national income. At least *initially* that was how the development picture was seen, i.e. that the essence of economic development should be or was to be the growth of GNP.

This was a direct application of ideas that had been developed in the industrial countries, by the industrial countries, for the industrial countries, and based on concepts that are relevant to the industrial countries. It was assumed that the same framework could be used for the analysis of the development problem of the poorer countries also and that the development problem consisted of how to achieve certain rates of growth of GNP. Therefore the idea was accepted that the Harrod-Domar model, which describes consistent rates of growth of GNP, should be applicable to the underdeveloped countries as well. The idea that the objective of development was to be measured in terms of GNP and growth of GNP and that this was a meaningful concept to apply to underdeveloped countries, was but rarely questioned initially. More recently, however, Myrdal and a number of other people have begun to question this application of the Harrod-Domar model. Nevertheless, the underlying concept of the Harrod-Domar model is obviously very influential, both in national planning and as the basis for the UN approach to the First and Second Development Decades. It is also the basis of the more econometric model which Tinbergen, Chenery, and a number of other people have developed as a foundation for the formulation of a more rational economic policy and also as a basis for research and collection of data and as a framework for development planning.

We have here an example of the transfer of concepts or economic technology from the developed countries to the underdeveloped countries through several intermediate stages at each of which serious questions might be asked. First of all, we have the Keynesian model of the 1930s. It is then assumed that this Keynesian model, applicable to the problems of the 1930s, might also be applicable to the rate of growth problem in the industrial countries in the 1950s. It is then assumed that the rate of growth problem of the industrial countries is the same as the rate of growth problem of the underdeveloped countries. It is further assumed that the rate of growth problem of the underdeveloped countries constitutes the essential part of their development problem. Finally, it is assumed that the Keynesian model, through the links established by a chain of identifications over these 4 or 5 stages, must be applicable to the development problems of underdeveloped countries. And taking all this for granted the Keynesian concepts have now become the traditional basis for development planning, for measuring the force of development progress in the underdeveloped countries, and for international approaches to the problems posed by the past and the coming development decades.

2. QUESTIONABLE CONCEPTS : THE DEMOGRAPHIC FACTOR

The elements of this Keynesian-Harrod-Domar system are the concepts of GNP and something which is supposed to be quantitatively measurable called the rate of growth of GNP; rates of savings; and a concentration on physical capital investment as a strategic key factor singled out in the formula. Then there is something called the capital-output ratio, which is taken more or less as a technological datum. Finally, the whole thing is modified by the fact that this formula relates to aggregate GNP, whereas we are interested in per capita GNP. Therefore, from the rate of growth in GNP, we must deduct as a minus item the rate of growth of population which gives us per capita GNP and *that* is economic development! Thus, the quantitative measure of the rate of growth of per capita GNP gives us our indicator of progress in economic development : growth of per capita GNP = economic development.

Now, like Myrdal and a number of other people, I am extremely sceptical of the validity of these concepts and of this approach to economic development, and here are some of the reasons that make me so sceptical.

Let us start off with the last item – population. Population in the Harrod-Domar formula appears explicitly as an entirely negative item. We deduct the rate of population growth from the rate of growth of GNP and we get the rate of development. Now this certainly does not seem to be adequate. The influence of the human factor as represented by demography (which is the only item in the Harrod-Domar formula which relates to people) is much deeper, much more strategic than this model suggests. Population is much more than a purely mechanical deduction. The implications of population are much more complex. It is true that the mechanical deduction view of the demographic factor in development has something to tell us. It is of interest to know, for instance, that in the First Development Decade the underdeveloped countries managed to achieve a rate of growth of GNP which was equal to or perhaps even a little higher than that of the industrial countries; so, judging by this indicator the expansion potential of underdeveloped countries is no less than that of richer countries. The essential difference comes in when we look at per capita GNP, if I might use this term in accordance with the negative sign that is used for population growth in the Harrod-Domar formula. The richer countries 'lost' only about $\frac{1}{4}$ or $\frac{1}{5}$ of their increase in production through population growth, in the sense of having to devote it simply to feeding more people and maintaining existing standards for a larger population. The rate of population growth, which, in the United States and Russia, and probably Japan, was no more than 1 per cent and in Europe generally often no more than $\frac{1}{2}$ of 1 per cent meant that only a small fraction of the aggregate growth had to be deducted. But in the case of the underdeveloped countries, out of the same average 5 per cent or so rate of growth of GNP, over half had to be deducted because the rate of population growth was $2\frac{1}{2}$ per cent or more. Therefore the notorious increase in the 'gap' can be largely attributed to demographic factors. Thus the formula at least serves the purpose of drawing our attention to the important role that the demographic factor plays in negating or in using up the increase in production, and in pointing towards an essential difference between the richer countries and the poorer countries.

The same result emerges when we try to compare the performance of the poorer countries during the various phases of the postwar period. What we find is that on the whole their performance in increasing aggregate GNP tends to decline gradually. That is to say, if we divide up the twenty years of the postwar period into four parts, during the first half of the 1950s the increase in production was pretty fast in the underdeveloped countries. Since then, on the whole, it has shown a slightly declining tendency. But the rate of population growth has increased over these four five-year periods. We find that in the latest period the rate of growth of per capita GNP was only half of what it was in the first five-year period of the early 1950s. Of that difference, most is attributable to the speeding up of the rate of population growth.

Again, it is a bold assumption to make that since population growth is quantitatively measurable, and since we have actual figures to quote, we 'know' the actual rate of population growth. The confidence with which we produce figures concerning the rate of population growth is often highly exaggerated. It is quite possible that the appearance of a speeding up of the rate of population growth is a statistical illusion, due to the fact that we have today more comprehensive measurements than we had twenty years ago for rates of population growth. Over wide areas of the world the rate of population increase is still a matter of guesswork. The registration of births and deaths remains a very rough-and-ready and incomplete affair. In many countries we simply cannot be as certain as the statisticians and demographers tell us we ought to be.

But my chief point is that the demographic factor is a lot more important than the Keynesian model would lead us to believe. To begin with, the rate of population growth is very intricately intertwined with the rate of savings, the rate of investment and the capital-output ratio, which are the strategic elements singled out in the model. When you have a high birth rate and rapidly increasing population, it is pretty clear that you must have a high rate of consumption and a low rate of savings. It must imply many large families with a low standard of living and that savings capacity is diminished, probably considerably diminished. Also, when you have simultaneously high birth rates and death rates, as was the case in practically all underdeveloped countries 10 or 15 years ago, is still true in many underdeveloped countries today, and is still true also with underdeveloped countries in general compared with industrial countries, this combination represents a situation which is obviously highly unfavourable to economic development. The average expectancy of life is short, and many children will die before they reach their productive ages. When the death rate is about 10 to 20 per thousand, it follows almost mathematically that half or more of the children will die before they reach the age of 16 or 18 or 20, that is, before they can start to produce or even complete their training. This means automatically that an extremely high proportion of the population will remain only consumers. They cannot become producers, or if they do, they cannot make a full contribution to production or development. They are excess consumers. Of those who start producing, again half or more die long before they have finished their productive life. That, in turn, means that it simply does not pay to give them a lot of training, or invest a lot of money in what might be called 'human investment'. Obviously, when people are often ill and away from work because they suffer from disabling diseases, above all if a high percentage die before they have produced for 40 or 45 years (as practically everybody in the richer countries now can be fairly confident of doing), it does not pay to invest as much in training.

Now these are facts of life that are important to economic development. They are not explicitly included, in fact they are excluded from the model because the model treats only physical capital investment and monetary savings and so on as strategic key factors. It leads us to assume that these factors are independent of demographic connections, since the demographic connections are relegated to a simple negative deduction from total income.

There is an even more fundamental point. The rate of capital investment is singled out in the model as a strategic key value. Yet in any worthwhile sense, the true investment of any country – and the early economists were very well aware of this – is the raising of a new generation who will be the producers of to-morrow. And the real problem of long-term development, surely, is to equip the present generation of children, to feed them, clothe them, house them, educate them, and train them in such a way that they become more efficient producers than their fore-fathers have been. That is the process of economic development in a much more significant sense than the process of physical capital formation. Yet this essential process is not dealt with by the model. The planner who studies the Harrod-Domar model, as all of them are now trained to do, will pay a lot of attention to physical capital accumulation, to capital-output ratios, the formulation and appraisal of projects in order to 'optimize the capital-output ratio' and so on. But the planner of today pays comparatively little attention to the conditions in which the children of the country live and grow up. The first is supposed to be a planning problem. The second is supposed to be a problem that concerns mainly social workers.

My suggestion is that this is a grotesque inversion of the true relative importance of these two problems. The conditions in which the children of a country live and are brought up and prepared for subsequent life as producers, and their life expectancy as producers – all of these are a lot more important and basic as the long-term strategic factors in the development process than physical capital investment. There is one aspect of this which is of fundamental importance and which is only just beginning to be realized. We now know that malnutrition of children between the ages of nine months and two or three years can have permanently handicapping effects, even if subsequently (i.e. after two or three years of age) they are properly fed. And these lasting effects can be mental as well as physical. We also know that the vast majority of children living in underdeveloped countries are in fact undernourished, partly because of poverty and partly because of ignorance and traditional food habits. These children are almost all undernourished not only in terms of calories, but more important in terms of proteins and vitamins. Now if the findings that malnutrition of children can have such permanent effects are correct, this is certainly a subject of key importance. It ought to be a more important problem for planners than the incremental rate of savings, for instance. Yet the neo-Keynesian model is not well designed to draw our attention to these problems, and in actual fact, as a result of their preoccupation and training on the Harrod-Domar model approach, even the planners in the underdeveloped countries are very rarely aware of the true importance of the demographic factor.

The proponents of the Harrod-Domar model are in the habit of replying to such criticism by claiming that the model is very useful in serving as a co-ordinating element to indicate to the planner what sort of information to collect, what to look for. This may be a good argument for the model approach but the model places emphasis on the wrong factor, it gives the planner and the statistician wrong guidance on what information to seek. We find great efforts being made in many countries to compile data on investments and savings, and many claims on the international organizations to give technical assistance through seminars on savings statistics, investment statistics, capital-output ratios and so forth. Yet it is only very rarely that we can get in any developing country reasonable information about the conditions in which the children live. The per capita GNP is completely useless for this purpose because obviously children have a lower average standard of living than the per capita GNP. The great majority of children, almost by definition, are members of large families where the average standard of living or income is lower, probably much lower, than the national average. Secondly, the birth rate usually is in negative correlation with social status, so that the birth rate is higher among poorer people. Thirdly, even if we had accurate data about per capita GNP in families with children, it still would not clarify the conditions in which children live, because it would not tell us how the family income is divided between the adults and children. Is it equally shared? Or do the children enjoy a preferential position as far as food is concerned? Or does all the food go to the breadwinner, the father? We do not know. Probably the last situation is more prevalent than the other two but except for some studies that have been started by UNICEF and which have given us some incomplete information, there is a blank in our knowledge. It is fortunate that UNICEF exists as it has a vested interest in drawing attention to the problems of children. It is not surprising that UNICEF saw quite early the need for a different type of development model and that they financed some statistical investigations about the nutrition of young children, and so forth. So the multiplicity of international organizations creates an opportunity for heretical views in model building to make themselves felt!

3. THE GNP CONCEPT

Let me now jump from the extreme right of the Harrod-Domar formula to the extreme left, which is GNP. Now, is this a useful concept for measuring economic development? Even in advanced countries we know that the concept is much less reliable and much more difficult to measure than enthusiastic national income statisticians tell us.

Even in industrial countries there are large subsistence sectors. The primary subsistence sector is housework. Everywhere a high proportion of a country's population, the housewives, are engaged in productive activities which are not in the market, which are not sold in the market, which have no monetary valuation. Pigou pointed out quite a long time ago that in most countries the national income could be doubled overnight if all men agreed to swap their wives! If you take two people, A and B, who are neighbours, and A hired out his wife as a paid housekeeper to his neighbour B and B hired out his wife as a paid housekeeper to A, of course the national income situation would be transformed overnight, although the level of productivity would not have been affected. Even in industrial countries, people do a great deal for themselves, quite apart from housework. Above all, what I consider in the light of the previous discussion to be the essential development function, namely the education and training of children, is still largely carried out in families, and thus is in the category of unpaid or subsistence work. There is no market mechanism which pays parents for bringing up their children; and there is no element in our income statistics to tell us about this.

In fact, the subsistence element in the richer countries is probably increasing rather than diminishing now. It is noticeable now in the United States and Canada and Europe that with increasing leisure, people do a lot more for themselves than they used to do thirty or forty years ago. To try to get their own car or house into shape is a very important preoccupation of many suburban householders. They spend a lot of time trying to produce a nice garden, or to improve their house, and many of them have a workshop in the basement in which they keep themselves busy building their own Hi-Fi sets and so on. This important element of the richer society, again, is left out of national income statistics.

When we turn to underdeveloped countries, obviously many further doubts arise. The market mechanism is a lot less descriptive of what is going on in the underdeveloped country; it covers even less. Above all, we have subsistence agriculture. Now, theoretically, subsistence agriculture can be included in national income data on a notional basis, but this is a very shaky business statistically – much shakier than the model makers and the planners who use these models are aware of or are willing to admit. We simply do not know what farmers produce for their own use in underdeveloped countries. The data are usually based on sample studies but it is always doubtful whether samples taken in one part of the country, or even one locality, at one point of time in the year, show what is going on in other places even a few miles away, and at other times of the year. Even when there is dependable information on subsistence production one is left with very little. This, by definition, is production that is not marketed. How can one value it? World market prices? Wholesale prices in the capital? Retail prices in the capital? Wholesale or retail prices in the provincial town nearest to it? We could try to calculate actual village prices because something is always being turned over, but the price at which subsistence farmers sell their output locally is not a market phenomenon – it is closely tied up with village institutions and events. The price varies enormously by season; it often includes credit transactions and the crop is often sold to the money-lender. In that case, the crop may be sold at a low price, which really should be called a high rate of interest for the money-lender. The whole business of valuing subsistence production is extremely shaky. And there is a further neglected factor : there is also a lot of subsistence investment. Even if we try to include it notionally, in practice we can never do so satisfactorily. The farmer engages in a lot of self-employment on his farm – and not just to produce food. He builds his house, he repairs it, he repairs his tools, he improves his land, he terraces it, he digs irrigation ditches, he uproots trees, he levels his land, he collects seeds, he engages in community development projects of various kinds and so on. All these are investment activities : part of the real national income, even though there is no market mechanism to record and value it. Yet it is outside the conventional monetary national income calculus. Above all, it is important because it directly vitiates the conventional measure of what the prevailing model singles out as a strategic variable, namely the rate of investment. The rate of investment itself is largely a subsistence phenomenon in underdeveloped countries. This is also the case in developed countries. If our previous proposition is accepted, i.e. that the real investment is the education of the young generation, then even in industrial countries this is very largely on a subsistence basis, and cannot be included in statistics of investment. But in under-developed countries even a lot of *conventional* investments are also on a subsistence basis, and cannot be included.

Perhaps I should make an even more basic criticism. The model is based on the assumption – or at least tends to suggest it – that economic development is a uni-directional, linear affair. This is what I might call a 'unistic' theory of development, where it is assumed that there is one single indicator, the GNP, which gives a satisfactory index of something which we call 'development'. There is one single direction – it either goes up or it goes down or it stays the same. Now my suggestion is – and I think this is also what Myrdal wants to say, although he may not say it in exactly those words – that development is *not* a uni-directional unistic affair. Rather development is multidimensional and certainly dualistic. In each country, we have a modern sector and a traditional sector. This is true of developed and under-developed countries; but we are concerned here with under-developed countries. The modern sector should grow – we must try to make it grow. But the growth of the modern sector, in turn, has an impact on the traditional sector. Now the impact of the modern sector on the traditional sector may be favourable or un-favourable. There may very well be – and not only theoretically – an unfavourable impact. This is what Myrdal calls a *back-wash effect*. Modern industry may be growing, but the growth of the modern sector may destroy traditional employment. Now what have we then? We have an economy with a modern sector that is growing, but at the same time it has growing unemployment, growing distress in the traditional sector, growing destruction of traditional industries. Is this development or is it not develop-ment? This illustrates the fallacy of working with a single indi-cator. If we look at the modern sector alone we can say that we have growth, yet if we look at the traditional sector we may see decay and increasing unemployment. Is this development or not?

I would suggest that it is misleading to pick out GNP, which is largely oriented towards the modern sector, and includes the market transactions, while employment as such is not included in the GNP. Employment is a very vital element in economic development. It is employment which keeps people linked to the growth of their country, makes them participate in its development, keeps them training for future jobs and presumably has value in itself. Employment, just as education and health, is not only an instrument for economic growth, but it is important in itself because it constitutes part of the very purpose of development.

If we adopt a multidimensional or pluralistic or dualistic view of development, whatever we may call it, we have a much more complicated picture. The development task is not just one, i.e. to increase per capita GNP. There are many development tasks to increase the size of the modern sector, but there are also many to improve the situation in the traditional sector whether it diminishes in size or whether it is increasing, and above all to achieve a better integration of the modern traditional sector, to provide some kind of transition by which people in the traditional sector can, in the course of time, become caught up and integrated in the modern sector. One can even have the modern sector growing and the traditional sector growing too, and *still* not get development because the two may grow farther apart with a hopelessly increasing gap between the two which makes it almost impossible for that gap to be bridged in the foreseeable future. It is very questionable whether this can or should be called economic development.

Economic development is a much more complex task, and a single indicator, particularly per capita GNP, strikes me as an utterly inadequate concept to measure what we are after. In any case, we are not only after production. In GNP, 'P' stands for production. Development is a lot more than production. Development is, one might say, growth *plus* change. Changes must occur in the society, even in the economy of a country before we can call it a developing country. Yet what do we see today in many underdeveloped countries in the total picture? Take industrialization – yes, we have industrialization, but what does it mean? We have industrial output increasing at rates of 7 or 8 per cent per annum in the underdeveloped countries; that is pretty good. It is enough to keep the model-builders happy because 7 to 8 per cent growth of industrial production is quite readily compatible with 5 per cent or higher targets of growth in GNP. But what do we find? We find that even with output or capacity increasing by 7 or 8 per cent, employment provided in the modern industrial sector is increasing at the rate of only 2 per cent or $2\frac{1}{2}$ per cent per annum in the total picture. And since the total population of underdeveloped countries is increasing at a similar rate of $2\frac{1}{2}$ or 3 per cent – in some countries even more, at least according to the official data – we also find that in the broad picture the percentage of the total population which is absorbed in modern industry is not increasing; it is often falling. Now this is something new in the history of economic development as we know it from England, from Japan, from Russia, from the United States. These are all different types of economic development which occurred in different periods of time. Yet they all had one thing in common – an increasing proportion of the people becoming engaged in modern industrial employment. That was an essential part of the process of economic development, one of the structural changes by which a society developed from a traditional and agricultural society into what we often call an industrial society. Although it is quite true that at later stages of development the percentage engaged in industry may cease to grow, in the past we have always identified the process of development over certain stages with an increasing share of the total population engaged in industry. We see something now which does not fit this picture. Is this development or not? Again the neo-Keynesian, Harrod-Domar formula tells us nothing about percentages of population engaged in industry. Like all other employment aspects and structural changes this is submerged or thrown out of the picture.

Yet can it be submerged, underneath the surface of 'output'? For again, what is output? The purpose of development is not output. The purpose of development is to produce a better life for people. Output is only a means to an end. It may be a suitable or unsuitable means to that end. Yet when people spend money on better health services, or when they spend money on better nutrition, that is called *consumption*. That is not supposed to be investment, which is treated as developmental and as a strategic key factor. But surely better nutrition is the whole purpose of development. Why on earth would we want to increase output? Presumably so that people can eat better, and otherwise improve their living conditions. So the distinction between 'consumption' and 'development' is quite questionable when one thinks about the purposes and the meaning of development. Secondly, in many underdeveloped countries, we have a situation where better nutrition, or more consumption generally, rather than investment, may be the truly productive factor, even in the strict investment sense. People may be too undernourished to be highly productive as workers. That, again, is a situation completely alien to the Keynesian model – and quite rightly so, because in industrial countries it is legitimate to assume that we can reduce consumption, increase savings, raise incremental savings, increase physical capital investment and so on, without affecting productivity. But in the underdeveloped countries we are making a very big assumption, at least implicitly, in applying a Harrod-Domar model. However if it is a very risky assumption that consumption can be cut without reducing productivity, why should physical investment be singled out as a key variable? Why not the nutrition of the people? Why should consumption, constructive consumption, developmental consumption, which is the purpose of development – why should that not be singled out as the key variable? In many countries, in many conditions, this might be more realistic than singling out physical investment.

Now, of course, those who develop or apply these models can and will say that all this is taken care of by the capital-output ratio. Obviously if people become more productive, this means more output, which in turn means a lower capital-output ratio. That is certainly true in the formal sense. I am not questioning the accuracy of the model. Any model of this structure must be correct. We could equally take the volume of writing pads existing in the economy as a strategic factor in economic growth. We could have a formula which would say that the economic growth rate is equal to the increase in the number of writing pads in the economy divided by the writing pad output ratio. That must always be true, because when we divide it we get output again, which is the left-hand side of the equation. Thus, in the formal sense, we can always say that everything is taken care of by the capital-output ratio, or the writing pad-output ratio, or whatever it may be. But the question under discussion here is not the formal accuracy of the model. It is whether or not the concentration on physical investment as a strategic factor makes sense and whether or not it draws the attention of planners, data collectors, aid donors and those in international organizations who form proposals for international action to the right or wrong areas, in a relevant or an irrelevant direction. My submission is that our minds tend to be pushed in a wrong or irrelevant direction by the model. We are being diverted from things which are really important towards things in the development picture which are of comparatively secondary importance.

If space permitted I would like to say more about the limitations of physical investment as a measure of development. The neo-Keynesian Harrod-Domar approach directs our mind very much toward financing of improved equipment as a key element in economic growth. This, of course, leads directly to an emphasis on aid and the terms of trade. I would be the last to argue against aid, or against better terms of trade as chief factors in international co-operation. These of course are key factors, matters that we can do something about. And I would argue as fervently as anybody else in favour of more aid and more useful aid and better aid, and more constructive trade between the underdeveloped countries and the developed countries. That is not in question. But within the total aid picture, for example, again I would maintain that the emphasis on the fixed-equipment factor tends to divert our attention from the really important things and may misguide us in our aid policy. What we have as a result, to mention only one aspect, is an aid system in which the prevailing method of giving aid is to finance specific projects and to finance only the foreign exchange component within those projects, and within the foreign exchange component only the direct requirements of imported equipment. This is in line with the emphasis of the Harrod-Domar model. But I am very doubtful whether in this way foreign aid really does the best possible job for underdeveloped countries. I believe it would be better if more aid were given not on a project basis, but on a programme basis, or a budgetary basis. I also believe it would be better if more aid were given for financing of local expenses, instead of financing of imported equipment. It would help to lead the underdeveloped countries into giving a lot more emphasis to labour-intensive technologies, to the employment of their own people, and to economies in the import of equipment. And I believe that would be a better approach to development for the underdeveloped countries and for the world, than the present system.

Let me give another illustration of the practical differences to which the two approaches lead. Take irrigation, which is clearly very important, particularly in Asia. Irrigation has two phases. One is the engineering phase, the construction of irrigation work. The other is the agricultural phase, the use of the water, of the secondary irrigation channels bringing water to the fields, and above all the arrangements for telling the farmer how to use the water, and enabling him to produce more and better food with the help of the additional water. The direct output of the project is water, and in most countries the water produced has a market value. So water is a revenue-producing item, and we can measure this contribution of the irrigation project to national income. But the real output of the irrigation project is not water – that is again only an intermediate goal. The real object is to produce more and better food. Yet, when you concentrate your attention on the physical investment, obviously it is concentrated on the engineering aspect. That is where you can bring into play all these appealing techniques of project appraisal that have developed on the basis of the model approach and fit so neatly into the emphasis on capital investment : cost-benefit ratios, capital-output ratios, internal rates of return, and so on. The other part, i.e. taking the water to the farmer and following through into what the farmer does with the water, that is an involvement with nature and with people, not an engineering project. But this is not so easily taught by any present model. It is submerged in the model, and the planners and project formulators and people who make feasibility studies, and the consulting engineers, the designers of the project, the contractors who carry out the projects, the aid givers – they all tend to limit their interest to the engineering aspect. That aspect lends itself easily to standard techniques based on the conventional model. Hence it is not surprising that we find in real life – and the situation just described is partly responsible – that all too many irrigation projects remain monuments. We have the irrigation works, but then there is a failure to follow through. Either the water is not taken to the farmer, or if the water is taken to the farmer it does not result in the increase in production one would expect because no attempts are made to tell the farmer how to use the water properly, either for traditional crops or for new crops. The farmer is not taught to combine the water with complementary inputs like fertilizers, pesticides and so on.

It is rather interesting to consider the one big contribution to progress that everyone is talking about now : hybrid seeds. This is expected to provide a great improvement in agricultural output. I hope it will : at the moment it looks hopeful in quite a number of countries. But let us take note of the fact that hybrid seeds are not physical investment items imported from other countries, which can be fitted into the Harrod-Domar formula. One cannot easily calculate the savings rate that is needed to pay for hybrid seeds, or the capital-output ratio for hybrid seeds. Hybrid seeds are an example of what happens when you *abandon* an imported technology, in this case plant genetics, which was developed for conditions of industrial countries with a temperate climate. Some hybrid seeds were developed with the recognition that the underdeveloped countries are different, because they are tropical and have different farming patterns, and that there was a need to study the specific conditions, climate, supply of water and the farming methods of each country specifically and come up with an indigenous tailor-made new variety of plant specifically adapted to the circumstances of each country. If the hybrid seeds are really the turning point it would be indicative of the importance of tailoring technology to local conditions. In any case, the new hybrid plants are not the result of conventional physical investment, but of Research and Development expenditure (pre-investment) with a rather different type of capital-output ratio.

It would correspond in other fields to substituting local resources, local equipment and local labour in a way specific to the circumstances of each country. This might even require an entirely different type of model for each country, not one generic model for all countries. Under the present system, it is more or less taken for granted that each country will be well served with the type of modern equipment that was developed in the industrial countries, which lends itself to one formula common to all countries and works equally well in Thailand and Kenya and Brazil and India. This corresponds to the idea that the process of development everywhere can be described by one single formula. The two ideas are linked, especially if the uniform technology considered essential is physical equipment of a modern kind. For it then lends itself to the Keynesian concept of investment and to the application of Harrod-Domar type formulae. But if the example of hybrid seeds teaches us anything, it is that the really important contributions to development may come in ways which do not conform to the emphasis of the model.

When it comes to matters of policy and what should be done, there is much less disagreement in what different economists advocate and want. I am certain that this would include both Tinbergen and Myrdal. We are all trying to move towards a new system of international co-operation and to introduce new approaches to development inside the underdeveloped countries. Both on the objectives, and also on the means, there is a broad measure of agreement. But when we discuss matters of economic techniques, there is a good deal of discussion and disagreement. My own view can be summed up by saying first of all that I find it difficult to believe that one single formula or approach can be applicable to all underdeveloped countries. Secondly, if there should be a generally valid and operationally useful model it would have to be of an entirely different type from the neo-Keynesian Harrod-Domar model.

3 The Distribution of Gains between Investing and Borrowing Countries*

HOW THE IMPORTANCE OF FOREIGN TRADE TO
UNDERDEVELOPED COUNTRIES HAS BEEN OBSCURED

International trade is of very considerable importance to under-developed countries, and the benefits which they derive from trade and any variations in their trade affect their national incomes very deeply. The opposite view, which is frequent among economists, namely that trade is less important to the under-developed countries than it is to industrialized countries, may be said to derive from a logical confusion – very easy to slip into – between the absolute amount of foreign trade, which is known to be an increasing function of national income, and the ratio of foreign trade to national income. Foreign trade tends to be proportionately most important when incomes are lowest. Second, fluctuations in the volume and value of foreign trade tend to be proportionately more violent in trade of underdeveloped countries and therefore *a fortiori* also more important in relation to national income. Third, and *a fortissimo*, fluctuations in foreign trade tend to be immensely more important for underdeveloped countries in relation to that small margin of income over subsistence needs which forms the source of capital formation, for which they often depend on export surpluses over consumption goods required from abroad.

In addition to the local confusion mentioned above, the great importance of foreign trade to underdeveloped countries may also

*Originally presented at the December 1949 meeting of the American Economic Association and printed in *American Economic Review, Papers and Proceedings*, vol. 11, no 2, May 1950.

have been obscured by the great discrepancy in the productivity of labour in the underdeveloped countries as between the industries and occupations catering for export and those catering for domestic production. The export industries in underdeveloped countries – metal mines, plantations, etc. – are often highly capital-intensive industries supported by a great deal of imported foreign technology. By contrast, production for domestic use, especially of food and clothing, is often of a very primitive subsistence nature. Thus the economy of the underdeveloped countries often presents the spectacle of a dualistic economic structure : a high-productivity sector producing for export co-existing with a low-productivity sector producing for the domestic market. Employment statistics in underdeveloped countries do not adequately reflect the importance of foreign trade, since the productivity of each person employed in the export sector tends to be a multiple of that of each person employed in the domestic sector. Since, however, employment statistics for underdeveloped countries are notoriously easier to compile than national income statistics, it is again easy to slip from the fact that the proportion of persons employed in export trade is often lower in underdeveloped countries than in industrialized countries to the conclusion that foreign trade is less important to them. This conclusion is fallacious, since it implicitly assumes rough equivalence of productivity in the export and domestic sectors. This equivalence may be safely assumed in the industrialized countries but not in the underdeveloped countries.

A third factor which has contributed to the view that foreign trade is unimportant in underdeveloped countries is the indisputable fact that in many underdeveloped countries there are large self-contained groups which are outside the monetary economy altogether and are therefore not affected by any changes in foreign trade. In industrialized countries, by contrast, it is true that repercussions from changes in foreign trade are more widely spread; but they are also more thinly spread.[1]

THE DRAIN ON THE BENEFITS OF INVESTMENT

The previously mentioned higher productivity of the foreign trade sector in underdeveloped countries might, at first sight, be considered as a cogent argument in favour of the view that foreign trade has been particularly beneficial to underdeveloped countries in raising their general standards of productivity, changing their economies in the direction of a monetary economy, and spreading knowledge of more capital-intensive methods of production and modern technology. That, however, is much less clearly established than might be thought. The question of ownership as well as of opportunity costs enters at this point. The facilities for producing export goods in underdeveloped countries are often foreign-owned as a result of previous investment in these countries. Again we must beware of hasty conclusions. Our first reaction would be to argue that this fact further enhances the importance and benefits of trade to underdeveloped countries, since trade has also led to foreign investment in those countries and has promoted capital formation with its cumulative and multiplier effects. This is also how the matter is looked at in the economic textbooks – certainly those written by nonsocialist economists of the industrialized countries. That view, however, has never been really accepted by the more articulate economists in the underdeveloped countries themselves, not to mention popular opinion in those countries; and it seems to the present writer that there is much more in their view than is allowed for by the economic textbooks.

Can it be possible that we economists have become slaves to the geographers? Could it not be that in many cases the productive facilities for export from underdeveloped countries, which were so largely a result of foreign investment, never became a part of the internal economic structure of those underdeveloped countries themselves except in the purely geographical and physical sense? Economically speaking, they were really an outpost of the economies of the more developed investing countries. The main secondary multiplier effects, which the textbooks tell us to expect from investment, took place not where the investment was physically or geographically located but (to the extent that the results of these investments returned directly home) where the investment came from.[2] I would suggest that if the proper economic test of investment is the multiplier effect in the form of cumulative additions to income, employment, capital, technical knowledge, and growth of external economies, then a good deal of the investment in underdeveloped countries which we used to consider as 'foreign' should in fact be considered as domestic investment on the part of the industrialized countries.

Where the purpose and effect of the investments were to open up new sources of food for the people and for the machines of industrialized countries, we have strictly domestic investment in the relevant economic sense, although for reasons of physical geography, climate, etc., it had to be made overseas. Thus the fact that the opening up of underdeveloped countries for trade has led to or been made possible by foreign investment in those countries does not seem a generally valid proof that this combination has been of particular benefit to those countries. The very differential in productivity between the export sectors and the domestic sectors of the underdeveloped countries, previously mentioned as an indication of the importance of foreign trade to underdeveloped countries, is also itself an indication that the more productive export sectors – often foreign-owned – have not become a real part of the economies of underdeveloped countries.

THE NONPROGRESSIVE NATURE OF TRADITIONAL INVESTMENT

We may go even further. If we apply the principle of opportunity costs to the development of nations, the import of capital into underdeveloped countries for the purpose of making them into providers of food and raw materials for the industrialized countries may have been not only rather ineffective in giving them the normal benefits of investment and trade but positively harmful. The tea plantations of Ceylon, the oil wells of Iran, the copper mines of Chile, and the cocoa industry of the Gold Coast may all be more productive than domestic agriculture in these countries; but they may well be less productive than domestic industries in those countries which might have developed if those countries had not become as specialized as they now are in the export of food and raw materials, thus providing the means of producing manufactured goods elsewhere with superior efficiency. Admittedly, it is a matter of speculation whether, in the absence of such highly specialized 'export' development, any other kind of development would have taken its place. But the possibility

cannot be assumed away. Could it be that the export development has absorbed what little entrepreneurial initiative and
domestic investment there was, and even tempted domestic savings abroad? We must compare, not what is with what was, but
what is with what would have been otherwise – a tantalizingly
inconclusive business. All we can say is that the process of traditional investment taken by itself seems to have been insufficient
to initiate domestic development unless it appeared in the form
of migration of persons.

The principle of specialization along the lines of static comparative advantages has never been generally accepted in the
underdeveloped countries, and it has not even been generally in-
tellectually accepted in the industrialized countries themselves.
Again it is difficult not to feel that there is more to be said on the
subject than most of the textbooks will admit. In the economic
life of a country and in its economic history, a most important
element is the mechanism by which 'one thing leads to another',
and the most important contribution of an industry is not its
immediate product (as is perforce assumed by economists and
statisticians) and not even its effect on other industries and immediate social benefits (thus far economists have been led to go
by Marshall and Pigou) but perhaps beyond this its effect on the
general level of education, skill, way of life, inventiveness, habits,
store of technology, creation of new demand, etc. And this is
perhaps precisely the reason why manufacturing industries are
so universally desired by underdeveloped countries : they provide
the growing points for increased technical knowledge, urban education, and the dynamism and resilience that goes with urban
civilization, as well as the direct Marshallian external economies.
No doubt under different circumstances commerce, farming, and
plantation agriculture have proved capable of being such growing points, but manufacturing industry is unmatched in our
present age.

By specializing on exports of food and raw materials and thus
making the underdeveloped countries further contribute to the
concentration of industry in the already industrialized countries,
foreign trade and the foreign investment which went with it may
have spread present static benefits fairly over both. They may
have had very different effects if we think from the point of

view, not of static comparative advantages, but of the flow of history of a country. Of this latter school of thought the 'infant' argument for protection is but a sickly and often illegitimate offspring.

To summarize, then, the position reached thus far, the specialization of underdeveloped countries on export of food and raw materials to industrialized countries, largely as a result of investment by the latter, has been unfortunate for the underdeveloped countries for two reasons : (1) it removed most of the secondary and cumulative effects of investment from the country in which the investment took place to the investing country; and (2) it diverted the underdeveloped countries into types of activity offering less scope for technical progress, internal and external economies taken by themselves, and withheld from the course of their economic history a central factor of dynamic radiation which has revolutionized society in the industrialized countries. But there is a third factor of perhaps even greater importance which has reduced the benefits to underdeveloped countries of foreign trade-*cum*-investment based on export specialization in food and raw materials. This third factor relates to terms of trade.

It is a matter of historical fact that ever since the seventies the trend of prices has been heavily against sellers of food and raw materials and in favour of the sellers of manufactured articles. The statistics are open to doubt and to objection in detail, but the general story which they tell is unmistakable.[3] What is the meaning of these changing price relations?

THE MEANING OF UNFAVOURABLE PRICE RELATIONS

The possibility that these changing price relations simply reflect changes in the real costs of the manufactured exports of the industrialized countries relative to those of the food and primary materials of the underdeveloped countries can be dismissed. All the evidence is that productivity has increased if anything less fast in the production of food and raw materials, even in the industrialized countries[4] but most certainly in the underdeveloped countries, than has productivity in the manufacturing industries of the industrialized countries. The possibility that changing price relations could merely reflect relative trends in productivity may be considered as disposed of by the very fact that standards of living in industrialized countries (largely governed by productivity in manufacturing industries) have risen demonstrably faster than standards of living in underdeveloped countries (generally governed by productivity in agriculture and primary production) over the last sixty or seventy years. However important foreign trade may be to underdeveloped countries, had deteriorated terms of trade (from the point of view of the underdeveloped countries) reflected relative trends of productivity, this could most assuredly not have failed to show in relative levels of internal real incomes as well.

Dismissing, then, changes in productivity as a governing factor in changing terms of trade, the following explanation presents itself : The fruits of technical progress may be distributed either to producers (in the form of rising incomes) or to consumers (in the form of lower prices). In the case of manufactured commodities produced in more developed countries, the former method, i.e. distribution to producers through higher incomes, was much more important than the second method, while the second method prevailed more in the case of food and raw-material production in the underdeveloped countries. Generalizing, we may say that technical progress in manufacturing industries showed in a rise in incomes, while technical progress in the production of food and raw materials in underdeveloped countries showed in a fall in prices. Now, in the general case, there is no reason why one or the other method should be generally preferable. There may, indeed, be different employment, monetary, or distributive effects of the two methods; but this is not a matter which concerns us in the present argument where we are not concerned with internal income distribution. In a closed economy the general body of producers and the general body of consumers can be considered as identical, and the two methods of distributing the fruits of technical progress appear merely as two formally different ways of increasing real incomes.

When we consider foreign trade, however, the picture is fundamentally changed. The producers and the consumers can no longer be considered as the same body of people. The producers are at home; the consumers are abroad. Rising incomes

c

of home producers to the extent that they are in excess of increased productivity are an absolute burden on the foreign consumer. Even if the rise in the income of home producers is offset by increases in productivity so that prices remain constant or even fall by less than the gain in productivity, this is still a relative burden on foreign consumers, in the sense that they lose part or all of the potential fruits of technical progress in the form of lower prices. On the other hand, where the fruits of technical progress are passed on by reduced prices, the foreign consumer benefits along with the home consumer. Nor can it be said, in view of the notorious inelasticity of demand for primary commodities, that the fall in their relative prices has been compensated by total revenue effects.

Other factors have also contributed to the falling long-term trend of prices of primary products in terms of manufactures, apart from the absence of pressure of producers for higher incomes. Technical progress, while it operates unequivocally in favour of manufactures – since the rise in real incomes generates a more than proportionate increase in the demand for manufactures – has not the same effect on the demand for food and raw materials. In the case of food, demand is not very sensitive to rises in real income, and in the case of raw materials, technical progress in manufacturing actually largely consists of a reduction in the amount of raw materials used per unit of output, which may compensate or even overcompensate the increase in the volume of manufacturing output. This lack of an automatic multiplication in demand, coupled with the low price elasticity of demand for both raw materials and food, results in large price falls, not only cyclical but also structural.

THE END RESULT : MALDISTRIBUTION OF GAINS

Thus it may be said that foreign investment of the traditional type which sought its repayment in the direct stimulation of exports of primary commodities, either to the investing country directly or indirectly through multilateral relations, had its beneficial cumulative effects in the investing country; and the people of the latter, in their capacity as consumers, also enjoyed the fruits of technical progress in the manufacture of primary commodities thus stimulated and at the same time, in their capacity as producers, enjoyed the fruits of technical progress in the production of manufactured commodies. The industrialized countries have had the best of both worlds, both as consumers of primary commodities and as producers of manufactured articles; the underdeveloped countries have had the worst of both worlds, as consumers of manufacturers and as producers of raw materials. This perhaps is the legitimate germ of truth in the charge that foreign investment of the traditional type formed part of a system of 'economic imperialism' and of 'exploitation'.

Even if we disregard the theory of deliberately sinister machinations, there may be legitimate grounds in the arguments set out above for maintaining that the benefits of foreign trade and investment have not been equally shared between the two groups of countries. The capital-exporting countries have received their repayment many times over in the following five forms : (1) possibility of building up exports of manufactures and thus transferring their population from low-productivity occupations to high-productivity occupations; (2) enjoyment of the internal economies of expanded manufacturing industries; (3) enjoyment of the general dynamic impulse radiating from industries in a progressive society; (4) enjoyment of the fruits of technical progress in primary production as main consumers of primary commodities; (5) enjoyment of a contribution from foreign consumers of manufactured articles, representing as it were their contribution to the rising incomes of the producers of manufactured articles.

By contrast, what the underdeveloped countries have to show cannot compare with this formidable list of benefits derived by the industrialized countries from the traditional trade-*cum*-investment system. Perhaps the widespread though inarticulate feeling in the underdeveloped countries that the dice have been loaded against them is not so devoid of foundation after all as the pure theory of exchange might have led one to believe.

It is, of course, true that there are transfer difficulties on the part of the underdeveloped countries which are avoided by production for export directly to the investing countries, but the above analysis may perhaps make a contribution to understanding why this traditional investment system broke down so rapidly and so irreparably in 1929 and 1930. The industrialized countries had already received real repayment from their foreign investments in the five forms described above, and in these ways they may have collected a pretty good return on their investments. When, on top of the returns received in those five forms, they also tried to 'get their money back', they may perhaps have been asking (in the economic though not in the legal sense) for double payment; they may have been trying to get a quart out of a pint bottle.

THE FALSE IMPRESSION OF RECENT CHANGE IN TERMS OF TRADE

There is a fairly widespread impression that this traditional trend towards deteriorating price relations for primary producers has been sharply reversed since prewar days, although this impression is not as strong now as it was in the middle of 1948. Even if we take that point of time, which represents the peak of postwar primary-commodity prices up till now, a detailed analysis does not bear out the impression that terms of trade have significantly improved in favour of the underdeveloped countries since prewar days.[5]

It may be suggested that the impression that price relations have sharply improved for primary producers can be attributed partly to the abnormal composition of primary-commodity imports into the United States, where coffee plays a predominating part (coffee prices have increased particularly heavily in the immediate postwar period), but specially to the widespread idea that foreign trade between underdeveloped countries and industrialized countries is an exchange of the primary commodities of the former for the capital goods of the latter. In fact, among the imports of the underdeveloped countries capital goods do not generally form the largest category, mainly because the import of capital goods from abroad requires a great deal of complementary domestic investment in those countries for which the domestic finance does not exist or is not mobilized.

The major proportion of the imports of the underdeveloped countries is in fact made up of manufactured food (especially in overpopulated underdeveloped countries), textile manufactures, and manufactured consumer goods. The prices of the type of food imported by the underdeveloped countries and, particularly, the prices of textile manufactures have risen so heavily in the immediate postwar period that any advantage which the underdeveloped countries might have enjoyed in the postwar period from favourable prices realized on primary commodities and low prices of capital goods has been wiped out.

A further factor which has contributed to the impression that relative price trends have turned sharply in favour of primary producers since the war is the deterioration in British terms of trade and the publicity which this deterioration has received because of the strategic importance of the British balance of payments in the network of world trade. It should not be forgotten, however, that the changes in British postwar terms of trade do not merely represent *ceteris paribus* price changes but reflect considerable quantum changes; namely an increase in the quantity exported and a decrease in the quantity imported. It may be suggested, perhaps, that these quantum changes rather than underlying price changes account for the adverse trend before devaluation of British terms of trade. Unless it is to be assumed that the elasticity of demand for British exports is infinite, it is obvious that an expansion in the volume of total exports of manufactured goods by almost 100 per cent will be reflected in lower unit prices for British exports; conversely, the reduction in the quantity of British imports is also reflected in higher prices paid than would otherwise have been the case, partly as a reflection of the diminishing bargaining strength of Britain in consequence of lower imports and partly as a necessary political concession to primary producers to enable them to maintain their incomes in the face of lower quantities sold. The supposition that the changed quantity relations in British trade (as well as deliberate colonial development policies) rather than price changes in world markets are largely responsible for the adverse trend in British terms of trade is greatly strengthened by the fact that other Western European exporters of manufactured goods did not seem to experience any deterioration in their terms of trade but, on the contrary, showed improved terms of trade.[6] The effect of quantum changes on British terms of trade is of course difficult to disentangle statistically. It is more in the nature of a gain missed through inability to exploit the postwar sellers' market price-wise to the full. It is surely a remarkable fact that in a world hungry for capital goods and with its two most important direct industrial competitors eliminated, England should have experienced adverse terms of trade in the years 1945 to 1948.

At this point it may be worth noting the curious ambivalent role which price relations in foreign trade play for the under-developed countries. Good prices for their primary commodities, especially if coupled with such a rise in quantities sold as occurs in a boom, give to the underdeveloped countries the necessary means for importing capital goods and financing their own in-dustrial development; yet at the same time they take away the incentive to do so, and investment, both foreign and domestic, is directed into an expansion of primary-commodity production, thus leaving no room for the domestic investment which is the required complement of any import of capital goods. Conversely, when the prices and sales of primary commodities fall off, the desire for industrialization is suddenly sharpened; yet at the same time the means for carrying it out are sharply reduced. Here again it seems that the underdeveloped countries are in danger of falling between two stools: failing to industrialize in a boom because things are as good as they are, and failing to industrialize in a slump because things are as bad as they are.[7] It is no doubt true that failure to utilize high boom export proceeds more deter-minedly for capital formation because of purely temporary price relations shows a deplorable lack of foresight, but this is hardly very apposite criticism of those underdeveloped countries which rely mainly on private development. All private activity tends to be governed by the price relations of the day.

NORTH AMERICA: A STRATEGIC CASE

If our view is accepted (namely that the traditional type of foreign investment as it was known prior to 1929 was 'foreign' only in the geographical sense and not in the relevant economic sense), does it then follow that foreign investment has failed to fulfil one of the functions traditionally ascribed to it (and hoped for from it for the future), i.e. to spread industrialization more widely and more evenly throughout the world? It would be premature to jump to this conclusion. What has been maintained in the preceding part of this argument is that past foreign investment and the type of foreign trade which went with it failed to spread industrialization to the countries in which the investment took place. It may be, however, that for a full understanding of the process we have to consider not merely the investing and the invested countries but a third group of countries as well.

It is an interesting speculation that European investment overseas was the instrument by which industrialization was brought to North America. Roughly speaking, the supplies of food and raw materials pouring into Europe as the result of the investment-*cum*-trade system and the favourable terms of trade engendered by this system enabled Europe to feed, clothe, educate, train, and equip large numbers of emigrants sent overseas, principally to the United States and Canada. Thus the benefits to the investing countries of Europe arising out of the system described above were in turn passed on to the United States – the converse of the Marshall Plan – and were the main foundation of the enormous capital formation the result of which is now to be observed in North America. This 'macroeconomic' analysis is, of course, in no way contradicted by the fact that the individual migrant was motivated by the prospect of raising his standards of living by the transfer.

Attention may be drawn to the interesting statistical computation of Corrado Gini that even the enormous capital stock characteristic of the United States economy is not more than the equivalent of the burden in consumption goods and in such services as health, education, and other provision for the immigrants – a burden which the United States was enabled to save by shifting it to the European mother countries of the immigrants. Perhaps in the final analysis it may be said that the ultimate benefits of the traditional investment-*cum*-trade system were not with the investing countries of Europe but with the new industrial countries of North America.[8]

If this analysis is correct, the industrialization of North America was made possible by the combination of migration and the opening up of underdeveloped overseas countries through European investment and trade. To that extent, Point Four and technical assistance on the part of the United States would be a gesture of historical justice and return of benefits received in the past.

POTENTIAL CONSEQUENCES OF THIS ANALYSIS

Rather than end on a wild historical speculation, it may be useful to summarize the type of economic measures and economic policies which would result from the analysis presented in this paper. The first conclusion would be that in the interest of the underdeveloped countries, of world national income, and perhaps ultimately of the industrialized countries themselves, the purposes of foreign investment and foreign trade ought perhaps to be redefined as producing gradual changes in the structure of comparative advantages and of the comparative endowment of the different countries rather than developing a world trading system based on existing comparative advantages and existing distribution of endowments. This, perhaps, is the real significance of the present movement toward giving technical assistance to underdeveloped countries not necessarily linked with actual trade or investment. The emphasis on technical assistance may be interpreted as a recognition that the present structure of comparative advantages and endowments is not such that it should be considered as a permanent basis for a future international division of labour.

In so far as the underdeveloped countries continue to be the source of food and primary materials and in so far as trade, investment, and technical assistance are working in that direction by expanding primary production, the main requirement of underdeveloped countries would seem to be to provide for some method of income absorption to ensure that the results of technical progress are retained in the underdeveloped countries in a manner analogous to what occurs in the industrialized countries. Perhaps the most important measure required in this field is the reinvestment of profits in the underdeveloped countries themselves, or else the absorption of profits by fiscal measures and their utilization for the finance of economic development, and the absorption of rising productivity in primary production in rising real wages and other real incomes, provided that the increment is utilized for an increase in domestic savings and the growth of markets of a kind suitable for the development of domestic industries. Perhaps this last argument, namely the necessity of some form of domestic absorption of the fruits of technical progress in primary production, provides the rationale for the concern which the underdeveloped countries show for the introduction of progressive social legislation. Higher standards of wages and social welfare, however, are not a highly commendable cure for bad terms of trade except where the increment leads to domestic savings and investment. Where higher wages and social services are prematurely introduced and indiscriminately applied to export and domestic industries, they may in the end turn out to be a retarding factor in economic development and undermine the international bargaining strength of the primary producers. Absorption of the fruits of technical progress in primary production is not enough; what is wanted is absorption for reinvestment.

Finally, the argument put forward in this paper would point the lesson that a flow of international investment into the underdeveloped countries will contribute to their economic development only if it is absorbed into their economic system, i.e. if a good deal of complementary domestic investment is generated and the requisite domestic resources are found.

4 The Distribution of Gains Revisited*

The contents of the preceding chapter were delivered to the American Economic Association late in 1949, some twenty-five years ago. Twenty-five years is a long time for reflection; and, although in the interval I had repeated chances in conference papers, articles and other publications to develop and revise my ideas, perhaps it will not be out of place to set down here some reflections on where and why Singer II (1974) would differ from Singer I (1949). I hope this will not be taken as an unduly schizophrenic exercise.

To begin with, Singer I discussed the problem very largely in terms of different *commodities* and their attributes. Quite specifically, like others of the day,[1] I thought of industrialization as the great saviour, as the escape from the dependency of the primary producer into true development as a producer of manufactured products. The proviso and obstacle towards truly *national* industrialization were seen in the enclave effects associated with foreign investment which Singer I pointed out. What Singer I did not foresee was the possibility that even national industrialization, and even import-substituting industrialization specifically geared to the home market, could take place in a context in which industrialization no less than the development of primary production for exports could become the basis of a continuing self-reinforcing relationship of dependency. With the benefit of hindsight, Singer II thinks that what Singer I failed to take into account was (a) the characteristics of a dominant technology based upon an R & D

* Paper presented to first Inter PAS Conference at the Institute of Development Studies, May 1971. I am grateful to my colleagues Michael Lipton and David Evans for comments.

monopoly of the investing countries; and (b) the structure of centralized decision-making in multinational corporations.

To put the point differently, Singer I assumed the central/ peripheral relationship to reside in the characteristics of different types of *commodities*, i.e. modern manufactures versus primary commodities. Singer II now feels that the essence of the relationship lies in the different types of *countries*. The investing countries are the seats of the multinational corporations, the homes of a modern autonomous appropriate technology, and are economically integrated societies in which the marginal groups are definable minorities (and even they tend to participate in the gains from progress, at least through social welfare). Being all this, the investing country will tend to be the chief gainer from *any* kind of relationship, whether the trade or investment or transfer of technology involves primary commodities or manufactured goods. Vice versa, the 'borrowing' country will not gain, for lack of a modern autonomous appropriate technology, except perhaps for groups which are geographically part of the borrowing country, but are being drawn into the nexus of the investing or dominant country. Singer I dimly outlined such relationships when he wrote about the investing country 'getting the best of both worlds' (as buyer and seller) and the borrowing country 'the worst of both worlds'. However, this again was seen in terms of the differences between factor markets, methods of price formation and the nature of product markets characteristic of primary production and manufacturing industries respectively, rather than in terms of a relationship between two different types of countries.

Although Singer I did explicitly visualize the possibility that foreign investment might be 'positively harmful' to the borrowing country, this was not much more than a wild speculation. Essentially Singer I assumed that foreign investment and the export sector might be 'enclaves', or 'outposts' of the investing country with a lack of interacting multiplier effects or spread effects to the rest of the economy. On his revisit Singer II would put this rather more strongly and more systematically. The interaction between the enclave or outpost and the rest of the economy is not absent – it is there all right and deserves the intensive study which it has recently received. But the interaction is of such a kind as to lead to polarization (or sharpened dualism) within the economies of the borrowing country. Hence it clashes with objectives of national planning and national integration, if these objectives are conceived in terms of reduction of poverty and more equal income distribution. To put the matter in different terms, Singer I felt that the mechanism of international trade *cum* investment was not an efficient engine of growth, because in fact it might be disconnected from the borrowing country and more connected with the industrial or investing country. Singer II now would go further than this : the engine of growth might in fact be effective, but pull the car in an undesirable direction, perhaps towards a precipice and catastrophe; or – an alternative metaphor – the engine of growth might work all right in the sense of taking the car at reasonable or even high speed, but at the same time the exhaust may fill the car with poisonous fumes, killing off the passengers (except perhaps the lucky one who sits at the steering wheel !).

Where Singer II is still rather pleased with Singer I is for the statement that 'economists have tended to become slaves to the geographers'. Of course, this was also a vague statement which could now be elaborated in much more systematic detail. But it did suggest that the geographical entity of 'country A' or 'country B' – beloved of the economic text books and the theory of comparative advantages – was a geographical fiction; and that the proper unit of analysis would be something else. This has become clearer through the rise of the multinational corporations which so clearly take the world as their stage. This has enabled Osvaldo Sunkel and others, in a series of recent books and articles, to base their analysis on systematically and graphically described global systems which cut across the units representing individual geographical countries, and to combine segments from different countries in more relevant systems of dependencies and balances.

Where Singer II on his revisit feels that Singer I failed was in putting the finger on the real source of maldistribution of the gains from progress between different types of countries. This is the nature of modern technology, and specifically the concentration of the power to develop new technology in the advanced countries, where it is naturally (and really unobjectionably) oriented towards solving the problems of the advanced countries by methods appropriate to *their* condition and factor endowment. As in trade, each partner exports and imports according to factor endowment, so in technology – but as distinct from trade, there is no other 'partner' in the present world picture. This goes much deeper than just the development of synthetic substitutes for primary commodities, or the emphasis on raw material-saving (as well as labour-saving) technologies. By submerging the older technologies this one-sided concentration creates a condition both of continued and sharpening technological dependency and of continued and sharpening unemployment and internal inequalities within the developing countries. Since this problem of concentration of technological power is quite particularly clear in the field of manufacturing industry, its disregard was another factor which misled Singer I into believing that the essence of the matter lay in the distinction between the primary commodities and manufactured goods. Singer II now would see salvation not in industrialization, but rather in the building up of indigenous scientific and technological capacities within the developing countries, or other ways of reforming the present system of concentrating R & D on problems and methods irrelevant or harmful to the developing countries. The target must be to bring the objectives of R & D expenditure into line with the distribution of the world's population. Given that, the uneven distribution of gains from trade and investment will begin to look after itself. Failing that, none of the remedies contemplated by Singer I will really work.

The traditional view, of course, is that the factor endowment of a country determines the production mix and at the same time the technology. For the developing country, this means that abundant labour and scarce capital would lead to (a) concentration and specialization on labour-intensive products; and (b) utilization of labour-intensive technology in the dual sense of (i) labour-intensive technology in the overall sense through specialization on labour-intensive products; and further (ii) choice of a labour-intensive technology within the available spectrum of choice for the production of individual commodities. This situation has the happy result for developing countries of tending towards full employment (or at least fuller employment), more equal income distribution, saving of scarce capital and gradual factor price equalization. It is, of course, recognized that the present trade restrictions concerning labour-intensive manufactured products, as well as the heavy tariff barriers against processing of crude commodities in the developing countries[2] prevent this advantageous process from operating in so far as it depends on the international division of labour. However, there is something much more fundamentally wrong with the idea that trade and investment benefit developing countries (as well as developed countries) by bringing into play their factor endowment. The logic of the preceding argument is that in fact we should look at this the other way round : it is the *technology* which imposes constraints and which determines the production mix and the factor endowment, at least in the sense of factor *use*. And since the given technology is *in fact* the 'modern' technology of the developed countries – capital-intensive, raw material-saving and raw material-substituting – this means that *in fact* neither the technology used nor the production mix corresponds to the factor endowment of the developing countries. Unemployment of labour and inequalities due to concentration of scarce capital on 'modern' products result as the natural outcome of this situation. In a sense, growing unemployment and inequality act as equilibrating factors which reconcile the prevailing technology (that of the richer countries) with the factor proportions of the poorer countries.[3]

Another way of putting the same point is that it seems misleading to put so much emphasis on the factor *endowment*. Rather, we should think more of factor *use*. As the unemployment situation and absence of labour-intensive technologies in developing countries indicate, the factor *endowment* as such does not seem to be very effective as a determinant of factor *use*. So, analytically, we propose that it would be more realistic to substitute for the chain : factor endowment – product mix – technology – factor use, the following sequence : technology – factor use – unemployment – unequal income distribution. Singer II would suggest that this change in approach is a deeper explanation of the maldistribution of benefits from trade and investment than the previous emphasis by Singer I on deteriorating terms of trade and foreign trade restrictions.

The previous point, i.e. that on a revisit Singer II would deal more with the characteristics of *countries* rather than the characteristics of specific *commodities*, can be further elaborated. The position of superior technology, and even more the monopoly of determining the direction of technological progress, possessed by the investing countries is but one aspect of their superiority and near monopoly in having access to all the relevant information necessary for discussion and bargaining. Here we clearly have a cumulative process at work. Information, like technology, feeds upon itself. If you do not have enough information to begin with to know where to look for the information that you need, or to know what new information could be assembled, your initial inferiority is bound to be sharpened and perpetuated. And if innovation becomes increasingly complex and difficult to comprehend, the information gap is bound to increase further. This unequal bargaining situation will affect *all* relations between the investing and borrowing countries, whether labelled aid, trade, investment, transfer of technology, technical assistance, or any other. The exception would be aid or technical assistance directed towards equalizing access to information by supplying relevant information to the developing countries, or strengthening their information-gathering capacity.

The finding that one should talk more about countries and less about commodities, is also consistent with the finding by Charles Kindleberger that the data which show a deterioration of terms of trade of primary commodities in relation to manufactured products – on which Singer I laid so much emphasis – really conceals a deterioration of terms of trade of underdeveloped countries, or more generally a deterioration of their position in all their dealings with more developed countries, and that the latter relation is the more significant of the two.[4] Even at that time, in 1957, Singer $I\frac{1}{2}$, as it were, already indicated his regret of having thought too much in terms of commodities and not enough in terms of types of countries.[5]

Another factor which leads to a systematic tendency towards an unequal distribution of benefits from trade and investment may be seen in the chronic foreign exchange shortage of developing countries (excepting the oil countries). Here I think Singer I failed to follow through on the implications of his thesis concerning the deteriorating terms of trade. The condition of foreign exchange shortage, caused by the tendency for lagging export proceeds, would make the typical developing country highly dependent on foreign investment or aid, even for its import-substituting industrialization programme. This is true, whether the 'equilibrium' exchange rate is established or the under-valuation of foreign exchange is dealt with by controls, licensing, etc. This position of dependency will tend to create a situation where the real net export proceeds or real net import savings, even from successful industrialization, will be low and insufficient, *after* allowing for repatriation of profits, dividends, management fees, salaries of expatriate staff, impact of internal transfer pricing by foreign investors, etc. All these factors (transfer pricing particularly clearly) will result in unfavourable terms of trade and other transactions for developing countries generally, in so far as even their exports of manufactured products and their imports of equipment, spares, materials, etc., will be at prices expressing the conveniences of transfer within mutlinational corporations rather than genuine market forces. And indeed, even their home production becomes an 'export' in providing resources for the payment of services real or alleged. The conveniences of transfer within corporations will usually be weighted – in the long-run sense at least – in the direction of taking money out of the developing country rather than vice versa, as a means of reducing taxation, beating controls, repatriating profits for free disposal and especially for new R & D investments. In this way, the export difficulties arising, perhaps initially, from the characteristics of primary commodities or simple manufactures, and their markets, lead to an on-going process in which the foreign exchange difficulties tend to be perpetuated, and the poor terms of trade generalized to *all* dealings between richer and poorer countries. Singer I saw the first link in this chain of events, but not the whole chain itself.

The classical (Ricardian) theory of income distribution, when applied to the international sphere, leads to optimistic conclusions for the developing countries in two respects :

(i) it assumes a tendency towards improvement of terms of trade for primary products as against manufactured products;

(ii) in assuming away technical progress, by postulating a stationary state, it suggests a higher marginal productivity of capital in the developing countries compared with the richer countries in which much capital has already been accumulated. This would lead to rapid capital accumulation in developing countries, equalizing the rate of profits.

The more realistic introduction of technical progress destroys both these favourable conclusions at the same time. Technical progress keeps the marginal productivity of capital in rich countries higher than in poor countries, because it is concentrated in the richer countries and capable of effective application only in them or by them. Moreover, by being specifically oriented towards raw material saving and substitution and thus counteracting the law of diminishing returns, it destroys the basic Ricardian assumption of better terms of trade for primary producers.

The establishment of the concentration of technical progress of a specific kind within richer countries, as *the* basic determinant of the uneven distribution of gains from trade and investment, has led Singer II to a realization that, for purposes of analysis, simple manufactured products (of the type capable of import-substitution in developing countries) share many of the characteristics which Singer I attributed to primary commodities ('unwrought commodities') as against manufactured goods ('wrought commodities'). The previous *dictum* that economists may have become slaves of the geographers, therefore, can perhaps be extended by saying that economists may have become slaves of the chemists analysing the physical nature of various commodities. The current 'product cycle' school in international trade theory has drawn attention to a different (and I think more relevant) principle of distinction. Import substitution shifts the geographical location of manufacturing plants, but the increasing technological dependence arising from the one-sided distribution of technical progress will ensure that the real terms of trade continue to go against the developing countries and in favour of the advanced countries from which the intermediate inputs flow. Where the relationship is that between a multinational corporation and its subsidiary in a developing country, the case is particularly obvious. If the developing country believes that it is developing because of a geographical shift in location of plants to within its own boundaries, this merely shows that the planners and politicians in the developing countries, no less than the economists, have become the slaves of geography. It has often been pointed out that when all the dynamic effects are taken into account, or counting in appropriate factor and market prices, the net marginal social productivity of import substituting production may well be zero or negative. This is but another way of expressing the idea that import-substituting industrialization becomes a part of the deteriorating terms of trade syndrome, rather than an escape route from it. Some kind of export-oriented industrialization might not be an escape, either, as has been shown by the work of Helleiner and others.

Singer I took it for granted that new manufacturing industries would prove to be the 'growing points' of a developing economy, in line with the prevailing 'infant' theory (that was the era of the Marshallian biological metaphor, pre-Rostow pre-space pre-take off!). To stay with the biological metaphor, the new industries turned out to be infants all right, but sired by another man – the developing countries find themselves cuckolded in their infants. And the *recherche de la paternité* leads us to the MNC and the RMT (Rich Man's Technology) as the parents. Singer I called the infant argument an illegitimate offspring – but meant this only in the purely intellectual sense of the genesis of ideas. Singer II would be more inclined to view the infants themselves with a critical eye as to signs of illegitimacy. Moreover, the domestic entrepreneurs and potential entrepreneurs displaced or aborted by MNC/RMT, were not as obviously 'marginal' characters, dinosaurs deserving extinction, as some of us were then inclined to believe. In this respect, Singer II on his revisit is rather pleased with Singer I for clearly having his doubts about the dinosaurs. However, he blamed the genocide of the possibly non-dinosauric potential entrepreneurs on export specialization in primary products rather than on MNC/RMT – induced import-substituting industrialization.

5 Dualism Revisited: a New Approach to the Problems of the Dual Society in Developing Countries*

SUMMARY

Dualism in the sense of persistent and increasing divergencies exists on various levels, internationally in relations between richer and poorer countries, and internally within the developing countries themselves. The following article focuses mainly on the internal dualism and growing inequalities within the developing countries, but links these to growing international inequalities in command over modern science and technology. Tendencies within the field of science and technology, including their increasing capital intensity and their increasing dominance by the needs of the richer countries and lack of direct relevance for the needs of developing countries are closely associated with growing unemployment and under-employment in various forms within the developing countries. More and more the relevant forms of dualistic fission run along the line of employed versus unemployed rather than the more traditional distinctions between rural and urban sectors, traditional versus modern sectors, etc. The tendency for technological developments to produce internal dualism in the underdeveloped countries is further strengthened by a number of factors, including the association of modern technology with foreign investment. The article also considers the argument by Professor Myint that dualism tends to be artificially induced and is due to prejudices in favour of a mistaken concern of

* Originally prepared for the Conference on the Dual Economy held at Glasgow in September 1969.

modernization. The article concludes that the forces making for dualism in the contemporary world are deeply rooted particularly in science and technology, and that much more radical action than a mere redress of discriminatory practices or correction of prejudices will be needed. The limited applicability of western concepts is illustrated by issues arising from the wage and income structure in the developing countries. The better utilization of existing capital is a problem parallel in importance with a more appropriate technology and both together hold out prospects of approaching development problems along more Keynesian lines than is often realized.

A FIRST DEFINITION

Without claiming any refinement of definition, the concept of dualism clearly embraces four key elements : (1) different sets of conditions (of which one can in some meaningful sense be described as 'superior' and the other as 'inferior') coexist in a given space at the same time; (2) this co-existence is chronic and not merely transitional, i.e. it is not simply due to a necessary gradualism creating time lags in the displacement of the 'superior' element by the 'inferior' element; (3) the degrees of superiority or inferiority show no signs of rapidly diminishing – they may be constant or even increasing; (4) the interrelations between the 'superior' and 'inferior' elements, or the lack of interrelations between them, are such that the existence of the superior element does not do much to pull up the inferior element (i.e. a weak 'spread'), or may even positively serve to pull it down ('backwash').

INTERNATIONAL DUALISM : DUALISM IN THE WORLD ECONOMY

When we reflect on this first definition, it becomes strikingly clear that these four elements also are an almost perfect description of the present situation in the world economy.

(1) Uudoubtedly great differences in *per capita* incomes or standards of living, however measured, coexist at the present time between the different countries, continents, races and climatic zones of the world.

(2) These differences are clearly not short-term but chronic. Comparing North-West Europe with say India, they have persisted now for at least a century or more, and compared with Africa for perhaps three or four centuries.

(3) The differences show signs of increasing rather than diminishing. Adopting the somewhat doubtful measure of *per capita* GNP, this increased during the last decade by about 4–5 per cent per annum for the more developed countries (taking East and West together) but only by about 2·5 per cent per annum for the less developed countries. Moreover, within the group of the less developed countries there was a marked tendency for the better-off among them to advance faster than the poorest group, thus satisfying another criterion of dualism within the group of the LDCs. This is in sharp contrast to the more developed countries where the tendency was for the best-off among the developed countries to grow more slowly than the less well-off among the richer countries.

(4) The interrelations between the richer and the poorer countries in the world economy, in the judgement of a number of economists at least, contain elements which make the rapid growth of the former only doubtfully helpful and possibly postively harmful to the development of the latter. Such backwash elements have been seen variously in the following: colonialism, capitalism, export of unsuitable science and technology, brain drain, private foreign investment, one-sided or harmful international division of labour, harmful trade policies, harmful aid policies (or even harm done by the concept of aid itself), creation of élites in poorer countries, unsuitable methods of training for unrealistic professional standards, demonstration effect in luxury consumption, etc. We need only mention the name of Boeke to indicate how from its very introduction into economic thinking the concept of dualism has been interwoven with questions relating to the international relations between rich and poor countries.

It is not surprising, therefore, that the concept of dualism within the underdeveloped countries has been examined by methods of analysis often directly borrowed from international economics. Such concepts as the internal terms of trade, net flows of resources from one sector to the other, internal migration, etc., come to mind in this connection.

The undoubted existence of dualism in the world economy must not be taken too far. Most economists would agree that the high rate of growth and the maintenance of reasonably full employment by the richer countries in the postwar period on balance has been immensely helpful to the poorer countries. It has enabled them to maintain a growth rate of output which is high by historical standards and would, if maintained over a long period of time, improve their situation considerably. However, at the other extreme, very few would now say that the rapid growth of the richer countries, or even a rapid expansion of their trade with the poorer countries if it were associated with it, would be a sufficient as well as necessary condition for their continued or rapid growth. Moreover, and this is more directly relevant to our present purpose, it is at least arguable that the very forces which are set in motion by the rapid growth of the richer countries – specifically the development of ever more sophisticated, costly and capital-intensive technologies, and of mortality-reducing health improvements and disease controls – are such as to create forces within the poorer countries – specifically a population explosion, rising unemployment and inability to develop their own technological capacities, which may in fact assure that they will not have the time needed for the continued maintenance of current growth rates, let alone their acceleration, so as to result in acceptable levels of development.

INTERNATIONAL TECHNOLOGICAL DUALISM

The international dualism in the world economy discussed in the previous section is mirrored in the crucial field of science and technology. Current discussion of dualism has concerned itself increasingly with this aspect, and this paper argues that it is the appropriate point of departure for an understanding of the nature of the problem.

International dualism in science and technology – in the sense of chronic widening inequalities can be seen in the following four dimensions :

(1) The process of scientific and technological advance in all

its stages – basic research, applied research and blueprinting[1] – has been heavily concentrated in the richer countries. The best estimate we can make at the present time is that measuring the distribution of advance by the distribution of inputs in the form of research and development expenditure, we find that 70 per cent of world expenditure is in the US, 25 per cent in Europe, and 2 per cent in the less developed countries.[2] This unequal distribution would not matter if the direction of advance, the scientific and technological priorities and the methods of solving scientific and technological problems, were independent of where the work is carried on. This, however, is patently not the case. The 98 per cent of research and development expenditures in the richer countries are spent on solving the problems which concern the richer countries, according to their own priorities, and on solving these problems by the methods and approaches appropriate to the factor endowment of the richer countries. In both respects – selection of problems and methods of solving them – the interests of the poorer countries would be bound to point in completely different directions. Yet the two-thirds of mankind with its different problems accounts for only 2 per cent of all expenditures – a discrepancy per capita ratio of no less than 100 : 1.

(2) The fact that the richer countries have such a virtual monopoly of research and development expenditures, as concretely expressed in terms of institutions, equipment, number of trained scientists and technologists, as well as a virtual monopoly of deciding where the existing frontiers of knowledge are, has the further consequence that the activities of the small number of institutions and people, represented by the 2 per cent of research and development expenditures in the poorer countries, is also itself largely devoted to the problems and methods determined by the richer countries. Much of the present expenditures of the poorer countries represent a hopeless attempt to compete from an inferior position in solving the same kinds of problems by the same methods, rather than those that would be suggested by their own conditions. In fact, the indigenous scientific and technological capacity of the poorer countries is even insufficient to determine the nature of their own problems and to determine how far they are

susceptible to solution by applied science and technology with appropriate methods.

(3) The existence of the richer countries, with their immensely superior facilities, and the glamour associated with work on their self-defined 'frontiers of knowledge' exert a powerful attraction resulting in the well-known 'brain drain'. Although this brain drain – the external brain drain – has attracted a great deal of attention, in actual fact the diversion of their own effort mentioned in the preceding paragraph – the internal brain drain[3] as we may call it – may in fact be a more serious and dangerous loss.

(4) The traditional remedy for the unequal distribution of research and development expenditures plus the two brain drains is, of course, the transfer of technology in ready-made form. However, this suffers from various difficulties. In the first place the technology is not always available for transfer, often being covered by secrecy, restrictive agreements, legal patent rights, etc. Perhaps underdeveloped countries may obtain this technological knowledge but only at an excessive price which they cannot afford for lack of foreign exchange, or perhaps only in the indirect form of imports of equipment or other commodities embodying the new technology which again possibly they cannot afford for lack of foreign exchange. The alternative of transferring technology as part and parcel of private foreign investment raises problems of its own, as will be seen in the next section. Perhaps most important of all, the transfer of technology may not be useful or even possible unless there is a domestic infrastructure available in the importing underdeveloped country capable of providing the capacity to select, adapt and introduce the appropriate technologies. This domestic capacity, as we have seen, is largely lacking.

FROM INTERNATIONAL TECHNOLOGICAL DUALISM TO INTERNAL DUALISM

This international imbalance, or dualism, in the field of science and technology explains to a large extent why the growth of the underdeveloped countries has not been as fast as one theoretically would expect. Theoretically – and a long line of classical as well as neo-classical economists were convinced of this – one would expect the development job to become progressively easier with the passage of time and the accumulation of knowledge. The late developing country would have an increasingly large stock of available scientific and technological knowledge to draw upon. Thus, the late-comers in development would be at an increasing advantage compared with their predecessors.

Now there is no doubt that the stock of available scientific and technological knowledge is increasing. In fact, it is increasing at an accelerating and unprecedented rate. Moreover, there can be no doubt that up to a point – perhaps we could say up to 1938 – the theory actually worked. The early developers, specific- ally Great Britain and France, developed at a slower rate than say Germany and the US in the second wave. The Scandinavian countries and perhaps Russia and Japan in the third wave developed even faster, and so again did the next wave of Australia, Canada, New Zealand, etc.[4] But in the last few decades one can- not say that this trend has continued or become more pronounced, as one would have expected.

Evidently the accumulation of scientific and technological knowledge has not played the role that was hoped for from it. The chief reason for this is closely related to international dualism : although the total *volume* of available knowledge has rapidly in- creased, at the same time its *composition* has changed so as to become increasingly less relevant for the underdeveloped coun- tries – and this in turn is due to international dualism, the fact that knowledge is accumulated by the richer countries, in the richer countries, and in respect of the problems of the richer countries. These are not the problems or methods of primary concern to the developing countries. The richer countries are mainly interested in sophisticated products, large markets, sophis- ticated[5] production methods requiring large inputs of capital and high levels of skill and management while saving labour and natural raw materials. The poor countries by contrast are much more interested in simple products, simple designs, saving of capi- tal and particularly land, reduction in skill requirements, and production for smaller markets. The potential impact of the in- creasing stock of knowledge – no doubt still very important and on balance useful to developing countries – has been largely offset by a tendency for each unit of this knowledge to become less and less useful to the poorer countries.

So far we have talked about the impact of international dualism in science and technology on the rate of development in the poorer countries. For our present purposes it is also necessary to state why these conditions lead to internal dualism inside the underdeveloped countries, apart from retarding their rate of growth. There are four main reasons which can be distinguished.

(1) Most obviously, since virtually no research and development expenditure is devoted to problems of special concern to the underdeveloped countries, we find that technology tends to be much more up to date in those sectors (typically, modern manufacturing industry) in which the activities in the poorer countries are most similar to those in the richer countries. By contrast, there is little or no technological progress in areas where the problem does not exist in the richer countries (typically, problems of tropical agriculture, problems of small-scale production, problems of utilization of natural raw materials specific to the underdeveloped countries, problems of subsistence farming and of subsistence crops). This will be obviated only by deliberate countervailing international action, e.g. such technical assistance in the field as the work of the Rockefeller and Ford Foundations towards the development of new seeds or the endowment of the Tropical Products Institute by the Ministry of Overseas Development in Britain.[6] Barring such special efforts – at present on a minute scale – the end result will be that agriculture, rural, small-scale production as well as production utilizing indigenous materials and local labour, will be technologically neglected and backward, while technology in industry or in fields otherwise corresponding to the situation in the richer countries (including also modern commercial farming) will be much more advanced.

(2) Since modern technology is imported from abroad by way of transfer, and for lack of an indigenous scientific and technological capacity inside the underdeveloped countries, the imported technology does not take root and is not adapted or sufficiently developed in line with the requirements of the country. This means that where modern technology is used its

use remains limited to the specific area where it has been introduced, but it thus becomes an enclave of modernity. This point
has been well expressed by Professor Stigler by saying that 'the
small economies that imitate us can follow our methods of
doing things this year, but not our methods of changing things
next year; therefore they will be very rigid'.[7] Although Professor Stigler attributes this rigidity more to the absence of a
supporting network of auxiliary industries and educational
facilities in the underdeveloped countries, this lack in turn is
closely related to the lack of an indigenous widespread structure
within the underdeveloped countries which could serve to
propagate the type of improvements required by the local
situation.

(3) The international dualism in technology leads to a situation where the transfer and foreign exchange difficulties are bypassed through modern technology being introduced into the
underdeveloped countries to a high degree as part and parcel
of the process of private foreign investment. In this way, the
whole process becomes internalized within the big international
firms. This arrangement, however, while it certainly helps
to introduce modern technology and obviate some of the consequences of the concentration of innovation in the richer
countries, has other drawbacks for the underdeveloped countries. Quite specifically, through the repatriation of profits and
dividends, a good deal of the reinvestment potential is lost to
the underdeveloped country. Moreover, a foreign firm (and
specially a large transnational company) is not likely to show
any great interest in developing labour-intensive technologies –
the handling of large masses of local labour is notoriously a
difficult, politically touchy and unrewarding job for such
foreign firms. In any case, the foreign firm is expected to pay
'decent wages' – the standard of decency being set with some
reference to the firm's wages to its staff in its home base in the
richer country or to the firm's size and profits – usually resulting in wages at a considerable multiple of average incomes
(and certainly of rural incomes) in the underdeveloped country.
This higher wage would in any case reduce much of the incentive for using local labour and for spending a lot of research
and development money on production methods directed to-

wards that end, even if the managerial and political reluctance to encourage masses of local labour did not exist. Moreover, in so far as the higher wage standards of foreign enterprise tend to spread to indigenous enterprise in the modern sector as well, the discouragement of indigenous labour-using technologies becomes even more general. A foreign firm also will normally have a preference for bringing in its skilled management and skilled personnel from abroad rather than to go through the lengthy process of training local people, particularly when it must assume that its days will be numbered. Management based on the assumption of getting out again or turning over to local management in a limited time will be weighted in the direction of using the known technology developed at its home base and its existing home-based staff rather than spending time and money on the necessarily gradual processes of local adaptation and local training. There is of course a danger of a vicious circle here : the foreign firms which do not develop local links or train local people, because they have only a limited time horizon, may find that the hostility which they thus generate will in fact shorten their days in the underdeveloped country; thus the initial short time horizon will have proved self-justifying. Enlightened foreign enterprise and enlightened governments can collaborate to break this vicious circle by combining confidence in long-term operation with application of development of local technology and local training (or alternatively providing for generous compensation for any expenditures on local research and development and training). But it would be short-sighted to deny that such a vicious circle does exist.

Thus it will be seen that there are many reasons why the association of modern technology with foreign firms may prove to be an obstacle to the spreading of modern technology into the economy of the underdeveloped countries beyond the original investment which will thus tend to remain an 'enclave'.

The need of the poorer countries for a wider spread of appropriate modern technology reveals one aspect of a 'divergence between the global planning of transnational corporations and the national planning of the various host governments' when on the part of the large corporation 'its main loyalty must be to the parent country'.[8]

(4) The fourth reason why international dualism in science and technology leads to internal dualism within the underdeveloped countries is perhaps the most important. This refers to the rising volume of unemployment in its various forms. Basically this is the combined result of a rapid increase in the population and labour force (itself largely a result of the progress of science and technology in the field of health and disease control) on the one hand, and the capital-intensive nature of modern technology with its limited power of penetration, on the other hand. This combination means that the total number of new jobs which can be created in the sectors reached by modern technology is insufficient to cater for the increase in population which cannot be productively absorbed in agriculture through the cultivation of more land. The artificially high wage rates in the modern sector already referred to in the previous paragraph and further buttressed by welfare legislation, trade union pressures, etc., also mean that it becomes quite rational, particularly for the younger people in the underdeveloped countries, to migrate to the towns even on a remote chance of a wage job in the modern sector. Since wage levels in the modern sector may be perhaps two or three times the level of average income on the small family farm – and many of the younger people might not even have the chance of sharing in this average income – it becomes rational to migrate even on a 50 per cent or 33 per cent chance of a job in the town.[9] Moreover, given the high skill differentials, the prospect, however remote, of obtaining further training or experience adds a further inducement, justifying the acceptance of even lesser chances of a present job. Thus the acceptance of even extraordinarily high rates of unemployment – far from being an irrational sociological featue of 'Eastern' society in underdeveloped countries, à la Boeke – becomes completely understandable.

This situation has created an employment crisis in the underdeveloped countries which is probably the most important and dangerous source of dualism in their economies and societies.

On the one hand, we find a small élite of regularly employed people. In sharp contrast with historical experience, the share of the total population and labour force in regular wage earning employment in the modern sector and using modern technology is not increasing in the underdeveloped countries, as it was decidedly doing in all the previous instances of development, from the UK to Japan and Russia. Typically, in an underdeveloped country today, industrial output is increasing at the rate of 7–8 per cent per annum which easily equals or exceeds the historical record of the now developed countries. Employment, however, increases only at the rate of about 3 per cent per annum – and even this may be a statistical exaggeration – hardly more than the increase in the labour force itself. On the other hand, we see an increasing number and an increasing proportion of the total labour force relegated to a marginal existence: either casual employment, intermittent employment, disguised unemployment or open unemployment in the town, or else as a landless farm worker or marginal producer on a small farm in the country.

This is the most dangerous dualism of all. The older discussion of dualism in its various categories – sociological, technological, economic etc. – seems to me to have faded in relevance by not focusing upon the central point, i.e. the employment crisis. This is perhaps understandable because the sharpening of the employment crisis and our realization of the seriousness of the situation are of comparatively recent origin. Professor H. A. Turner in a recent study[10] has found that, in fourteen underdeveloped countries studied, unemployment is increasing at the rate of 8·5 per cent per annum. My own estimate is that the present level of unemployment in the underdeveloped countries on a moderate definition – not of course including low productivity employment except where the disguise of the unemployment is quite transparent – is 25 per cent or so, more or less equivalent to our own experience in the depths of the Great Depression. At that time we would have had no doubt where the source of dualism in our own societies was: it was between the men with work and the men without work. This is the situation in the underdeveloped countries today, except that the situation is statistically concealed since the notion of a 'job' is more complicated in countries where self-employment is dominant. If my estimate of a starting level of 25 per cent and Professor Turner's estimate of an annual rate of increase of 8·5 per cent are both correct, a projection into the future would yield frightening percentages of unemployment: 43 per cent by 1980 and 73 per cent by 1990. No doubt, drastic changes in policy, including the field of science and technology, would become inevitable in the face of such unthinkable exercises in futurology.

In the face of this present situation much of the previous discussion of where the lines of dualism should be drawn seem rather obsolete. Some of the dualistic models or theories contrast the urban and the rural sector; some the industrial and the agricultural sector; some the cash and subsistence sector; some the large-scale and small-scale sector, etc. All these distinctions are relevant for many other purposes, and they all place the activities with a prevalence of capital-intensive technology mainly on one side, with wage employment important, and on the other side activities carried out with little capital and with self-employment vastly predominant. However, in the light of the new situation it seems clear that the line of division does not run cleanly between the rural and urban sectors. Open and disguised unemployment of all types is as rampant in the towns of the underdeveloped countries today as it is in the countryside, and no simple rural/urban dichotomy will do. Similarly, those whom the available supplies of capital and land provide with reasonably full employment are to be found both in the country and in wage employment in the towns. It would not be easy to say whether the urban or rural proportions are generally higher on one side of the division or the other.

DUALISM – NATURAL OR ARTIFICIALLY INDUCED?

Some authors, including Professor Myint, maintain strongly that dualism tends to be artificially induced and is due to discrimination shown by planners and policy makers in the underdeveloped countries, and by aid donors and investors in the richer countries, in favour of a mistaken concept of 'modernization', mistakenly identified with 'capital-intensive' and 'large-scale'. One can comment on this at various levels, in the light of the preceding analysis.

At the most superficial level, one can question whether this alleged discrimination really exists. There are certainly countervailing forces at work which one should also not fail to mention. For instance, surely taxation is much more effective in the case of the urban modern sector, specially perhaps foreign enterprises, while it is very difficult to collect taxes from traditional producers? Surely also, while in the past very often a pro-urban and anti-rural bias existed among the planners, there has now been a considerable swing in the opposite direction? Surely, the policy of high urban wages squeezes the profits of the modern urban producer and helps to maintain the demand for agricultural products and other products from the traditional sector? Surely, while over-valued exchange rates and the tariff policies of developing countries may favour the import of capital at artificially cheap rates, other cases could also be cited where the balance of payments pressures on the developing countries result in general import difficulties which must hit the modern organized sector more severely than the traditional sector centred upon local inputs, and may in fact open up sales possibilities for the traditional sector? Surely, in many underdeveloped countries the social and political pressures arising from mass unemployment are now strong enough to enforce policies in the direction of creating employment by rural and urban public works, building of industrial estates for small-scale producers, etc? Surely, the restrictive trade practices of the richer countries, such as the prohibitively high implicit tariffs on the processing stages, or their protectionist agricultural policies, may also bear as harshly or more harshly upon the development of the modern sector in the developing countries, and in some ways favour the traditional as against the modern sector?

But while at a superficial level one can debate whether the discrimination in favour of the capital-intensive sector is really as clear-cut as it is sometimes presented, at a somewhat deeper level the argument certainly carries much weight. Our own analysis has placed the emphasis on factors which could be defined as 'artificial' or 'discriminatory'. It was pointed out that the scientists and technologists of the developing countries are

themselves trained and conditioned to accept the frontiers of
knowledge as being where they are for the richer countries –
frontiers which may be as far removed from the problems of
the poorer countries as the moon. This point certainly has much
more general validity. It applies not only to the scientists and
technologists but also to the economists, planners, skilled workers,
business men and indeed the general population of the poorer
countries. This used to be known as the 'demonstration effect'. Because the richer countries have come closer to the desired goal of
development, their products, their way of life, their approaches are
considered as superior, and it is forgotten that these approaches,
products and technologies did not spring ready-made from the
head of these various Zeuses, but rather are the end product of
a long and painful development. When these standards are taken
over, dualism results for two reasons : (a) the non-modern sector
is excluded as being unworthy of attention and thus falls farther
and farther behind; and (b) the resources of the poorer countries
– both physical and human – are insufficient to do more than
spread the forces of modernity over more than a limited and
often exogenously controlled part of their economies. Thus, the
discrimination involved in applying a concept of modernization,
based on such a demonstration effect, does go a long way towards
explaining the prevailing dualism.

Yet at an even more searching level one must say that it is not
sufficient to change discrimination in day-to-day policies in order
to avoid dualism. Rather, our analysis is aimed at maintaining
that the forces making for dualism are deep rooted, particularly
so in the field of science and technology. Much more positive
action than a mere redress of discriminatory practices will be
needed before balanced and widespread advance, indigenously
fed and sustained, can permeate the economies of the underdeveloped countries in all their sectors.

Apart from the abandonment of mistaken concepts of modernization, mistakenly identifying progress with physical capital and
with the large-scale unit, a positively new and different concept
will have to be developed. Hence, the insistence in the earlier part
of this paper on the vital necessity of creating an indigenously
based problem-solving capacity in the field of science and technology. If the rising pressure of unemployment enforces on all

D

of us reconsideration of present approaches it may yet turn out to be a blessing in disguise.

DUALISM – DO 'WESTERN' CONCEPTS APPLY?

In Boeke's original introduction of the concept of dualism into development analysis, this was closely linked with the idea that traditional western concepts, and quite specifically conventional western economics, do not apply to the underdeveloped countries particularly not to their traditional sectors. 'East is East and West is West and never the twain shall meet.' Any attempts to modernize the traditional 'eastern' (we would now call them southern) economies by the introduction of western ideas, western techniques or western-trained men only result in difficulties and in sharpening the dual character of their economies.

This viewpoint certainly has fallen into disfavour. Particularly such phenomena as the alleged backward sloping supply curve of labour, whether in agriculture or industry, or the alleged reluctance of the traditional farmer to migrate or accept new ways for raising his crops are fairly widely discredited, and rightly so. Obviously, east and west are in fact meeting in many places and many ways (although not always successfully), and the most ardent desire of the east does seem to be that the west would meet it more frequently and more intimately (although again not always in the same ways that it does now).

Our previous presentation of dualism as arising from the cleavage between the limited sector where modern regular wage employment obtains, and the sector where unemployment or underemployment in its various forms obtains, based on the lopsided nature of technological advance, in some ways serves to vindicate Boeke's position that conventional western concepts should not be applied too directly or uncritically. It was Keynes who demonstrated in 1936 with his General Theory that in a labour surplus condition many familiar and established tenets and relationships have to be re-thought, or even turned upside down. This is even more true in the special type of a labour surplus economy found in the underdeveloped countries of today.

A few illustrations may be given of how some apparently 'universal' economic propositions will have to be modified in the dual economies characterized by labour surpluses. The most obvious illustration can be provided in connection with the very first step in dealing with this unemployment problem. The 'universal' (including Keynesian) answer would be that the cure for unemployment is to create additional jobs by more public investment, more private investment, or by increasing the number of jobs connected with a given unit of investment through labour-intensive technologies, better utilization, etc. Ultimately that may be the answer – but more immediately and within the results of what can realistically be done, the creation of additional jobs may actually increase rather than diminish unemployment. This seemingly paradoxical or 'perverse' result follows directly from the previous explanation of high unemployment rates as arising from a willingness to accept a fractional share or chance of a wage job in exchange for marginal employment in agriculture or in other self-employed traditional occupations. This means that for any actual new job there will be a penumbra or cluster of the workers (larger than one) either actually sharing the job (through under-employment or intermittent employment or disguised under-employment in overstaffing), or sharing the earnings from the job (extended family-kinship-tribal system), or accepting un-employment or disguised unemployment (marginal employment) in view of the imagined chance of a future job. In the frame-work of this model[11] one can quite reasonably say that the creation of additional jobs creates more unemployment because for every available job two or three people are attracted by the prospect of obtaining it. It could be argued that this is not a real net addition to unemployment because the migrants would otherwise be unemployed in other forms either in rural unem-ployment or under-employment or else they would have migrated in any case even without the prospect of an additional job be-cause of the attraction of the city lights, etc. This, however, is not necessarily so, and the Todaro model has a certain degree of realism.

Another economic relationship which looks to us perverse from the point of view of conventional economics, but which may well be true in the specific type of dualistic surplus economies with which we are now dealing, is that an increase in the supply of labour instead of reducing wage and salary levels, has the opposite effect of actually increasing them. Dr Jolly has pointed out that 'when salaries and qualifications are linked directly, increasing the supply may actually raise average remunerations'.[12] The point here is that remunerations are determined not by the functions and requirements of the job actually performed, nor by market forces relating to supply and demand, but rather by the qualifications of the man holding the job. These qualifications may often be needlessly high, or have no relation to the job to be done, as a result of previous standards set by expatriate employees or colonial officials, under different types of administration or job classifications.

In the British-associated developing countries, the piling up of high educational or professional qualifications resulting in high standards of pay, can often be traced to the standards set by professional associations in the UK, for instance the Society of Chartered Accountants, the Institutions of Civil, Mechanical and Electrical Engineers, the Joint Medical Council, the Royal College of Veterinary Surgeons, etc. The high standards set by these institutions – however unnecessary or even harmful in their application to underdeveloped countries – are to a large extent understandable. It must be remembered that under conditions of free Commonwealth migration persons having the required medical/engineering/accounting, etc., qualifications were also entitled to practise in the UK.[13]

Additional training of skilled persons would tend to raise average educational standards, and thus average remuneration, since new trainees are likely to have higher formal qualifications than the existing stock of local jobholders – the first post-independence generation of jobholders. Furthermore, the higher the rate of unemployment, the more would trainees tend to postpone the date of entry into the labour market and pile up additional qualifications instead, thus further increasing the already high average rates of remuneration.

The high differentials in favour of skilled workers observed in the labour surplus underdeveloped countries – much higher differentials than in the richer countries – are conventionally supposed to encourage training and the acquisition of qualifications and thus serve to reduce the differentials to more reasonable proportions. Apart from other doubts on the effect of increasing supply previously discussed, this assumption further fails to take into account that many of the jobs are in the government sector where the present high differentials may often inhibit any further expansion of additional training on the grounds that it would be too expensive to employ the products when trained.[14] Moreover, in the case of governments specifically, but also of firms, the high salaries paid out to the middle and upper levels of their employees may absorb the funds that otherwise would have been available for the training of more people. In these and other ways, the effect of the skill differentials tends to become perverse rather than functional.

Another strand of 'western' theory which has played a long and important role in the development of economic analysis has derived from the idea that labour supplies arising from increases in population excessive in relation to demand for labour must produce something like a constant or subsistence wage level. This idea governs the development model of Ricardo with the proviso that wages, although remaining constant at subsistence level in real terms, would have a rising tendency in terms of wage cost to the industrial producer (as a result of diminishing returns in agriculture); this would exert a squeeze on profits and in the long run result in a slowing of development (the stationary state). In the analysis of Karl Marx, the industrial reserve army (labour surplus) would keep wages constant at or near subsistence level; but the squeeze on profits would be on the profit rate due to competition among producers while total profits would be constantly increased through constant replacement of labour with reproducible capital; this would go on until the situation became so antenably 'dualistic' (as we would now say), with rising unemployment and impoverishment, that the whole system of organizing production would have to be changed. In the work of Arthur Lewis, a much more optimistic turn appears. While also starting from a hypothesis of constant wages due to unlimited supplies of labour, Lewis assumes that the constancy of wages will lead to high and possibly rising rates of profits as the result of technical progress. This will increase capital formation and continuing reinvestment, thus raising the demand for labour and finally exhausting the labour surplus in agriculture. The era of constant wages will then be superseded by one of rising wages;

and the whole process would be accompanied by rising production, rising capital formation and modernization of technology, i.e. development. Moreover, wages, according to Arthur Lewis, while constant, would not be at subsistence level, but would include a differential over and above agriculture incomes – with rates of 30–50 per cent variously mentioned as minimum differentials.

In the light of the present situation in underdeveloped countries with a marked dualism governed by the existence of surplus labour, how does this major stream of western thinking look today? Superficially, facts do not agree at all with the theory. As previously stated, in spite of the existence of surplus labour wage rates in the modern sector are by no means constant but seem to be rising at a smart pace. Moreover, and as a result of such rises, the differential between urban wages and agricultural incomes seems a great deal higher than 30–50 per cent, although statistical comparisons of real agricultural incomes and real urban incomes are notoriously tricky. However, on the analysis presented earlier in this paper, and following the Todaro model logically through, the facts may not be as much in discord with the assumption of constant urban wages as we might think. We should perhaps take as our unit of labour, over which the wage rate for one job has to be divided, not only the person actually and regularly employed, but instead include also the penumbra or cluster of semi-employed or unemployed people connected with each job. If we then divide the going wage rate not by the one person who does the job, but by the number of persons who are either doing the job or hold themselves available to do the job (and who may in fact be directly sharing the earnings of the employed person), then our urban wage rate should be divided not by one but perhaps by two or three. And in that case the wage rate would in fact be pretty close to subsistence, pretty close to rural incomes, and (because of rising unemployment) pretty constant, even in Africa.

Thus, the classical Ricardo/Marx/Lewis analysis is not so much at variance with events as might be superficially thought. But what is happening, although not anticipated by the existing models, is that in fact the family system of self-employment which Boeke emphasized as leading to divergencies between average and marginal product and hence to divergencies for neo-classical marginalism, has in some ways invaded also the modern or urban sector in the underdeveloped countries. This leads to deviations in the allocation of resources away from marginal productivity which are similar to those always known to apply to family farms in a framework of extended family or communal systems.

Where Ricardo does seem to have gone wrong is in his projection – made, of course, for a closed economy – that rising wage costs would exert a squeeze on industrial profits. Wage costs have risen – just as he projected although not for the same reasons – but the squeeze was not on profits. Instead, it was partly on the farmers (this is where the anti-rural bias and discrimination emphasized by Myint and others comes in) and partly at the expense of the workers themselves, namely those not in regular employment. The effect of the squeeze on profits has been obviated by the capital-intensive technologies and by technological progress biased in that direction, both making high wage costs unimportant and acceptable as long as they served to avoid any labour troubles constituting threats to the spreading use of physical capital.

Where the Lewis model seems to have been wrong (at least in the earlier versions of his model), is in the assumption that unemployment and under-employment in its various forms and disguises would remain bottled up in the rural sector while development proceeded. The analysis of this paper, following Todaro, has on the contrary emphasized that in the urban sectors of the underdeveloped countries situations have arisen which are closely similar to and as serious as the structures which used to be associated with overcrowded farming communties on a family and communal basis under conditions of acute land shortage. In the light of this development, the old rural/urban dichotomy is no longer satisfactory as a basis for the analysis of dualism in the underdeveloped countries of today.

SOME FINAL REFLECTIONS

A further conclusion on the basis of the analysis of the type of dualism described here, is that it superimposes an additional type of inequality in income distribution over and above the familiar ones based on the categorization of factors of production or social classes. This additional inequality between the regular wage-earners and fully-employed farmers – i.e. those with sufficient capital and land – on the one hand, and the 'marginal' population of the unemployed and under-employed in town and country on the other hand, is largely dysfunctional. A high share of profits or high professional skill differentials could be justified as serving the functions of increasing the rate of investment and capital formation or encouraging skill formation, although some analysts have expressed doubts about these justifications. By contrast, the inequalities inherent in the cleavage between the fully employed and the marginal population can hardly be said to serve any such purpose. In fact, the fully employed urban group in the under-developed countries is specially privileged in the sense that for historical and sentimental reasons it is still considered to be among the 'economically under-privileged', and as such in need of special protection against exploitation and special consideration in social service legislation, etc. This includes also external support by international trade unionism and international organizations promoting minimum wage legislation in the developing countries. In fact, however, the regularly employed wage-earner represents a comparatively privileged group in his own country by comparison with the broad masses of the population, mainly marginal farmers. The real justification for high minimum wages might be seen in the fact that the benefit of the privileged full employment condition does often in practice not go to the individual employee but is shared by him with unemployed or under-employed relatives, kinsmen or neighbours. In this case, the high minimum wage can be defended as an essential part of the social service system, and the receiver acts more as a social service agent than as an income-earner. In that sense the dysfunctional equality is eliminated and can be *ex post* justified. But this is not the ground on which the minimum wages are proposed.

In the preceding discussion, the main weight of the argument has been upon lopsided development in the field of science and technology. In the short run, however, there is another important factor producing high capital intensity and explaining the heavy incidence of unemployment and under-employment. I refer to the under-utilization of existing capital. It seems paradoxical that in situations and countries in which the shortage of complementary capital is such an obvious obstacle both to the increase in production and to fuller employment of labour, existing capital should be so heavily under-utilized. This is not the place to analyse the reasons in detail. They include an identification of development planning with new investment – symbolized by the Harrod-Domar model with its associated notions of the ICOR;[16] the availability of external aid for new capital investment under the fetish of 'project aid', but not for the utilization of existing capital, thus artificially lowering the apparent costs of new investment from the point of view of the receiving country; the balance of payments difficulties prevalent in the underdeveloped countries which prevent the import of replacements, spare parts, etc.; inexpert management or absence of complementary infrastructure such as transport, etc., which prevents continuing operation at full capacity; failure to exploit the possibilities of shift work, etc. All of these play their role here.

Those who identify the need for new technologies more appropriate to the underdeveloped countries as the fundamental problem in reducing dualism and achieving national integration in the underdeveloped countries, must also feel under an obligation to pay equal attention to the short-run problem of better utilization of existing capital. Although the concept of capacity utilization is statistically as tricky as the concept of employment in the underdeveloped countries, all the available evidence points in the direction of an extremely heavy degree of under-utilization of existing capacity – perhaps as high as the degree of under-utilization of labour. It is a commonplace for development economists to explain that the unemployment problem in the underdeveloped countries is not the Keynesian problem of lack of effective demand, because of the lack of complementary factors and inelasticities of supply. In some respects, however, the situation is much more Keynesian than we would imagine, and the complementary factors which are lacking to make Keynesian solutions relevant may be more in the field of planning policies and aid practices or in the field of entrepreneurship and administration than in inescapable shortages of physical capital. The utilization of existing capital together with the development of more relevant technology holds the key to solving what is presented in this paper as the most important type of dualism in the underdeveloped countries today.

6 Trade Liberalization and Economic Development*

The central objective of this chapter is to direct attention to the employment and income distribution effects both between and within developing countries of trade liberalization measures in international negotiations. This aim involves a departure from the usual analysis of trade policy changes in terms of export and import values or volumes only, and towards selectivity according to local effects within the developing world. Within the overall objective particular attention is focused on the potential benefits of trade liberalization for :

(a) the poorer developing countries;
(b) the poorer groups within all developing countries, and specifically the present unemployed through additional employment creation.

It is clear that the latter two categories may conflict with each other. In benefiting a poor developing country the gains may go to the rich within that country; to multinational corporations operating within that country; or to the government of that country; or to the government of that country through taxes. Vice versa, benefits for a richer or intermediate developing country may benefit a poor region or poor groups.

In spite of these complications, the approach proposed seems better than the simplistic assumption that any pound's worth of extra trade by any developing country, in any commodity, is equally helpful.

* From 'Trade Liberalization, Employment and Income Distribution – a First Approach' by H. W. Singer, with Richard Blackburn, Frank Ellis, Peter Hadji-Ristic, Angus Hone, Percy Selwyn, Nick Stamp, Richard Stanton, Ann Zammit. Institute of Development Studies Discussion Paper No. 31, Oct 1973.

THE CONCEPTUAL FRAMEWORK

The benefits to any developing country from trade liberalization are broadly twofold. These are :

(a) The additional employment and income created by addition *exports*.

This should include both the direct employment effect in the industry concerned, and the indirect effect through local employment linkages. It should also include the multiplier effect resulting from the use made of extra incomes, though this may often be difficult to quantify. In practice an assessment of the direct and linkage employment effects may be the closest approximation achievable.

For convenience we shall term these the primary effects.

(b) The additional employment and income generated through additional *imports*, made possible as a result of the extra foreign exchange made available by the additional exports. These we will term the second round or secondary effects.

In the case of primary effects (additional exports) we may identify four main determinants of whether a particular trade liberalization measure has the desired effect in terms of employment creation and improved income distribution. These determinants relate to certain key distinctions between alternative institutional organizations of trade, and alternative kinds of commodities.

(1) The first distinction relates to alternative forms of organization and ownership of production. It is clear that it will make a considerable difference whether a commodity is produced by a multinational corporation or a domestic enterprise; or (in the case of agricultural commodities) whether it is produced on large plantations or by small farmers. *A priori* one would expect greater benefit to occur when trade liberalization is directed to commodities produced mainly by domestic enterprises, and particularly in industries where there is a high degree of participation by the local population (for example, handicrafts, small farming).

(2) There is a distinction commonly made between 'capital-intensive' and 'labour-intensive' activities. This distinction is

to some extent ambiguous unless it is specified whether direct or total labour requirements (including linkage effects) are included. In general, empirical evidence seems to support the view that there is positive correlation between industries which are relatively labour-intensive in respect of direct employment, and those that remain so when linkages are taken into account. However, this positive correlation is by no means strong enough in most cases for us to be certain that the 'labour-intensive'/'capital-intensive' distinction is very useful for our purposes.

Perhaps a more relevant categorization from the viewpoint of employment potential lies in the distinction between 'resources-based' and 'technology-based' activities. An activity (such as the processing of primary commodities) which requires predominantly local resources of all kinds will have greater linkage and multiplier effects than an activity (such as electronics) which uses the relative abundance of labour only in the production of a commodity for which all other inputs are imported.

(3) A third distinction concerns the role of government in trade. It is clear that the primary effects of trade liberalization will be lessened to a greater or lesser extent depending on the extent to which the tax policy of a particular government is regressive.

On the other hand increased local effects may derive from the use made of the revenues which the government obtains from taxing increased exports and increased imports. Where the additional exports are produced by subsidiaries of foreign firms with 'enclave' aspects, the tax and other revenues of the government may provide the *main* benefit to the local economy, because the direct employment provided is small. This is especially true of some of the mineral and extractive exports, such as oil. Whether such trade expansion benefits the poor and results in additional employment, will depend entirely on the use which the government makes of increased revenue.

(4) Arising out of these latter three distinctions we can arrive at a broad classification of commodities in terms of their employment and linkage potential. In spite of specific examples

where the institutional organization of trade inhibits widespread local effects, increased exports of primary commodities would still seem to be a very worthwhile goal of trade liberalization. Semi-processed and processed primary commodities, and handicrafts, should also receive priority attention as these are resource-based activities. The case for 'modern' manufactures is somewhat less convincing on the basis that these are very often 'technology-based' and may therefore have limited indirect or multiplier consequences.

In regard to the secondary effects (increased imports) the long run effect of increased inflow of foreign exchange and relaxation of foreign exchange constraints upon development, is an analytically controversial matter and one that has proved difficult to quantify in spite of a number of attempts. As with the analysis of increased exports, we may distinguish certain key factors which will determine whether increased foreign exchange will have the desired effect on increasing employment and income. These are (1) the impact of additional foreign exchange on savings and investment; (2) the impact on income distribution; (3) the impact on government resources.

(1) Much depends on whether increased availability of foreign exchange leads to increased local savings and local investment (involving the import mainly of capital goods); or whether it leads to increased consumption (involving the import of consumer goods). In earlier analyses, it was simply assumed that additional foreign exchange inflows were directly added to domestic savings. Subsequently, this view has come under challenge and it was pointed out that additional inflows of foreign resources could reduce the domestic savings rate, either through the destruction of local investment possibilities or through relaxation of government savings and taxation efforts. However, statistical evidence for this view was never very convincing or unmixed and some of the results of quantitative correlations between additional availability of foreign exchange on the one hand, and savings and investment rates on the other, are capable of quite different interpretations.

Moreover, these studies relate to additional foreign exchange availabilities through aid and one might assume that additional foreign exchange which has been *earned* through additional exports is less likely to have a negative effect on local savings and investment rates than foreign exchange obtained through aid.

It has always been recognized that inflows of additional foreign exchange would increase rather than reduce savings and local investment in developing countries where the relevant constraint is a foreign exchange bottleneck. Empirical evidence suggests that in about half the developing countries foreign exchange, rather than domestic savings, is the operationally significant constraint.[1] For our own analysis this would imply that the additional import capacity resulting from trade liberalization for those countries would further add to the employment created directly and through linkages and multipliers, in producing additional exports.

It has recently been shown in a study of twenty developing countries that additional foreign exchange inflow will lead to more investment rather than more consumption where it leads to exchange appreciation and/or relaxation of import barriers by developing countries. It is less likely in countries where the inflow of foreign exchange leads to expenditure – increasing fiscal and monetary policies (expansion of government expenditure and bank credit), 'in particular where expansion of bank credit is the main adjustment tool'.[2] These results appear intuitively plausible. The degree of additional long-term growth of employment due to relaxation of foreign exchange constraints would seem to depend largely on the mechanism of adjustment in the various benefiting developing countries.

(2) The impact of additional imports on income distribution is more difficult to analyse. Additional foreign exchange available for imports may in the nature of things largely accrue to the higher income groups who have access to foreign exchange allocations and have a demand for foreign exchange. The easier availability of foreign exchange may also lead to more capital-intensive techniques than would otherwise have been used, thus reducing the impact on employment and leading to more unequal income distribution.

(3) The impact on government resources is less equivocal. Both the increased exports as well as the additional foreign

exchange obtainable for imports give the government greatly strengthened opportunities to raise revenue. Traditionally and administratively, exports and imports offer better bases for tax collection by the government than domestic production. The allocation of foreign exchange (sometimes at over-valued domestic exchange rates) offers additional opportunities for government revenue. If we assume that the government has an effective and beneficial income distribution policy, the effect of increased government revenue would work in the direction of better employment, better income distribution, and more development.

The general failure of quantitative studies and analytical discussions, to make explicit allowance for the increased import capacity of developing countries arising from trade liberalization has some justification. When we try to measure the indirect and multiplier effects from increased exports in addition to the direct employment provided, a main factor which sets limits to such effects is in fact a 'leakage' into imports. It is precisely because the additional output requires inputs from abroad, and because the increased incomes due to increased employment result in increased demand for imported consumption goods that the degree of indirect employment creation of all sorts is limited. In this way it can be argued that the increased import capacity resulting from expansion of exports is already absorbed in providing the inputs for the production of the additional export goods, and to satisfy the increased demand arising from increased incomes. Indeed the direct impact of additional imports may be to *reduce* employment rather than to increase it. This is what we assume to be the immediate impact on rich countries of additional imports from developing countries though this effect can be compensated for in rich countries by internal adjustments within the framework of a full employment policy. In developing countries such compensation can rarely be achieved. Additional imports by developing countries *can* have a seriously destructive effect on employment and income distribution if the imports consist of goods competing with products of local industry and agriculture, and particularly where these competing local goods are produced with simple labour-intensive techniques.

Nevertheless, in our view there is a specific restraint due to foreign exchange shortage in a large number of developing countries, and additional foreign exchange could be made to be complementary with domestic resources given the right kind of policies. When we hypothesize that the additional imports *add* to employment, we assume in fact that they consist of developmental inputs (intermediate goods, raw materials) required to activate latent local resources and to increase the pace of development. In other words we assume that the additional imports are complementary to, rather than competitive with local resources.

The interrelationships between these various effects of trade liberalization are summarized in the following diagram.

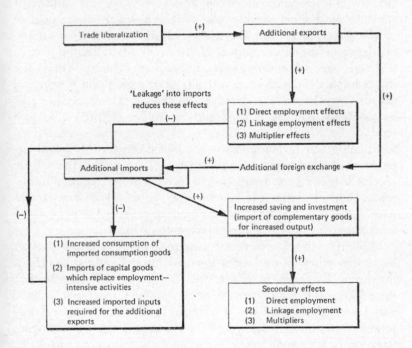

All those who have studied these matters either analytically or quantitatively, seem to agree that the *direct* employment and income effects of producing additional exports are only a part, and often a comparatively small part, of the total benefits overall. This is certainly true wherever the nature of the exports concerned prevents production from being of the 'enclave' type and where the removal of foreign exchange bottlenecks is important for the growth rate and development of the country. Even disregarding the effect of additional imports, one observer after detailed quantitative studies assumes a domestic multiplier (including what we have called linkages) of 3 : 1.[3]

This means that if trade concessions are selected so that the direct production of the additional exports benefits poorer sections (perhaps small farmers or a less developed region of a developing country), care must be taken to trace what happens to the bulk of the benefits – through linkages, multipliers and the use of enlarged import capacity. Both the magnitude and incidence of these indirect effects and even more the impact of the enlarged import capacity will depend as much on the policies of the government and the nature of the economy, as on the incidence of the direct impact of the trade liberalization.

There are, of course, some qualifying factors. Where the direct impact is mainly in a specially poor region of a developing country (say North-East Brazil or North-East Thailand), it might be assumed that the linkage and multiplier effects would also tend to be weighted in favour of that particular region. Unfortunately this presumption is not borne out by the actual experience of poor regions in many parts of the world. Indeed the reverse is true : poor areas tend to have very low regional multipliers. And of course the benefits may go to the richer sections within the poor region – for instance, as a result of patterns of land ownership and local control of production.

Similarly, when the direct benefits go to poorer sections through being concentrated on labour-intensive products thus creating a maximum employment effect, one might generally assume that the additional demand created, being exercised by poorer groups, will be more oriented towards other local, simple and labour-intensive products[4] than would be the case if the direct impact were on richer producers or on more capital-intensive products. But here again the general assumption must be subject to modification depending upon the nature of the economy, and the nature of the government and its policies.

Hence, in both cases only direct study of concrete cases could assure that the desired selectivity is attained.

A SUMMARY OF EVIDENCE

Economists are divided as to the overall importance of trade expansion in helping to solve problems of unemployment, and related problems of income distribution and poverty in the developing countries. On a purely aggregative and static approach, a general assumption must be that the impact could be considerable. The view has been intuitively expressed that the sustained fall in the share of developing countries in total world trade could account for a significant part of the typical unemployment and under-employment rates in the region of 25 per cent in many developing countries.[5] This view, which is indeed the natural corollary of considering trade as the chief engine of growth, was described as 'startling', but has since been supported by more quantitative analysis.[6]

Tyler estimates that the drop in the share of developing countries in total world trade between 1955 and 1970 has been equivalent to the loss of about 72 million additional jobs, or 14·5 per cent of the total 1970 labour force.[7] In arriving at this estimate he assumed a certain cost per job as a basis for estimating direct employment creation, and he estimated a multiplier effect of 3 : 1 (including what we defined as linkages). Both figures are based on his own detailed quantitative studies. Even these figures may be an underestimate since he does not expressly allow for the removal of foreign exchange bottlenecks and the impact of aditional imports. Even so, 14·5 per cent of the labour force would be more than half of an estimated 25 per cent under-employment rate.

A similar estimate can be arrived at as follows. Total exports of developing countries at $55·4 billion in 1970 were about 16 per cent of their estimated aggregate GNP of $354 billion.[8] A 15 per cent increase in their total exports would therefore add about 2·4 per cent to their total GNP directly, and 7·2 per cent if we assume Tyler's multiplier of 3. If the developing countries had maintained their 1955 share in world trade their exports in 1970 would have been 43 per cent higher than was actually the case which would have involved a total expansion of GNP by 6·9 per cent directly, or 20·7 per cent including Tyler's multiplier effects. If employment had increased in proportion to the expansion of GNP this would have accounted for the bulk of the employment problem on the 25 per cent estimate. Even the more modest assumption of a 15 per cent increase in exports would have quite a sizeable impact, equal to almost one-third of the total problem.

It is accepted that the assumption that employment would increase *pari passu* with output and GNP is only a rough and ready one. However, one can think of as many reasons why employment should increase more than proportionately as there are reasons to the contrary. The first group of reasons in favour would be based on the assumption that the developing countries should have a comparative advantage in exporting relatively more labour-intensive products, and that their main loss of share in world trade between 1955 and 1970 has been in agricultural products which are more labour-intensive than manufactures. In manufactures the developing countries have more or less held their own. On the other side, one should also take into account that the most labour-intensive sectors, i.e. subsistence agriculture, services, rural handicrafts and the urban informal sector do not normally participate in export activities. The case for assuming a proportionate increase in employment seems therefore broadly justified.

Similarly, the FAO on the basis of a world trading model has estimated that the removal of all agricultural protection alone would raise the national incomes of the LDCs by close to 6 per cent.[9] Since the capital/labour ratio in agriculture is much below the average, the corresponding increase in employment should be more than 6 per cent. Again, this would make a very substantial contribution to the solution of the developing country employment problem.

But this conclusion, that trade expansion could play a very important role in employment creation, does not necessarily hold when applied to the expansion of manufactured exports only. Manufactured exports still only represent some 20 per cent or so of the total exports of developing countries. Moreover a proportion of them represents exports of international corporations with limited linkage or multiplier effects; and some of the manufactured exports are necessarily of a fairly capital-intensive nature. Empirical study has confirmed[10] what seems evident from this qualitative statement, i.e. that the rates of expansion of manufactured exports alone would have to be unrealistically high before they could become a major answer to the unemployment problem.

For every job which is being lost in a rich importing country as a result of shifting production to a developing country in the form of liberalized imports, it can be assumed that more than one job is being created in the developing country concerned. This is simply the result of labour intensity of production being greater in developing countries than in rich countries. The impact of trade liberalization on employment is not a zero-sum game. Even the direct employment loss in the rich countries and the direct employment gain in the poor countries as a result of trade liberalization is a gain in employment rather than a simple shift.

The preliminary results of a major study in this area would seem to indicate that the correlation between employment intensity in the production of given commodities and the size of *per capita* GNP is in fact quite significant.[11] Thus, for manufactured commodities the displacement of one employee in the EEC by additional imports from the development countries may be estimated to result in additional employment for as many as three employees in a developing country with a *per capita* GDP of $50, and as many as almost five employees for very poor developing countries with *per capita* GDPs of around $100.

In the case of agricultural commodities the difference in employment intensity as between rich countries and developing countries would generally be expected to be even greater since the gap in labour productivity between agriculture and manufacturing industry tends to be more pronounced in developing countries.

NEGLECT OF DEVELOPING COUNTRIES' INTERESTS IN
DEVELOPED COUNTRY TRADE POLICIES

(1) *The Kennedy Round*
The Kennedy Round achieved fewer and smaller reductions for resource-based processed commodities than it did in general for manufactures. In particular little was achieved for processed

primary commodities which are of special interest to developing countries.

In many cases it seems a logical step for a developing country to include in its development strategy the processing of an exported primary commodity with a high domestic employment linkage. This can serve the dual purpose of increasing foreign exchange earnings and adding to the employment potential of a particular sector. However, this step is often denied developing countries because effective rates of protection on such products are notoriously high. The nominal tariff on a processed product is typically much higher than the corresponding tariff on the raw material from which it is derived – a consequence of developed country protection of their own processing industries. The failure of the Kennedy Round to make equivalent reductions on processed products has resulted in an increase in the ratio of effective to nominal tariffs, making it even more difficult for developing countries to contemplate moving into the processing stage. Fifteen to twenty per cent nominal and 30–40 per cent effective would be fairly typical figures – and this does not include nontariff barriers.

Even in 1964, before the Kennedy Round, the weighted average of effective tariffs in industrial countries on imports from developing countries[12] escalated from 22·6 per cent for processing Stage II to 29·7 per cent for Stage III and 38·4 per cent for Stage IV of fabrication – compared with only 4·6 per cent for Stage I (primary). Both the nominal and effective rates of protection for imports of manufactures were much higher for developing countries – 17·1 per cent and 33·4 per cent respectively than for other industrial countries – 12·3 per cent and 21·7 per cent respectively. It will be noted that not only the level but also the degree of escalation was greater for imports from developing countries.[13]

According to UNCTAD calculations, the Kennedy Round reduced average tariff rates by 21 per cent for products of interest to developing countries but by 39 per cent for other products.

The House of Commons Select Committee on Overseas Development has, therefore, specifically recommended that negotiations in the forthcoming GATT Round should pay special attention to reductions in MFN rates of duty on products in which the developing countries have a strong export interest. In the light of the preceding discussion, such an emphasis is indeed needed, if only to compensate for the opposite emphasis in the Kennedy Round and other arrangements so far.

The fact that products in which rich countries dominate world trade have received larger cuts in the Kennedy Round than other products,[14] is given further significance for employment in developing countries by the natural association between items for which developed countries dominate world trade and items produced by high-level technology and characterized by high capital intensity.[15]

(2) *The European Community's generalized system of preferences*

The generalized preference scheme, apart from its other weaknesses, operates against an emphasis on employment in the poorer countries in a variety of ways. In the first place, agricultural products are hardly covered : only to the extent of 5 per cent of all dutiable agricultural imports. Manufactured goods are somewhat more widely covered, although even there the share is only about one-third of dutiable imports. Since it is the poorer countries which rely more on agricultural exports, and since agricultural products are more employment-intensive and benefit rural and poorer producers, this feature of the GSP should be modified if a greater impact of trade upon employment is sought. Within manufactured goods the coverage of processed and semi-manufactured goods is less than that of fully manufactured goods, adding further to the bias against poorer countries and more labour-intensive exports. This is superimposed on the tendency inherent in any preference scheme of the EEC type – with tariff ceilings, country quotas, etc. – to operate against the latecomers (again normally the poorer developing countries). Moreover, the uncertainty about the duration of the schemes and the operation of the escape and disruption clauses further handicap countries where the supply of the exports would have to be newly developed. The extreme limitation and concentration of the benefits of the GSP on a few semi-developed countries has been amply documented.[16]

It would certainly be necessary to liberalize and extend the GSP, to relax and regularize the safeguards procedures, and to protect the scheme from erosion arising from further liberalization of trade among rich countries, before it became a serious weapon against poverty and unemployment in the developing countries.

(3) *Agricultural protection*

It is not only integration – EEC and all that – and trade liberalization among the rich trading nations which in effect militate against developing countries. The other major causes are, of course, the protectionist agricultural policies pursued by all the rich countries, culminating in the Common Agricultural Policy of the EEC. Here not only the policies themselves – with total public expenditures on agricultural support by rich countries increasing at the rate of 10 per cent per annum during the past decade – but also the method of agricultural protection (particularly the spread of price support instead of income deficiency payments) seem designed to impose increasing burdens on the poorer developing countries and the poor producers within all developing countries, depending as they do on agricultural production and exports. And as a final twist, a disproportionate part of the barriers in the way of agricultural trade is of the non-tariff variety.

Non-tariff barriers (NTBs) are notoriously very difficult to deal with by the poorer developing countries. Over 40 per cent of all items in the food and beverages group face such NTB handicaps, as distinct from 28 per cent for all developing countries' exports and only 11 per cent of all world exports. The escalation involved in these figures is again directly counter-productive to the reduction of developing countries' poverty. It should be eliminated and, if possible, reversed. It seems well established as a general observation that NTBs are inherently more complex and more difficult to deal with than 'straight' tariffs. This again places the developing countries at a handicap with their richer competitors, and the poorer developing countries at a handicap compared with those better equipped to deal with such complexities, and better connected internationally. Health regulations concerning meat and other food may serve as an example, whether genuine or used as a protective device.

All these preceding points – to which many more could be

added – have not been made for the purpose of lamenting the inequities of the world trading system for developing countries, but in order to show that the reduction in the share of world trade falling to the developing countries has not been due only to inevitable natural or structural reasons, nor to the policies of the developing countries alone, but that it is closely associated with the trade policies of the rich countries. The value of any preference is eroded through the extension of free trade areas, and the continuing success of developing countries in liberalizing trade between themselves. It is difficult to avoid the conclusion that the very bargaining system, under which negotiations take place bilaterally with 'principal supplies' and concessions are subsequently extended through most favoured nation treatment to other countries, introduces a systematic tendency to neglect items of special interest to developing countries. Developing countries will rarely be 'principal suppliers'.

These matters should be capable of being dealt with in the coming international trade negotiations. Indeed, if we are seriously concerned with employment and poverty in developing countries as a major world problem, these matters would seem to deserve a high place on the agenda.

POLICY IMPLICATIONS

(1) *Agricultural and processed primary commodities*
One general rule or presumption might be that overall trade liberalization in respect of agricultural products and processing of agricultural products would tend to do more to benefit poor countries and poor people within countries than concessions in relation to modern manufactured products. This is so because :

(a) rural producers are poorer than urban producers;
(b) poorer countries have less manufacturing and more primary exports than better-off developing countries;
(c) manufacturing production in developing countries tends to benefit more foreign investors who expatriate their profits and where linkage effects may be smaller, while primary producers tend to be nationals with less expatriation, more local linkage, etc.

Naturally there are many expectations to this overall rule; primary producers may be foreign-owned plantations, manufacturing producers may be small-scale nationals or public enterprises. However, in the broad sweep – the kind of broad sweep which may be necessary in approaches to generalized trade negotiations – the rule could be supported. Taken together with the fact that present trade restrictions seem overall more severe in the case of primary products and particularly in the case of processed commodities and semi-manufactures, this represents a strong argument for focusing attention in the trade negotiations upon agricultural and processed primary commodities (as well as on the removal of non-tariff barriers).

All the available quantitative studies have shown particularly strong linkage and employment effects from the processing and fabrication of a country's own primary commodities. Even where the processing stage itself is capital-intensive, the indirect effect on employment when the production of the primary input is taken into account has invariably been to convert the process into a highly labour-intensive one. There is, admittedly, a statistical problem involved which in quantitative studies may tend to exaggerate the effect due to such linkages : when the additional exports of processed or semi-manufactured goods take the place of previous exports of the primary commodity in unprocessed form, the *additional* employment effect is limited to the direct effect due to processing plus such other inputs as are directly attributable to the processing stage as such.

In concrete cases it may not always be easy to determine to what extent the processed export would take the place of the raw product or be additional to it. But it is certain that the bias against processing in developing countries through the escalation of effective tariffs is harmful to employment. It is also harmful to income distribution in developing countries. Processing often takes place in a rural environment, particularly when it has to be physically contiguous with the production of the primary commodity. In other words, the prevention of processing in developing countries is often harmful to rural development which one wishes to see promoted for the sake both of employment and more equal income distribution. 'Primary processing industries may be more important for rural development than simple farm development.'[17]

It has also been suggested by Angus Hone that by offering free entry to all developing countries for handicraft products, leather products and floor-coverings, much of the benefit would go to the poorest or least developed countries.

The rise in primary commodity prices has possibly made multinational corporations and other processors and fabricators in rich countries more inclined to leave processing to be done in the developing countries. This is because primary commodity prices now form a higher part of the combined price of the product, and also conceivably because processing margins are squeezed between higher commodity prices and competition or price controls on the finished manufactures. In addition, the developing countries may be readier in a seller's market to withhold the raw product from the market and offer only the processed product. These, however, are long-run speculations based on the assumption of a continuation and perpetuation of the present boom in primary commodity prices. They would hardly constitute an argument against doing what the Kennedy Round failed to do, i.e. to concentrate on a reduction of the escalation in effective rates of protection against processing and semi-manufacturing within developing countries as a priority objective for the coming international trade negotiations. In any case, the effect of higher commodity prices on the location of processing under present trade rules is by no means clear.

(2) *Special problems of the least developed countries*

For the purposes of this study, we define the least developed countries as those which combine very low incomes per head with low levels of industrial production and export. This is not a clear-cut group; it would include the 25 countries in the UN's list of 'hard-core' least developed countries, but it would also include others. An accurate definition is, however, unnecessary if we recognize that there are *some* poor countries which have scarcely begun the process of industrialization and whose earnings from primary production are very low. For such countries, access to foreign markets may not be a central problem; internal structural problems and a lack of resources may be more immediately relevant. But questions of market access are likely to be an important element in any policies designed to raise income levels and promote structural change.

The Third Session of UNCTAD *unanimously* adopted a resolution[18] on special measures in favour of the least developed countries. The main elements of the resolution in the context of the present study were as follows :

(a) Efforts should be made to initiate and accelerate the elimination or reduction of revenue duties and other specific fiscal charges on the consumption of tropical products of special interest to the least developed countries. (These would be principally coffee and tea.)

(b) Developed countries should undertake, in so far as possible, to avoid domestic support policies which might adversely affect the interest of the least developed countries. (The product most affected under this heading is beef.)

(c) Developed countries should make their best efforts urgently to reduce and progressively to eliminate quantitative restrictions and other non-tariff barriers affecting trade in processed and semi-processed products of the least developed countries.

(d) Special consideration will be given, in the review of the GSP, to the possibility of extending it for a long enough period to permit the least developed countries to derive equitable benefits from it.

(e) The GSP should include processed and semi-processed agricultural and mineral and handicraft products of export interest to the least developed countries.

(f) Escape clause measures introduced by preference-giving countries should remain exceptional, and should be decided on only after due account has been taken, in so far as their legal provisions permit, of the interest of the least developed countries.

The resolution also recognized that trade measures per se would be insufficient to increase substantially the least developed countries' export earnings, and complementary proposals for financial and technical assistance were included.

This resolution is broadly in line with our own proposals, except in so far as we consider that a general reduction in levels of effective protection on processed goods and simple manufactures would be of substantial benefit to such countries.

The EEC supported this resolution; the forthcoming GATT negotiations would appear to be a suitable opportunity for putting it into practice.

It is possible to rank traded commodities according to degree of poverty of the exporting country, based either on actual exports for some recent data or on projections of potential export expansion (when such projections are made in quantitative terms). Such exercises can be made with varying statistical techniques and varying degrees of sophistication. The results can be suggestive as a general first indication as to what commodities are most likely to deserve special weighting for trade liberalization on grounds of being of special interest to the poorest developing countries.

An UNCTAD study[19] lists the following 12 commodities in which the share of the 25 countries designated by the UN as least developed exceeds 10 per cent. The commodities are listed in descending order of the share of the least developed countries: Fur skins (48%), dried fruits (41%), zoo animals, pets (31%), cotton (20%), live animals (19%), cheese and curd (18%), crude vegetable materials (17%), oil seeds, nuts and kernels (16%), vegetable fibres other than cotton or jute (16%), undressed hides and skins (14%), natural and manufactured gas (14%), fuel wood and charcoal (13%). Free and unhindered access in these commodities would benefit the least developed countries in a disproportionate degree.

(3) *Measures in addition to trade liberalization*

One problem arising is the limited capacity of the developing countries generally, and of the poorer of the developing countries specifically, to take advantage of trade liberalization opportunities. In other words, supply constraints may reduce or prevent benefits even when demand constraints are removed. If, therefore, we want to concentrate benefits from trade liberalizations upon the poorer developing countries, supplementary measures to reduce supply constraints may be necessary. Such possible measures could include the following:

(a) Special guaranteed long-term market access for those

countries, i.e. renunciation of escape clauses, tying of low tariffs or zero tariffs for longer periods of time.

(b) Specific assistance with export promotion such as is already tentatively given – but not specifically tied to trade liberalization – by the International Trade Centre in Geneva. One could think of a strong intensification of such assistance in various directions with export marketing much more specifically linked with specific opportunities arising from trade liberalization.

(c) Such export promotion could extend into related areas such as the actual organization of the production of exportable goods rather than merely the use of already existing productive capacity for export purposes. Other examples might be the financing of potential exporters, or of national export credit guarantee schemes, in the poorer developing countries, through international action. This could also be supported by mobilizing the importer interests of all richer countries more effectively (retail stores, trading companies, consumer organizations, etc.). Many of these matters transcend the conventional area of trade negotiations. Yet if there is a serious desire to concentrate benefits from trade liberalization in the way here discussed, they might have to be included from the very start.

Another possible measure would more directly come within the scope of trade negotiations : special favourable country quotas for the poorer among the developing countries under the EEC-type of GPS, or one-way transferability of unused country quotas of richer developing countries to the poorer developing countries within this category.

Trade liberalization provides opportunities, but the effectiveness of an economy and of a government to seize such opportunities is itself a function of development. This has been well documented and analysed for the GSP and a number of remedies have been proposed to enable the less developed among the developing countries to take better advantage of the terms, e.g. longer duration of GSP commitments, or specially long-term commitments to the poorer among the developing countries. Perhaps the most direct and effective proposal (by Angus Hone) is that of free floor quotas in which the poorer among the developing countries obtain free access without conditions or limitations, on an equal footing, for minimum quotas (preferably fixed on a *per capita* basis rather than a *per country* basis).

Thus some of the measures needed to make certain of the incidence of benefits from trade liberalization may take us well beyond the traditional range of trade policy. These measures are, however, a second-best solution to reducing and simplifying non-tariff barriers.

Another example concerns non-tariff barriers. These affect the poorer developing countries more than the others for two reasons : (a) they affect food and primary commodities more than manufactures, and (b) the less developed a country is, the more difficult it will be for it to cope with the complexities of non-tariff barriers, or meet the objective criteria of non-tariff barriers such as health regulations. Hence, the House of Commons Select Committee on Overseas Development (para. 73) has suggested using British aid to help developing countries to bring their beef production up to Community health standards. This recommendation could be generalized in suggesting that British aid – and aid from other donors, including multilateral agencies – should be used for overcoming non-tariff barriers. This would only place them in a more equal position with richer countries affected by such barriers.

(4) Inflation and monetary problems of developed countries
Two other current problems may be mentioned as affording new opportunities. They are emphasized here because their relation to the employment problem in developing countries is not usually realized. The first is the problem of inflation, and the resulting problems of wage and income policy in nearly all industrialized countries, including specifically the UK. Obviously, more liberal import policies would help to lower prices. In so far as the import liberalization would refer specifically to food and simple manufactured products which are items of mass consumption in the rich countries (such as clothing or footwear), such liberalization would concentrate the benefits on the poorer among the developing countries and the poorer groups within developing countries and provide a maximum of employment and rural development. It would also concentrate the benefits of lower

prices, and reduce the impact of inflation, within the importing countries precisely upon those least able to carry the burden of inflation (the lower paid workers, the large families and the old age pensioners). Through its effects on the lowest paid workers, the impact of such a policy would help to promote wage restraint. If the rich countries who share inflation and income policy problems could, perhaps through the OECD, examine systematically the potentialities of trade liberalization within the framework of policies to combat inflation, a new set of priorities and a new additional urgency might arise for the international trade negotiations. It does not seem that such a systematic examination has yet been made.

The second problem relates to the international monetary troubles, the solution of which also occupies a high priority, in their own interest, for the rich countries. The fundamental reason for these international monetary troubles is the disequilibrium in balances of payments between the chief partners in the present world system, with special reference to the two key currency countries, i.e. the US and the UK. But the solution of these underlying disequilibria offers an opportunity to combine it with an attack on unemployment and poverty in the developing countries through trade liberalization. If the US balance of payments has to be strengthened in relation to Japan and the EEC, one way of doing this is to promote US exports to Japan (EEC) and cut US imports from Japan (EEC). But another and perhaps more commendable way of doing this would be for Japan and the EEC greatly to increase their imports from the developing countries, with the developing countries placing (either in the natural course of trade business or by special arrangement) a high proportion of their additional foreign exchange earnings as additional import orders in the US. The monetary aspect of this idea is, of course, expressed by the proposed link between the SDRs and aid which at last is under serious international examination now. However, it may be pointed out that even if such a link should be rejected or delayed, there are possibilities of solving the disequilibria underlying present international monetary instability through trade shifts benefiting the developing countries. This might achieve the same objective in ways perhaps more acceptable than the link between SDRs and aid. Obviously these two approaches should not be competitive and certainly one need not exclude the other; any danger that the proposed link should be delayed indefinitely merely to await the outcome of the international trade negotiations is something to be avoided. But the suggestion made here is based on the presumption that this approach to international monetary instability has not yet been examined by the international community seriously.

E

7 Some Problems of International Aid*

1 VOLUME TARGETS FOR AID?

The best-known volume target is the 1 per cent of national income adopted by the United Nations and accepted, at least in principle, by all the aid-giving countries. Such a target raises a number of obvious questions. In the first place, it obviously would be a minimum target. It is equally obvious that it requires some definition of 'aid' to be of any meaning. Should private investment be included? Short-term credits? Suppliers' credits? Should grants and loans be equally counted? Should any distinction be made between the flow of aid and financial resources? If so, where should the line be drawn? Should aid be counted as gross, or as net of repayment? If the latter, what repayments should be taken into account? Should trade concessions be counted as aid? Should trade, tourism, etc., be disregarded when comparing the aid performance of countries? If commercial transactions such as private investments are not excluded, on what grounds can we distinguish between trade and aid? Should aid be measured as the cost to the donor or the value to the recipients – by no means identical concepts? The logic of meeting the need for such further definitions and precisions has been unmistakably at work in OECD discussions following upon the acceptance of the 1 per cent target.

As an international income tax, the 1 per cent target is obviously crude since it makes no allowance for the differences in *per capita* incomes, in the balance of payments situation and perhaps also in the internal needs and employment situation in the various aid-giving countries. This statement applies if the

* Originally written for the Founding Conference of the Institute of Development Studies published in *Journal of World Trade Law*, Vol. 4, No. 2, Mar/Apr 1970.

1 per cent target is treated as a national target for each aid-giving country, rather than as a collective target for the whole aid-giving community (or perhaps western community). Whether the target is intended to be national or collective is also not clear although it seems to be assumed implicitly that the target applies to each individual country. On the other hand, discussion of international burden-sharing in aid has proceeded on the opposite (perhaps more realistic) assumption that different circumstances (e.g. income, rate of growth of income, state of balance of payments, etc.) are relevant in determining the national aid level. The contradiction can be removed or mitigated in several ways: the 1 per cent can be treated as the actual target for countries with lower incomes, sluggish income growth or balance of payments difficulties, while aid-givers in a better position are expected to exceed it; this brings us back to the question of minimum versus actual target. Or it could be stipulated that aid-givers in a better position should give their aid in softer forms than others; this brings us back to the need for defining aid. The aid recipients can justly claim that balance of payments difficulties and surpluses will cancel each other out almost by definition for the aid-giving community as a whole, since they – the recipients – do not build up surpluses; this brings us back to the question of collective or national targets.

While raising a host of questions such as these, the international 1 per cent target has obvious virtues to recommend it. It embodies the international recognition of a world responsibility and world interest in the advancement of the poor countries – a reflection, however faint, of the unity of mankind. It embodies the principle of burden sharing, of comparing and measuring the performance of individual countries – the same principle that at the country level of aid recipients is recognized in the establishment of consortia and consultative groups. It embodies the principle of relating aid to aid-giving capacity, even though the national income is at best only one element in measuring this capacity. Further, the 1 per cent target shows up the relatively modest burden of the kind and volume of developmental aid which the richer countries are expected to provide and which the poorer countries are assumed at present to be in a position to use effectively – only a fraction of the quasi-automatic annual increase in national income accruing to the aid-giving world. (But, of course, aid at 1 per cent of the national income represents a larger burden for the slow growers, if the burden is measured by the fraction of the increment in national income syphoned off into aid; nor is there any guarantee that national incomes will grow year by year everywhere!) The 1 per cent target has the further advantage of protecting the aid target against erosions due to falls in the value of money and, beyond that, of creating a built-in growth factor within the aid total.

With all these arguments in its favour, one feels that the 1 per cent target should be taken as a point of departure. Our task is to give meaning or 'put teeth' into this or some similar target. How to do this would be fruitful to discuss (but it is not attempted here). It can be argued that even the problems and difficulties of interpretation to which such a target gives rise (only some of them mentioned here), show the value of such a target since it forces us to face these difficulties. The alternative to an aid target would be either, at one extreme, the calculation of aid requirements through some macro-economic calculations of 'gaps', or, at the other, the limitation of aid to a figure arrived at by some standard of what constitutes 'effective use' of aid. While the former procedure opens the floodgates, and is also subject to great uncertainty depending upon the projection model and the data used (e.g. Prebisch *v.* Balassa!), the latter procedure places the aid recipients at the mercy of more or less arbitrary standards established by aid donors.

2 AID LINKED WITH TRADE?

For the developing countries, aid is only one possible method of acquiring the resources and the foreign exchange which they need to finance their economic development. Even on the most generous definition of 'aid' (equating it with financial resources), it is still the junior partner, about a quarter of total exports. In this sense, the developing countries are more interested in the expansion of trade than of aid. However, it does not necessarily follow that they would or should prefer £1 million of additional trade to £1 million of additional aid. That would be a tricky question for them to answer. It really depends on the kind of trade and the kind of aid which is compared. It may be argued that the question of 'more trade or more aid?' is a non-question, in the sense that aid is not intended to divert resources from export use. This, however, would not be realistic since in international life aid concessions may often be obtainable as a substitute ('soft option') for trade concessions, and the alternative does exist in real life.

The extra trade has the advantage that it gives additional foreign exchange without repayment obligation and thus does not add to indebtedness. But so does aid in the form of grants and really soft loans and in any case some trade, such as the bilateral type, sets up its own kind of indebtedness in the form of import obligations. The extra trade has no strings tied to it – it leaves the developing country in sovereign charge of its policies. *But:* (a) some trade expansion may also have to be bought with policy concessions or political alignments, and (b) the 'strings' may, in fact, be beneficial to the developing countries if the policy leverage of aid is used solely with the interests of the recipient country in mind. On the other hand, extra trade, if it is in the form of additional volume rather than a higher price for exports, ties down the resources of the developing country, while with corresponding aid these resources would be available for alternative developmental home uses. Against this, the resources absorbed in the production of exports may be specific and have no alternative home use, and, besides, aid is normally not supplied to enable a country to direct resources away from export use. Moreover, aid may also tie down a country's own resources, particularly if it is supplied in the form of project aid and if the developing country has to divert its own resources to an aided project which would not have been undertaken otherwise. Trade is considered by liberal economists as the time-tested engine of growth with a built-in compulsion to efficiency, while aid enthusiasts have corresponding faith in the possibilities of using aid as a leverage for more effective and forceful development policies. So we can go round and round – and the only reasonable conclusion is that the question 'more trade *or* more aid?' *in a general sense* is more or less unanswerable, although it must still be decided in innumerable concrete cases and circumstances.

For a developing country, trade has the presumption of being a more lasting relationship than aid under present arrangements. Combined with the skeleton of truth in the free trade doctrine, i.e. that trade forces countries to be efficient and to specialize on lines of comparative advantage and appropriate factor propor- tions, this is probably sufficient to make us look at trade as the normal and primary matter under review in the dialogue with the developing countries, with aid as the supplementary. However, even this general liberal presumption becomes doubtful if the trade matters under review refer to *prices* rather than *volumes,* and to *preferences* rather than to *access,* and of course much of the UNCTAD dialogue does exactly this. Moreover, the *governments* of the western aid-giving countries may be able to do more in fact about aid than about trade, which is a matter of private enter- prise, except where governmental interference such as tariffs, quotas, preferences, etc., can be brought into debate.

If trade is the primary foreign exchange earner and aid a supplementary factor, then the idea of compensatory or supple- mentary financing naturally comes to mind. It has proved a fertile idea since it was thrown into the international debate by Sr Olano of Argentina in the United Nations Committee on 'Commodity Trade and Economic Development'. It is now being operated on a small scale by the IMF – the 'fifth quarter' now in fact being expanded into a 'sixth quarter' – and a wider-ranging scheme has been worked out by the World Bank on an Anglo-Swedish initiative in UNCTAD; it seems to have good chances of leading somewhere, its attractions reinforced by the obvious difficulties of negotiating and operating commodity agreements. The country aid consortia have pointed the way here, since the amount of aid needed is usually arrived at as a residual after more immediate trade possibilities are exhausted. It is perhaps surprising that the aid consortia have not done this more systematically, and that no trade consortia have developed alongside the aid consortia. The proposals for supplementary financing are certainly sufficiently promising on the one hand, and still sufficiently full of unsolved problems and unresolved difficulties on the other, to deserve considerable attention in the current aid discussion.

Apart from supplementary financing, aid can be used to stimulate trade. Among aided projects, projects with an export potential could be specially emphasized, technical assistance with export promotion can be given, aiding countries can prevail upon their private firms establishing branches of subsidiaries in developing countries, or licensing production there, to permit exports of the new production lines more freely. Also, aid could be given more on a regional basis and for multinational projects or groups of projects, thus encouraging the trade of developing countries with each other; this could be associated with the use of regional banks such as the new African and Asian Development Banks. The techniques of regional or multinational aid are still practically unexplored, and may be suggested for study now. Preferential aid for export projects or export promotion or in general support or leverage for export-minded development policies can be justified on general welfare grounds since the shadow price of foreign exchange for nearly all developing countries is higher than its market prices. This would also justify aid for import-substituting projects or policies as far as that argument goes, but aid-givers may have other valid reasons for preferring to see their money used to help export promotion rather than import substitution. But when all is said and done, one still feels that a policy by aid donors of using aid to help trade – the recipient's trade this is, not the donor's! – would be hypocritical unless accompanied by a trade policy giving easier access to their markets and reducing the current discrimination against processing and fabrication inherent in (and often concealed by) tariff structures. Only in this sense would aid be truly supplementary to trade. Of course, if the trade policies of donors are taken as unchangeable, it may be better that aid should help trade rather than that trade should not be helped at all – but this would be very much a second best world, and certainly not the world of UNCTAD with the 'T' in it.

Returning for a moment to the 1 per cent target discussed in the first section of this paper, the relationship between trade and aid suggests the possibility of a more realistic combined target, with the aid-givers being given the option to count agreed additional imports from developing countries resulting from agreed new trade concessions as part of their aid target. Combined targets of this kind, presumably larger than 1 per cent of national incomes in that case, may perhaps be worth discussing.

The most dramatic link between trade and aid would be for

the aid to be given in the form of subsidy on imports from developing countries – a negative tariff (assuming that the subsidy is larger than any tariffs and is not simply given as a full or partial tariff kickback). This is, of course, a more generalized version of the tariff preferences proposed by Dr Raùl Prebisch and probably much more effective since the subsidy would give preference over the local producer as well as over the rival exporter from richer countries, but also for the same reason politically more explosive. Looked at from another angle, such a subsidy across the board would be considered as a generalized series of commodity arrangements for the exports of developing countries, but resulting in a fixed addition to the market price obtained by the exporter rather than a fixed price itself. Yet another angle would be to think of such subsidies as an agreed partial devaluation of the currencies of the aid recipients, without the devaluers having to pay the penalty on import prices. It is not clear whether these different angles help to make such an approach of direct 'aid to trade' debatable in terms of practical possibilities at the present time, nor indeed whether it is an economically sound approach.

Some kind of active complementary relationship of aid to trade is inherent in the aid situation. It arises from the fact that an entirely passive relationship would mean that the foreign exchange bottleneck would be widened by aid, and the recipient country would be less keen to export (as well as keener to import). This can only be avoided if the development programme is enlarged, at least by the full amount of the aid ('at least', because of the catalytic effect of aid in mobilizing local resources). The assurance and demonstration that the aid finances truly *additional* development, so that the shadow price of foreign exchange is not reduced by the aid, and the recipient does not relax his exports in any way because of the aid, will also be politically necessary in order to persuade the tax payers of the aid-givers that their money is properly spent. The fact that an active relation to trade is inherent in any test of effective use of aid may, perhaps, help to develop more directly trade-linked forms of aid in the future. It is of course, conceivable to think of situations where the aid donors positively *want* the recipient to relax his export effort. This situation although unadmitted is not entirely unrealistic – for instance aid as an alternative to abandoning the textile quotas!

3 TERMS OF AID : SOFT OR HARD; INDEBTEDNESS

The rapid rise in the indebtedness of the developing countries, especially in Latin America, but also elsewhere, has created a burden which begins to conjure up the ominous shades of the nineteen-thirties. This burden can be pictured either as causing real terms of trade – deducting the debt payments from export proceeds – to be much worse for the developing countries than their statistical terms of trade and easily the worst of the post-war period; or else it can be pictured – deducting the debt payments from gross aid received – that net aid has been rapidly shrinking, and is now negative for quite a few countries. Once we correct the often-quoted plateau which aid has reached, both for the fall in the value of money and the mounting debt obligations arising from past flows, the plateau is tilted sharply downwards and begins to look more like a chute than a plateau. It is also clear that the interpretation of the 1 per cent target – gross or net, and net of what? – is of crucial importance. The principle of a net basis of definition has been widely accepted, following the UNCTAD recommendation, but this principle still leaves many open questions.

The indebtedness of some of the developing countries can be dealt with in several ways. One basic question likely to be asked is whether the indebtedness in any concrete case is due to a failure of the country concerned to use the previous inflow of financial resources properly for the earning or saving of foreign exchange. A positive answer may or may not lead to the conclusion that the payment of the debts must be insisted upon even at the price of slowing future development. If the answer is that the burden is due to an excessive hardness of the terms of previous aid rather than failures of the recipient, the argument for insisting on debt payment would be correspondingly weakened. But it might still make sense to argue that debt payment is essential for the maintenance of international financial confidence and co-operation, and to prevent a new era of beggar-my-neighbour. The indicated policy, then, would be to learn the lesson of softening aid terms in order to prevent a recurrence of such situations in the future, and meanwhile avert the danger of bankruptcies by special advances through the IMF or bilateral action; or by *ad hoc* agreements to spread out ('re-schedule') repayments; or by accepting repayment in the form of surplus or export commodities. In the longer run, repayment difficulties can be avoided by (i) a combination of trade concessions, (ii) easier or more flexible aid terms, (iii) supplementary aid arrangements made in advance in the case of declining export proceeds, (iv) more effective use of aid to guide developments in the direction of export promotion and genuine import saving, or (v) by accepting repayment in terms of commodities on the presently typical Eastern aid model. The term 'genuine import saving' is meant to convey the need for combining import substitution with measures and policies to maintain productive efficiency, and the development of local supplies for the import-substituting industries. Much of present import substitution is not genuinely import-saving.

The consortium technique can also be helpful here. Debts of developing countries can be taken into account as reducing import capacity, thus increasing the need for aid to import the goods and services essential for the target rate of economic development. The necessary increases in aid can be shifted either formally or informally to those aid-giving countries with most of the claims arising from debts arising from earlier transactions, or those which stand most to gain from the maintenance of imports.

An internationally agreed scaling-down, phasing out, or forgiving of debts is clearly preferable to unilateral default. One could picture a system in which effective use of aid or vigorous growth is rewarded by leniency in debt collection on public claims, and perhaps even by help on the part of aid-giving governments directly to their own firms and citizens in respect of debts owed to them by developing countries. Theoretically, such a scheme could be defended on the grounds that the developing country has really repaid its primary debt to the world community by promoting or laying the foundation of its own vigorous development. In practice, however, there would be serious objections to any such proposal which also could hardly be protected from abuses. One feels that this whole field of debt re-scheduling, in view of the great variety of national causes and circumstances, will continue to call for a good deal of 'ad hoc-ing', indirect approaches, face-saving formulae, and the active use of the IMF as the ideal cushion.

There is no clear evidence that aid is becoming softer. It is true that the terms of loans have shown a tendency to become softer (in a time of rising interest rates, too!) but, on the other hand, the share of straight grants has declined and shifted to loans. The two trends have largely cancelled each other out in their net effect. The OECD recommendation for specified shares of softer loans is certainly pathbreaking, and shows a willingness both to put teeth into the 1 per cent target and at the same time develop more equitable international burden-sharing in aid.

The most direct and explicit proposal to soften aid terms and at the same time maintain or increase the total flow, is the Horowitz proposal. The pros and cons have been amply set out in recent discussion and are not repeated in this paper. But the proposal is clearly both deserving and in need of further international examination, and should be on the agenda of current issues and current research in the field of aid.

Soft aid, clearly, has greater leverage effect in influencing the policies or selection of projects of the recipient country. Since the aid-giver offers a *quid pro quo* in the softness of the aid, the use of aid as leverage will be more natural and less resented. On the other hand, the re-negotiation or re-scheduling of debts can offer the aid-giver a new leverage. The use of hard aid as a lever will, however, appear to the recipient as an attempt on the part of the aid-giver to have his cake back and eat it, too. In given situations, the leverage effect of soft aid can become either an argument for soft aid, if the leverage is wanted by the giver and accepted or even welcomed by the recipient, or for hard aid if the leverage effect is not wanted by either or both sides.

4 FORMS OF AID: PROJECT AND NON-PROJECT AID*

This is an important issue at the present time, and the pros and cons of both forms of aid are considerable. Some of the advantages of financing 'high priority projects' by aid are illusory, if they neglect the substitutability of the recipients' own resources, or of resources supplied by other donors of aid. However, it is likely at the present time that aid-givers, as well as aid-recipients,

* For an extended treatment see H. W. Singer, 'External Aid: For Plans or Projects?', *Economic Journal*, No. 299, Sept 1965.

are no longer victims of the cruder forms of this illusion. This at least seems indicated by the fact that aided projects are often discussed and selected within the framework of a general review of the broad policies of the recipient and the use of the overall resources at his disposal. Such broader information can be obtained by the consortium technique initiated by the Colombo Plan, or by the annual consultations or confrontations characteristic of IMF and International Bank staff procedures, or by *ad hoc* survey missions, or perhaps more satisfactorily by the maintenance of field missions in close touch with general developments in the aided country. The latter method has so far been most developed by the US Agency for International Development (AID) but can obviously not be matched by smaller aid-givers, specifically, and in smaller aided countries generally.

Non-illusory project aid of this type still has certain disadvantages, especially from the recipient's point of view : the rate of disbursement of aid may become erratic and will be reduced well below the rate of commitment of aid as projects are delayed or changed or original aid estimates are revised, etc.; long 'pipelines' develop, and slow disbursements may reduce the aid total by discouraging new commitments of funds; much time and money may be wasted by overlapping independent assessments of projects; the friction generated by different assessments, and the delays inherent in projects, may undo the political goodwill and the spirit of co-operation and understanding which aid is designed to promote; the taxpayers of the aid-givers and their parliamentary representatives may then conclude that aid is not worthwhile; any bungling of projects becomes associated in the public mind with the bungling of aid itself, etc. It may be said with little fear of contradiction that these dangers just described are far from being hypothetical and speculative. It may well be asked to what extent the present widespread sense of disillusionment with aid and the present stagnation of aid is attributable to the prevalence and characteristics of project aid. Could it be that the disillusionment and stagnation can be overcome by emphasizing more the broader progress and issues of development, and shifting away from the project basis?

In the tangled world of aid policies and aid economics, one cannot be certain of the answer. Perhaps the taxpayers and parliamentary representatives of the aid-givers need the concreteness of aided projects to continue to approve aid, even if it be the fallacy of misplaced concreteness. Perhaps the long pipelines of aid make it easier for aid-givers to make fresh commitments, in the knowledge that actual disbursement may still be a good way off in the future – so perhaps in this way the aid total is larger than it otherwise would be. Perhaps the educational and political value of working together, donors and recipients, on the formulation, appraisal and execution of specific development projects is sufficient to justify the drawbacks. Perhaps the aided projects are of higher and more genuine priority than anything the recipients would have done with their own resources or with general programme aid or budget support. Perhaps project aid has helped to bring down development planning from the lofty heights of macro-economic exercises to the brass tacks of concrete projects. Perhaps – perhaps! We cannot be certain. Our uncertainty is a measure of a lack of data and a failure to record and analyse experience bearing upon the effectiveness of different methods of rendering aid.

In the field of manufacturing industry, there is some ground for feeling that non-project aid has been unduly neglected, relatively to project aid. The rate of growth of industrial output in most developing countries has been vigorous in recent years, and even more so the rate of growth of industrial capacity. But this increase in output and capacity has been achieved in wasteful and expensive ways. New capacity has been created, capital intensive and at high cost (often inflated by sales pressures on one side, and a naïve belief that the largest and newest must be 'best', on the other), profitable, if at all, only under strong protective cover. At the same time existing capacity, which could produce at lower additional cost and in the process provide more employment and cost less foreign exchange, stands idle for lack of finance, lack of repair and maintenance facilities, lack of spare parts or components, lack of consideration in foreign exchange allocation or import permits, and also for lack of proper interest on the part of managers and development planners. In this way, industrialization has failed to carry over into general development. On the contrary, it has drained the rest of the economy, especially agriculture, of resources; failed to provide the necessary employment and training, and remained a high-cost enclave in a high-cost economy. Aid and investment tied to new 'projects' – with emphasis on the larger projects – is only a part of this story, and probably not the most important part. All the same, one feels that a shift to non-project aid, providing the leverage for import liberalization for the requirements of existing firms and greater attention to existing capacities in output planning, would be a change for the better. A survey of existing industrial capacities and a concerted approach to their proper utilization – typically by multiple-shift working – could be a method of aid in the industrial sector with a higher pay-off than at present.

Where project aid is at the same time tied to the goods and services of the specific aid-giving country, this double tie can greatly reduce the value of the aid to the recipient. If tied aid – in the sense of aid tied to the use of goods and services of the aid-giver – is accepted as necessary or at any rate a fact of life, the reduction in the value of the aid to the recipient can at least be mitigated by making the limited range of goods and services available for all possibe uses in the development process, rather than for specific new projects only. Where the range of goods and services is further limited by the availability or surplus situation in the aid-giving country, the case is particularly strong for providing such 'aid in kind' on a non-project basis. This has been recognized in the US food aid programme under Public Law 480, which has, in fact, been a main source of non-project aid for many developing countries.

Abandonment of the project basis does not, of course, exclude control of the uses, purposes and sectors to which the aid is to be applied. On the contrary, non-project aid in many ways provides more effective leverage to the aid-giver since it is eagerly sought by many developing countries (India is a case in point) and the release from project tying would often be accepted as an aspect of softness.

5 TIED OR UNTIED AID : BALANCE OF PAYMENTS OBSTACLES, MULTILATERALISM

The individual aid-giving country has a good enough case for limiting or reducing its total aid and also the export of private capital in times of balance of payments difficulties, as well as for tying aid more closely to national goods and services. The tying of aid will statistically remove the balance of payments impact of aid, but we can only be confident that this is really so if the indirect effects can be ignored. The aid-supplied goods and services may directly take the place of commercial exports, or require imports for their production, or divert scarce factors of production away from exports or even from domestic production, thus intensifying domestic shortages and increasing the degree of pressure in the economy and so cause new balance of payments difficulties, etc. With total aid at less than 1 per cent of national income, these indirect effects of tied aid, and even more of those of marginal changes in the aid flow, can perhaps reasonably be neglected. The statement that tied aid does not affect the balance of payments, even though not strictly accurate, may be sufficient to justify the minor element of a 'white lie' in a good cause.

Where the balance of payments trouble is assumed to be strictly temporary, it makes sense to limit short-term aid such as suppliers' credits, commercial banking facilities, etc., but it does not make sense to harden the terms of aid which can benefit the balance of payments only in a future when the trouble is assumed to be removed, and vice versa, if the external payments trouble is assumed to be chronic. This distinction is perhaps not always made clearly and systematically enough.

In the world as it is, balance of payments troubles will be used as an argument to shift aid away from multilateral channels into bilateral channels which permit tying of aid. However, this need not necessarily be so. One could imagine arrangements under which the multilateral institutions would give some priority in supplying aid goods under their loans and investments to those of their member countries in balance of payments difficulties, or would accept tied contributions from such members (as in the case of the Russian contribution to the UN technical assistance and pre-investment programmes), perhaps in the form of special funds, etc. However, such arrangements are not easily accommodated within the framework of truly multilateral organizations, particularly those of more or less world-wide coverage within the UN system. In view of balance of payments troubles in important aid-giving countries on the one hand, and the desire to maintain and extend the advantages of multilateral co-operation on the other hand, perhaps more thought could be given to techniques of combining the advantages of multilateralism with aid tying, in spite of the difficulties. Certain variations of the Maxwell Stamp Plan would also have an effect in this direction.

The United Kingdom and the United States, where the balance of payments problem is most acute among the aid-givers, have made great efforts to exempt the flow of aid from balance of payments restrictions, including private investment in developing countries in particular. It is not clear, of course, in such complex matters as international business operations, to what extent it is really possible to exempt operations in developing countries from restrictive measures generally imposed or 'voluntarily' observed. But broadly speaking, the developing countries have no real complaint that balance of payments troubles take an undue toll of aid, except, of course, in the sense that balance of payments troubles have clearly intensified the tying of aid, and tied aid is clearly less valuable.

However, where there is a very genuine and compelling cause for complaint is that the aid-givers in balance of payments surplus do not show any signs of compensating by an expansion of aid or any untying of aid, or softening of the terms of aid. It can be legitimately argued that the aid-givers, collectively, should have no balance of payments problem. Any appearance to the contrary could only be due either to an overall shortage of international liquidity and/or to an asymetrical behaviour of countries in deficit and surplus, respectively. This is true almost by definition since the aid-givers account for the bulk of world trade and other payments items, and the developing countries do not collectively build up major foreign exchange reserves. It follows that the balance of payments deficits of some aid-givers will always be offset by balance of payments surpluses of others. Moreover, as long as the needed goods and services financed by aid are bought in the advanced countries, the aid given by aid-giver A will benefit the balance of payments of aid-giver B, and vice versa. Thus, simultaneous untied aid by A and B can be expected, roughly, to leave their individual balances of payments unaffected unless, of course, their ability to supply aid goods differs markedly from their ratio of untied aid funds.

Thus, the developing countries can strongly argue : (a) for them the present aid situation is of the 'Heads you lose, tails I win' variety – balance of payments trouble being a case for restricting aid in one way or the other, while a balance of payments surplus does not seem to provide a case for corresponding expansion; (b) this is essentially a matter for the aid-givers to settle and specifically for the balance of payments surplus countries among the donors – since the developing countries essentially do not cause any balance of payments deficits of others, since the aid-givers collectively have no balance of payments deficit, and since only the aid-givers can deal with any overriding liquidity problem; and (c) mutual agreements among aid-givers to expand or untie their aid in step with each other may not cause any major new balance of payments problems for any of them, while increasing the value of the aid. This case – which seems as clear as the case for freer access and again against discriminatory tariff structures – is, in fact, seldom clearly made by the developing countries themselves. Perhaps it is too delicate a subject for them. But it is a real issue at the present time, and economists are not restrained by delicacy from examining it, and suggesting ways and means of improving on the present situation. This involves co-ordinated moves on the liquidity front by the surplus countries, and joint action on the part of all aid donors. There are four possibilities, or stages, in untying aid :

(i) Individual donors should be asked to untie their aid in respect of specific other developing countries which they are also assisting at the same time;

(ii) Individual donors should untie aid in respect of all developing countries;

(iii) Bilateral arrangements should be made between two aid-donors to agree to mutual untying;

(iv) All donors should abandon tying and reach agreement among themselves on the necessary payments adjustments. The aim is the expansion of aid; the burden of additional aid should fall on surplus countries.

On the liquidity front, reform could provide an even more

direct impetus to aid if proposals to link the expansion of international liquidity in one way or another with aid to the developing countries should be acceptable. The Stamp Plan and the Report of the UNCTAD Expert Committee are two proposals in this direction. These also are live issues (since in any case the planned extension of international liquidity is a live issue), which deserve attention and discussion at the present time.

6 CRITERIA FOR ALLOCATION AND EFFECTIVE USE OF AID

This issue is too important to be omitted, although no more will be done here than to list some of the questions arising. The principle that the aid should go where effective use is made of it, is now widely proclaimed although, in practice, modified by the multiple purposes of aid and by politics. Another modification with important implications is that where conditions are such that aid is not effectively used, aid itself can be used to improve the situation and lay foundations for more effective use in the future. This is true not only of aid in the form of technical assistance (which is not itself dealt with here), with its extension into project preparation, pre-investment, training and pilot production, and the management and operation of aided projects, but also of aid used as a lever to induce the recipient to improve existing policies and machineries. Perhaps it is easier for multilateral organizations to set up, and report upon standards of effective use of aid, and to pioneer in the use of technical assistance to increase the amount of aid which can be effectively used.

This opens up a number of issues, but even if we stay with the mainstream of analysis, i.e. that aid should go where it is 'effectively used', and even if the 'effective use' can be defined as strictly economic or developmental, we are by no means out of the wood. It must be said that in spite of the sophistication introduced into this field, mainly by research initiated by the US AID, the concept involved is by no means clear. What is 'effective use'? Should aid go to the 'good performer' (whatever that may mean), or to the 'improving performer', or to the 'bad performer' who can be reformed and improved by aid? Should aid be given on an assessment of past performance or on the prospects of future performance? Or can we identify the two? Should 'good performance' be assessed in terms of a country's use of its total resources or of the additional resources provided by aid? Should the tests of performance be the same for Bolivia and Mexico, the Chad and Greece, India and Malaya? Should aid be concentrated on the upper range of countries where it can be self-terminating with effective use, or should it be concentrated on the poorer countries where its effective use will have the greatest impact in terms of welfare? Should effective use be measured in terms of the volume of saving or investment achieved, in terms of the efficient use of this investment, in terms of increase in output regardless of the volume of investment, or in terms of the human potential as a source of future output? (It is clear that the followers of different development models will give different answers to this question.) Should the test of 'effective use' be applied to all forms of aid, including multilateral and bilateral, and if so should the same test be applicable? Should the test of 'effective use' apply to the aided project or to the economy as a whole? What are the best techniques for measuring and improving effective use : studies by international organizations, consultations, confrontations, consortia, aid field missions, *ad hoc* surveys; quantitative indicators, judgements, intuition; evaluation missions, or built-in progress assessment?

Or is this whole business of devising tests of 'effective use' merely a device to rationalize decisions reached on other grounds, or to sell aid to taxpayers and parliaments? Is the real test to place maximum orders at inflated prices with influential sellers of equipment, to recruit the right kind of spokesman or lobbyist, or to take the right kind of journalists or officials on the right kind of publicity tour?

All these questions have to be answered within the framework of specific constraints : multilateral aid must be fairly widely and thinly spread so that all member countries benefit in some reasonable and fair degree – and with 'countries' as units of measurement this on a *per capita* basis probably operates in favour of the smaller and against the large countries. Bilateral programmes, on the other hand, must be concentrated on the friends and associates, perhaps with some thought to potential enemies who may be prevented by aid from becoming actual ones. Within this framework of constraints, how much real scope is there left for the exercise of objective criteria of effective use of aid?

8 Employment Problems in Developing Countries*

As a result of our experience and increased knowledge of the facts acquired during the 1960s, the conviction has emerged that much more attention needs to be paid to the human factor in the theory of economic development. Until recently the Keynesian or neo-Keynesian approach has dominated the theory of development. In the Keynesian model, the problem of development is identified with the growth of *per capita* GDP or national income. This growth is explained as the combined result of the rate of saving and the resultant physical capital accumulation on the one hand, and of the capital/output ratio (the productivity of new capital investment in terms of physical output), on the other. This picture of growth or development leads to the identification of certain capital requirements, and helps to identify deficiencies or bottlenecks in terms of foreign exchange requirements, domestic savings and capital inflows. The resulting aggregate growth rate is then transformed into a *per capita* growth rate by the simple expedient of deducting the net rate of population increase (excess of births over deaths) from the aggregate growth rate of production. Although this appears a somewhat inhuman economic construction, it actually arose from concern with the problems of mass unemployment which emerged as the dominant economic problem in the industrial countries during the early 1930s. The new framework of thinking devised by Keynes enabled the industrial countries to cope successfully with this particular problem – at least in the aggregate sense of escaping the overall mass unemployment of the 1930s. Yet when it was discovered that even full employment (in this aggregate sense) did not open up the

* Condensed from a paper with the same title prepared for the Human Resource Conference of the ILO, Philadelphia, May 1969.

gates of economic paradise, concern arose about other problems, including the economic growth rate, of the industrial countries.

When the colonial era came to an end and the world turned to the problems of the two-thirds of mankind living in the poorer countries, we perhaps inevitably applied the same intellectual process to the developing countries, identifying their problem as economic growth, only to discover that the real problems lay elsewhere, and prominently in the field of human resources, including those of employment and unemployment. Even in the more advanced countries the success which has been achieved in banishing mass unemployment is more apparent than real. While it may be true that overall unemployment levels are down to tolerable figures, say 3 per cent or so in the US, this conceals serious pockets of heavy unemployment among specific vulnerable groups of the population. The likelihood of finding employment depends on educational achievement; age (higher unemployment being associated with older members of the labour force and with those newly arrived at working age); race (in the US, unemployment is higher among negroes and Puerto Ricans than among the whites); and the location of the region.

To live in an underdeveloped country places one automatically within the vulnerable group. The overall unemployment rate in underdeveloped countries is probably in the range of 25 to 30 per cent. This figure can only be given with some hesitation, since unemployment in developing countries takes forms which do not lend themselves to statistical precision, at least not by conventional statistical categories, and figures are in any case often lacking even where precision might be possible. Since the developing countries comprise two-thirds of the world's population, it is therefore the non-vulnerable resident in a developed country who is the exception rather than the rule. Particularly tragic is the fact that in underdeveloped countries there is some evidence that the correlation between educational level and unemployment points in the opposite direction from that in the industrial countries : in the developing countries there is some evidence that the unemployment rate is higher the more previous education the person concerned has had. This suggests many possible causes such as the structure of education which alienates the resident from the actual jobs which his simple society can offer; a higher prestige of non-technical occupations for which the educated believe themselves to be predestined, and factors such as the brain drain, high wastage rates in education and the small size of countries, which makes more specialized training difficult.

Our old modes of thinking, based on the Keynesian model, do not enable us to deal with the problems in the developing countries. To give an illustration; in the economic model, the prescription for reducing unemployment is simple. You must increase aggregate demand – increase either the demand for consumption or the demand for investment and employment will increase and spread, so long as there is any slack in the economy to take up. However, in the developing countries of today we find that this simply will not work. If you create additional jobs by increasing aggregate demand, the new jobs will be created in the modern sector, probaby in industry or in modern infrastructure, and therefore in the urban areas. But for any new job created in the town, two or three people are attracted from the countryside in order to compete for it. Urban wages are so much higher than the marginal income from traditional farming, that even a 50 or 30 per cent chance of an urban job will be sufficient to attract a migrant from the countryside. Thus, the creation of additional jobs through familiar economic policies, which may work well in the industrial countries, will increase unemployment in the poor countries' expanding towns, and quite possibly even overall national unemployment, instead of reducing it! This must appear like Alice in Wonderland economics to anybody who thinks in terms of the traditional economic model. But the situation falls into place as soon as we abandon the model's over-simplification.

We cannot possibly disregard the fact that the developing countries of today have a rapidly increasing population, a traditional and mainly rural sector, as well as a modern and mainly urban sector. The relentless pressure of population combined with a low rural levels of living creates pressure on the land, a situation which has added enormously to the influx of people into the cities, exploding them into gigantic accumulations of unemployed or only marginally employed people, and creating almost insuperable problems of maintaining them as places to live. Unfortunately, it is particularly for the younger and more educated people that the city lights burn bright, and the country seems a dismal place. This deprives the rural areas of precisely those elements which would be particularly important as spearheads of agricultural innovation and of improvement in the quality of life. On the other hand, the heavy representation among the urban unemployed of these younger and more educated people introduces an element of additional danger and disruption into the already explosive mixture of seething cities with insufficient facilities and rising unemployment. The problem is further intensified where the educational process, as is so often the case in developing countries, is ill adjusted to the needs of the economy. Confronted with this reality, the traditional model of economic development has little or nothing to suggest, and thus is of very limited operational value, where it is not positively misleading.

What then are the reasons for the lack of employment opportunities in the cities? The relentless increase in population is certainly an essential part of the story; the technology and sociology of death control has proved very much easier to introduce and spread across the globe than the technology and sociology of birth control. Secondly, there is the great problem of agricultural stagnation, combined with the unattractive quality of life in the countryside. The importance of agriculture and of rural development is now much more clearly recognized than it has been in the past and new hope is centred on the agricultural breakthroughs based on new high-yielding hybrid varieties of crops.

The third and most obvious reason is the failure of employment in the urban sector, to increase in proportion to the demand for jobs. They even fail to increase in proportion to the actual increase in production in the modern/urban sector. This can be seen most clearly in the case of modern industry. The typical or average picture in the developing countries is of a regular annual increase in modern industrial production by some 7–8 per cent. This rate has been maintained more or less steadily over the last twenty years. Modern industrial capacity has in fact increased even faster than actual production. All this looks satisfactory from the point of view of the traditional model. It makes a big contribution, especially when valued at the high domestic industrial prices within developing countries, to the statistical GDP or national income; it creates plenty of concrete tangible physical capital. However the trouble, so far as employment is concerned, is that industrial employment in the modern sector is not increasing at the rate of 7–8 per cent but at the far lower rate of around 3 per cent. Since total population also increases at a similar rate of close to 3 per cent per annum, this means that there is practically no structural change in employment at all. The share of total population engaged in modern industry does not increase. This is in the sharpest possible contrast to the historical experience of the now industrialized countries. In their development the shift in the structure of employment from agriculture to modern industry has been very marked, and development economists have declared this to be an essential feature of economic development in the earlier and middle stages. This raises an alarming and fundamental question. Is economic development without the historical structural change in employment towards modern industry feasible, and can it be sustained?

What then is the reason for this absence of structural change in employment? The answer in simple terms is as follows: it lies in the nature of current technology. When the new industrial countries developed, historically led by Britain, they were able to develop on the basis of an evolving technology suited to their problems and conditions. At the beginning the prevailing technology was labour-intensive but gradually, as crude labour became relatively less abundant in those countries and higher skills and capital became more abundant, the technology changed in the same direction of requiring less labour and more capital and higher skills.

The developing countries of today have no choice but to use the capital-intensive technology developed in, by and for the richer industrialized countries and imported from them. Essentially this is a fact of life, and the developing countries, as well as the rest of us, must live with it as best we can. This is not to say that there is nothing we can do about it, and some possible lines of action will be shortly indicated. As Professor Hirschman has remarked in a slightly different context, to expect the developing countries of today to develop, and specifically to achieve full employment, on the basis of modern capital-intensive technology, is the same as advising a young man from a poor family who is looking for a prosperous career to go and get himself a rich grandfather. The employment-intensive modern technology which the developing countries would need, simply is not there. It has been thought that, as more and more technical knowledge accumulates, the development of new countries must become progressively easier since the newly developed countries have progressively more technological knowledge at their disposal on which to build. To some extent this has been true : the US developed faster than Britain, Japan faster than the US. Moreover, even for the developing countries of today it is undoubtedly true that certain parts of current new technological advances can be of great value to them, particularly those parts which, against the general trend, are capital saving or skill saving rather than labour saving. It is the instinctive feeling of this, as well as an instinctive identification of development with 'modernization', which makes many people in the developing countries suspicious of any talk of a labour-intensive technology. What we must clearly do is to find and select those parts of modern technology which are of value, and combine them with developments oriented in a labour-intensive, yet modern direction. This should be the real meaning of the search for an 'intermediate' technology.

At the present time, everything seems to conspire to give technology a capital-intensive rather than a labour-intensive twist, and thus reduce the employment potential of the limited capital resources of developing countries. Aid donors, as well as private foreign investors, have tended to put the accent on supplying imported capital equipment of a sophisticated kind for specific large projects; technicians, advisers, planners, consultants and contractors are either imported from abroad, or trained abroad, or even when trained at home they still tend to be steeped in the knowledge evolved in the industrial countries. Moreover the planners, politicians and the people of the developing countries themselves take pride in big capital structures which come to symbolize progress and modernization. Thus true development comes to be retarded, while the landscape is littered with engineering monuments which fail to provide employment, and thereby fail to enable the people of the country to learn by doing. Often, for lack of proper utilization of capacity, such monuments even fail to make a contribution to the fetish of '*per capita* GDP'. The preference of the developing countries for 'modern' capital-intensive technology is perhaps all the more striking since in other ways there is a good deal of local or national resistance to the features of Western industrial society which advanced technology inevitably brings. Thus, while the 'hardware' of technological colonialism is eagerly sought, its social effects are often bitterly resisted.

What can be done about the problems and pitfalls of techno-logical choice and transfer? Several approaches suggest them-selves, and it is clear that several or all of them will have to be pursued simultaneously. The most obvious approach but not necessarily the most helpful one is the direct approach : to create more modern labour-intensive technology. This can be done in several ways : the first is to persuade the advanced industrial countries, with their virtual monopoly over technological progress, to take the needs and special conditions of the two-thirds of man-kind living in poorer countries more fully into account, in their Research and Development expenditures, than has been the case in the past. A second possibility would be to undertake more autonomous technological research inside the underdeveloped countries themselves. This, however, is difficult because of the lack of research facilities, the absence of a research environment, the difficulties of securing the required high-level personnel, and the constant brain drain of such personnel into the industrial centres. A third possibility is that more can be done to adapt technology imported into developing countries to local needs. This is at least the intended or declared purpose of much tech-nical assistance, but for reasons already explained this policy is faced with an uphill task.

Perhaps more hopeful than these direct technological approaches are the more indirect approaches. The planners and statesmen of the developing countries show welcome signs in recent years of realizing the limitations of the monumental approach to development, and of understanding the importance of the human factor, i.e. not only big dams but also the small irrigation works, and not only the small irrigation works; and at a more 'micro' level still, taking the water to the fields; teaching the farmer how to manage the water, etc. A greater emphasis on agriculture and rural development has also been associated with this shift. Progress has recently been achieved by the development of high-yielding hybrid crop varieties. But it is important to note that this has been done by studying in detail in each location the specifications of climate, soil, geographical location, etc., so that a new package of new plants specifically designed, water supply, fertilizer, and insecticides, was devised. The new emphasis on agriculture and on rural development can help to slow down the big exodus from the countryside and thus make the problem of urban unemployment more tractable. The new plant varieties, with their shorter growing periods, may also create more direct employment in the countryside by making possible the introduction of double cropping. But on the other hand the new agricultural breakthroughs may merely result in high profits for the larger farmer and the dispossession of the smaller farmer, thus intensifying rather than mitigating unemployment. Or else the improvements may result in unmanageable surpluses, with intolerable financial losses to the exchequers of the developing countries.

The reform of aid practices should be even more feasible, at a time when these are in any case under review as a result of the work of the Pearson Commission, the Development Assistance Committee of the OECD in Paris, and other bodies. It is to be hoped that aid techniques will be amended in the direction of aid being more readily available for the financing of local expenditures and for the payment of the wage bills of additional personnel absorbed in labour-intensive projects, particularly perhaps in rural public works. Food aid, whether under PL 480, or the multilateral programme under the Kennedy Round, or the UN World Food Programme, is particularly suited to the financing of local employment through labour-intensive public works.

It would be of particular importance to move away from the tying of aid to a system of freer or more untied aid. At present, aid is largely tied, both in respect of being available only for specific projects, and also in respect of being available only for commodities, mainly capital equipment, coming from the specific donor country extending the aid. Both these ties greatly reduce the value of the aid in helping to cope with the employment crisis in developing countries. The tragedy of the situation is that these ties also reduce growth in general, and in actual fact are largely illusory even from the donor's point of view. Thus, the competitive tying of aid by projects and by source of supplies, on the part of specific donor countries, does not even fulfil its intended purpose of protecting the balance of payments. Nor does it promote the trade interests of the donor countries or give them leverage for changing the programmes of the developing countries in the direction of the priorities emerging from the judgement of the donor countries. To extend aid under the auspices of an international consortium or consultative group in which all the donor countries sit together with the developing country under impartial or rotating chairmanship usually is a great improvement. But we have so far failed to exploit this improvement by placing all aid agreed in this way within a multilateral framework on the basis of approved plans and policies by the recipient country and on the basis of a complete untied programme. This would make aid available to the developing countries for the implementation of employment-oriented growth policies, without forcing them into distortions in the direction of capital-intensive monumental projects, frequently not even reflecting their own true priorities.

However, as an economist I am bound to say that the main avenue along which one would look for a major contribution to the solution of the unemployment problem in developing countries lies in trade. Traditionally, trade has been the method by which each country exports, through the commodities produced and traded, those factors of production which it has in relative abundance. At the same time it imports, again through commodities, those factors of which it is relatively short. For the developing countries this would mean that through trade they would find an outlet for their abundant labour, and be enabled to remedy their deficiencies in capital through imports.

Unfortunately, trade has not in fact played this major role conceptually attributed to it. But it still remains true that potentially this could be the case. The developing countries, with a good deal of support in the industrial countries as well, are putting forward in UNCTAD and elsewhere requests that their labour-intensive manufactures should be admitted to the huge markets of industrial countries on a duty-free or preferential basis. Similarly freer access of agricultural commodities and other raw materials is also under debate. When we think of the tremendous markets involved, and the tremendous rate of expansion of international trade as a whole, in which the developing countries have so conspicuously failed to participate, one cannot help being impressed by the vast potential improvement in the employment picture of the developing countries which expanded trade could produce. It may be worth reflecting for a moment how far, in our discussion of the employment crisis in the developing countries, we have moved away from the narrower and more specific field known as 'employment policy'. The answer to the problem lies, I believe, perhaps mainly in such fields as trade, aid, technology, planning, etc.

It should not be inferred from this that there are no equally important, or perhaps more important, internal factors which are more directly under the control of the developing countries themselves. Some of them have in fact been mentioned above, such as the predilection of planners in developing countries to identify development too much with big capital structures. Additional internal factors of great importance include the failure to utilize existing capacity more fully before embarking upon extensions of such capacity. Athough definitions of excess capacity are very tricky, the data that exist enable us to state with a high degree of confidence that at least 50 per cent more industrial output could be produced with existing capacities, providing in the process perhaps 75 per cent more industrial employment. In particular, the working of additional shifts should be possible and defensible as a way of economizing capital. Often the failure to utilize capacities more fully is due to weaknesses in repair and maintenance of capital plant. It is to be hoped that the employment-creating agricultural techniques of double cropping will be matched by similar employment intensification in the industrial, transport and other fields.

Among the internal factors which prevent the adoption of more labour-intensive technologies, one should also mention the prevailing fiscal system and prevailing fiscal incentives. All too often in developing countries, the planners and policy makers jump from a correct premise, i.e. that capital is the scarce factor and that its accumulation must be fostered, to a quite possibly incorrect conclusion, that the best way of promoting capital accumulation is to give fiscal and other incentives to enterprises based upon the volume of capital which they employ. An example of this is the tax exemptions which desirable new enterprises in priority categories are frequently given in developing countries. Such exemptions and privileges are based on the amount of capital employed rather than upon the volume of employment provided. It should be clear that the overall or macro-economic objective of capital accumulation is not necessarily best served by a micro-economic or project application of this principle.

Of even greater and more far-reaching importance as an obstacle to better employment is the income or wage structure in the developing countries. The urban wage rate is usually a high multiple of the average rural income of the small farmer or farm labourer, and even more so of the income of the small farmer or farm labourer who is in surplus as a result of over-population or landlessness or for other reasons. Part of the rural/urban income differential represents a skill premium for the urban worker. Such skill premiums can be extremely high in the developing countries. To a large extent, these high skill premiums reflect economic realities, i.e. the actual scarcity of such skills, and to that extent they are necessary and desirable as an incentive to provide the training and acquire the skills. But other factors give rise to great difference between the urban and rural income. The disparity reflects another contrast between the development of the older now industrialized countries and that of the newly developing countries. At the time of the development of the older industrial countries there were no notions of a welfare state, nor of social security, nor of minimum incomes required for an acceptable subsistence. To some extent, the existence of such a trade union and welfare structure in the developing countries of today reflects a 'demonstration effect', due to the infectious example of the modern industrial countries. It also reflects in some degree the operation of foreign firms from the more advanced countries which tend to bring higher standards of minimum wages with them from their own industrial base, and in any case there are strong political pressures to pay higher wages than more traditional indigenous firms. And once foreign firms set such a high wage standard, it tends to spread also to local firms which are placed under pressure not to fall too far behind the new standards.

Where producers, particularly foreign producers, are worried about dealing with raw labour fresh from the countryside, and perhaps unruly, undisciplined or politically volatile labour, this could constitute yet another reason why management may prefer to rely upon machinery. Machinery, of course, may break down or be prematurely worn out by inexpert handling; but at least machinery does not strike, demonstrate, riot or present new wage claims. Finally, the level of urban and industrial wages may simply be too high for the producer, because the production value represented by each unit of labour is so low in terms of skills, experience or industrial tradition. In this case, the wage rate may look low in money terms, but it is high in effective economic terms. And once again the natural result will be a choice of capital-intensive methods, to the detriment of employment.

The best and most constructive way of dealing with this rural/urban disparity of income and wage levels, is on the one hand to raise rural income levels by increased agriculture production and rural development, and on the other hand, to raise the economic value represented by urban wages through better training and increase in the productivity in the urban and industrial sector. However, both ends of this constructive approach represent long-term solutions. Meanwhile, measures of income policy and wage policy will be necessary and have been tried in many developing countries, although such policies have been found as difficult to execute successfully in the developing countries as in the older industrial countries.

9 International Policy and Its Effect on Employment*

It is notoriously difficult to measure unemployment in LDCs in terms which make it comparable with unemployment in the richer countries. Its forms and apparitions are too different, and I agree with Gunnar Myrdal, Michael Lipton, Paul Streeten and others that we must be wary of transferring uncritically western concepts to the different Third World. However, we must be equally careful not to jump from the legitimate refusal to apply First World concepts – or Second World concepts for that matter – to Third World problems, to the illegitimate assumption that unemployment and under-employment in open and disguised forms do not exist, or are not serious, merely because they cannot be measured by familiar concepts and caught by familiar definitions, or because the data are lacking. Without labouring the point, for my present purposes I shall simply assert:

(a) that unemployment is extremely serious in the LDCs;
(b) that it is much more serious at present in the LDCs, than in the richer countries;
(c) that on reasonable definitions unemployment is of the order of magnitude of 25–30 per cent in many LDCs and 20–25 per cent in the overall picture;
(d) that it is serious, more or less equally so, both in its rural and urban manifestations;
(e) that unemployment has become increasingly serious in the last 10–20 years;
(f) that on present indications it is bound to increase further, unless counter-influences appear (which must probably include

* From Ronald Robinson and Peter Johnson (eds.) *Prospects for Employment Opportunities in the Nineteen Seventies*, London: HMSO, 1971.

F

a vigorous and balance development of science and technology in directions more relevant to the LDCs and their factor endowments, and in the longer run a slowing down of population growth).

All this amounts to saying that the present context of relations between richer countries and LDCs has been at least consistent with a global disequilibrium in the incidence of unemployment in the two groups of countries; say 3–5 per cent in the rich countries and 20–30 per cent in the poor countries. The thesis of this paper is to suggest :

(i) that the present relations between rich and poor countries are not only *consistent with*, but also *contributory to*, this disequilibrium, with heavy persistent unemployment in the LDCs; and
(ii) that reforms in the present relations of the two groups of countries are among the counter-influences, mentioned in (f) above, which are required to improve the situation, or even to prevent it from worsening.

We shall consider the possible contribution of rich/poor countries' relations to LDC unemployment under the headings of (1) Trade; (2) Aid; (3) Private Investment; (4) Science and Technology; and (5) International Liquidity.

1. TRADE

It is no accident that trade has been placed first. As an economist I am bound to say that the main avenue along which one would look for a major contribution to the solution of the unemployment problem in developing countries lies in trade. Traditionally, in the thinking of economists, trade has been the method by which each country exports, through the commodities produced and traded, those factors of production which it has in relative abundance, while it imports, again through commodities, those factors of which it is relatively short. For the developing countries this would mean that through trade they would find an outlet for their abundant labour, and be enabled to remedy their deficiences in capital through imports.

Unfortunately, trade has not in fact played this major role conceptually attributed to it. But it still remains true that potentially this could be the case. The developing countries, with a good deal of support from enlightened opinion within the industrial countries as well, are putting forward in UNCTAD and elsewhere requests that their labour-intensive manufactures should be admitted to the huge markets of industrial countries on a duty-free or preferential basis. Similarly, freer access of agricultural commodities and other raw materials is also under debate. When we think of the tremendous markets involved, and the tremendous rate of expansion of international trade as a whole, in which the developing countries have so conspicuously failed to participate, one cannot help being impressed by the vast potential improvement in the employment picture of the developing countries which expanded trade could produce.

It is not easy to quantify hypothetical situations which cannot be isolated from other events and trends. However, I am going to stick my neck out and risk the guess that if the share of LDCs in world trade had been kept up since 1955 by a reduction of agricultural protectionism and trade barriers in the richer countries, the employment volume in the LDCs could be about 10 per cent higher than it is now. That would be say $82\frac{1}{2}$ per cent of the labour force instead of 75 per cent and unemployment would be $17\frac{1}{2}$ per cent instead of 25 per cent. Moreover, if this hypothetical assumption of a fully maintained share in total world trade could be projected into the future and if world trade should continue to expand as rapidly as in the past decade, the establishment of this condition might prevent unemployment in the LDCs from rising in the next decade, even in the presence of a capital-intensive technology and a certain rapid increase in the labour force. But this is a big and extremely hopeful assumption to make. Notwithstanding favourable votes in UN bodies and acceptance of global targets which really depend upon such action, are we in the richer countries really ready for it? No doubt we could ourselves benefit in the long run by concentrating on the more sophisticated lines of production (but by the same token perpetuate global dualism and technological colonialism). But the case of aid should warn us that demonstrations of long-run advantage do not seem to be particularly compelling in eliciting from taxpayers, parliaments, civil services and politicians of richer countries any great willingness to make what looks like one-sided 'concessions' even though the sacrifice may be more apparent than real, and transitional rather than lasting. Perhaps real sacrifices could be more readily elicited than the inconveniences of adjustment?

The trouble of course is that the burden of adjustment, if not properly handled, will tend to fall on vulnerable groups most directly in line of competition with the potential exports of the LDCs – the elderly textile worker in Lancashire, the farmer, the older more labour-intensive firms. The necessary adjustments and compensations should certainly be within the power of the richer countries, as well as being in their own interest. Nobody wants to solve the problems of the LDCs on the backs of the poorer people within the richer countries – but then we should also stop trying to solve the problems of our poorer (or simply more vocal!) sectors on the backs of the even poorer LDCs.

In this paper which deals with 'International Policies' we naturally look at the action required by the richer countries, but let us remind ourselves that the LDCs may also have to make painful and difficult adjustments in their present policies and outlook to take better advantage not only of the present, but also of any potential larger future export opportunities. This requires outward-looking policies, willingness to take risks, to study foreign markets and tastes. It takes two to export, and perhaps it takes a dash of Japanese! And the mentioning of Japan could serve as a reminder that the development of a prosperous home market base has never yet hurt a country in developing its exports as well. But there is also a counter-lesson from Latin America : the building up of a pseudo-prosperous home market under the banner of import substitution may be more of a hindrance than help in export development.

Hal B. Lary of the National Bureau of Economic Research in New York has found that the following industries stand out as particularly labour-intensive in relation both to skills ('human capital') and to physical capital : apparel and related products; leather and leather products; lumber and wood products; textile mill products; furniture and fixtures; miscellaneous manufactures; rubber and plastic products. Trade concessions in these products (which I have listed in more or less descending order of employ-ment-intensity in terms of unskilled labour) would have particu-larly strong employment impact in the LDCs, and relieve wage pressures and tight labour markets in the richer countries. Is there not a ready-made agenda here for international action? If the LDCs can only provide the skills, even while lacking the physical capital, a number of other industries could be added as being employment-intensive in the LDCs : fabricated metal products; printing and publishing; electrical machinery; non-electrical machinery. This list of eleven employment-intensive industrial groups prima facie suited for export from the LDCs would still leave the richer countries with nine industrial classes which are both skill- and capital-intensive, and hence prima facie suitable for *their* exports.

The case made here for international trade concessions to the LDCs specifically directed towards employment promotion is of course additional to the more general case for trade development as a way of reducing their foreign exchange bottlenecks and speed-ing up their general rates of growth and investment. This more general case has been amply made in UNCTAD, the Pearson Report, and elsewhere, but by comparison perhaps not much attention has been given to how to obtain maximum employ-ment impact through trade concessions. The scope is certainly enormous, considering that imports of labour-intensive products from the LDCs are only a small fraction of rich countries' total imports of such products, and only a fraction of that fraction when related to their total consumption of such products. Even a target of say 10 per cent of the total *increase* in the consumption of such products to be imported from the LDCs would have highly important employment impact.

But all this is 'potential', i.e. pie in the sky. Meanwhile the ugly skeleton of the scandalous international cotton 'agreement' rattles its bones to remind us of reality, and of *one* reason for 25 per cent unemployment in the LDCs. To this we should add, as equally misleading, the moderate-looking nominal tariff rates on pro-cessed and manufactured products from the LDCs which con-ceal the real, and much higher, effective taxes on value added by employment.

2. AID

Here once again we must distinguish between the general case for additional aid, as contributing to fuller employment in the LDCs, and the specific case for adjusting the forms and methods of aid so that a given volume of aid becomes more 'employment-intensive' in its impact. The general case is no doubt valid (within certain limits and with certain qualifications): increased aid, say the achievement of the Pearson targets of 1·0 per cent and 0·7 per cent of GNP for total financial flows and public aid, would increase the rate of investment and growth, and *ceteris paribus* increase employment.[1] Improvements in the terms of aid, untying, more grants and anything that leads to more effective use of aid would have the same presumptive favourable effect on employment. The limits and qualifications mentioned include a possibility such as the following : if the additional growth and employment created by more aid are in the urban/modern sector, then the increase in the number of urban jobs created might swell the flood of migration to the cities to such an extent that unemployment, at least in its open and urban forms, could actually increase. This possibility, based on East African conditions, is inherent in Michael Todaro's much-discussed model.[2] Another possibility would be that the higher growth rate and investment rate in the urban/modern (and capital-intensive) sector could be accompanied by such a change in the overall *composition* of investment, by drawing complementary domestic resources out of the rural/traditional/service sector (largely labour-intensive), that overall employment is diminished rather than increased. The possibility of this applying to Colombia has been pointed out by the ILO mission under the World Employment Programme, led by Dudley Seers.[3] However, broadly speaking, more aid, or more effective aid = more employment, although the conventional aid/employment ratio is almost certainly unimpressive.

How can the aid/employment ratio be improved? This is the special relationship between international aid policies and employment with which we are concerned here. Space limits us to an enumeration of changes in international aid policies which could improve the employment impact of a given volume of aid.

(a) Aid is now available predominantly for the *import component* of projects, largely equipment. This puts an artificial premium, as far as the LDCs are concerned, on preferring capital-intensive projects to more labour-intensive ones, or for any given project preferring a more capital-intensive (import-intensive) to a more labour-intensive technology. Both these effects reduce (or possibly pervert) the employment effect of aid. Aid should be equally available for local expenditures on projects (including local equipment). This could be done either by giving aid as a fixed percentage of *total project costs*, whether 100 per cent or 50 per cent or 25 per cent of the total cost, or alternatively by giving aid on a programme or general budgetary basis. The Pearson Commission has recommended that aid-givers remove regulations < which limit or prevent contributions to the local cost of projects, and make a greater effort to encourage local procurement wherever economically justified.[4] This recommendation deserves full support. In particular, it is to be hoped that the multilateral aid sources will pay full attention to it; so far they have been more in the rear than in the van of the faint movement in this direction.

(b) Aid is more readily available for investment in the urban/modern sector than in the rural/traditional sector. This has the dual effect of raising the overall capital/output ratios by changing the investment mix in the direction of the more capital-intensive urban/modern sector; and of intensifying rural/urban migration by increasing the rural/urban income differential and the job attractions of the towns. Both these effects tend to reduce the employment impact aid. The aid/employment ratio could be improved (lowered) if more aid were available for the rural/traditional sector (not necessarily agricultural but inevitably much of it directly agricultural and most of it agriculture-related). Here again, we are pushing at an open door in so far as most aid programmes, especially the World Bank, have announced an intention to shift more aid into the agricultural sector, and into rural development. However, the implementation of such a policy will be more difficult than the policy-farmers realize. Often the aid would have to be on a programme or budgetary basis, and channelled through local financial institutions in order to overcome the logistic difficulties of channelling aid into a multitude of small widely dispersed projects conducted under unfamiliar and unsophisticated conditions of book-keeping, expenditure control, etc.

(c) Aid is more readily available for a few large projects rather than for a variety of smaller projects. Smaller projects however are both more likely to be employment-intensive and also more likely to be found in rural or small town locations where they reduce migration to the cities and consequently urban unemployment. There is of course a certain fungibility in that external aid for large projects may release local resources for smaller-scale projects (or vice versa). This fungibility however may work in reverse if the external aid covers only a relatively small part of the total cost of the large-scale project while the rest may have to be covered from complementary local resources. The best approach would be either to channel aid through local financial institutions or to place it on a programme of budgetary basis.

It will be seen that the policy prescriptions under (a), (b), and (c) above coincide quite closely. In fact it may be said that present aid practices form an anti-employment syndrome, while the corrective measures required also form a single syndrome.

(d) The employment impact of aid also suffers from a confusion within the present aid system of promoting new growth or development as distinct from promoting new development *projects*. It is a great deal easier to obtain aid for a new project rather than for the expansion of an existing project, or the repair and maintenance parts needed to keep existing projects going, or the import of raw materials required for their operation, or the additional expenditures (largely local wages) which would be needed to utilize existing plant more fully by multiple shift work. There has been some improvement particularly in the direction of providing aid for import of required raw materials, but the statement is still broadly true. As a result we have the extraordinary spectacle of scarce capital standing idle or under-utilized although no doubt deficiencies in management, income distribution, planning, etc. also play a large part in this. Aid given for the more effective utilization of existing capital would nearly always be much more employment-intensive than aid given for the introduction of new capital. In fact the kind of aid here advocated would represent the best kind of intermediate technology – capital-saving yet without arousing the antagonisms conjured up by the idea of a 'different' technology.

(e) Aid for the financing of public works, and especially of rural public works, is almost impossible to obtain, partly because there is no single project and partly because the expenditure involved is local. Food aid is a form of aid particularly useful for the financing of public works and labour-intensive development in general. No doubt food aid can be harmful if it depresses prices for local farmers or leads to a slackening of domestic effort in food production. But it would be throwing out the baby with the bath water to go slow on food aid rather than administer it in such a way that it has no undesirable side effects. It is to be hoped of course that food aid, which essentially does not impose any real sacrifice on the donor of the surplus food, would be considered as additional to other aid rather than competitive with it. Perhaps for this reason it should not be counted within the 1 per cent and 0·7 per cent Pearson targets.

3. PRIVATE FOREIGN INVESTMENT

The present employment impact of private foreign investment is reduced by a number of factors and could be increased by changing them. A bare list must suffice here.

(a) A foreign firm, particularly a multinational firm, will almost automatically fall back on the capital-intensive technology available to it internally through the research products, know-how, patents, etc. of the head office or parent company.

(b) A foreign firm will not wish to be troubled with the incomprehensible and politically-charged problems of handling large masses of local labour, deciding who should be employed and who should be refused employment, etc. The employment of capital is the line of least resistance.

(c) A foreign firm will be faced with a demand for wages much higher than the prevailing local labour situation and the resource endowment of the country would justify. To push up wages against foreign firms is almost a patriotic duty, and will understandably be supported by the local government as one way of keeping the money in the country and reducing the repatriation of profits.

(d) Where one of the original motives of the foreign investment was to use the local subsidiary or licensing agreement as a foothold for selling equipment, spare parts, operational raw material, etc., the provision of secondary local employment by ordering locally will be absent or greatly reduced.

This is by no means a full list, and no doubt there are also countervailing factors at work – including deliberate policies of a number of foreign firms – but it will help to indicate some of the changes in foreign investment policies which might be needed if we are to increase its impact on local employment.

4. SCIENCE AND TECHNOLOGY

Although problems of science and technology are less discussed (at least by economists and politicians) than trade, aid or investment, in fact this is the area in which the rich countries have perhaps the most powerful impact – for better or worse – on employment in the LDCs. The dominant fact of international life is that it is the richer countries, with one-third or less of the world's population, which account for 99 per cent of the world's scientific and technological innovation. Admittedly, R & D expenditures (on which the 99 per cent figure is based) is a less than satisfactory input proxy for the output of innovation, and in addition it covers only one segment of the relevant inputs; but it is the best we have. In some ways, it even understates the dominance of the richer countries : such is this dominance that even the R & D expenditures of the LDCs are largely devoted to making a marginal contribution towards 'extending the frontiers of knowledge', in ways and in directions automatically determined by the conditions and factor proportions of the richer countries.

In the Sussex Manifesto – prepared by a group of consultants to the UN Advisory Committee on Science and Technology meeting at the University of Sussex in 1969[5] – we described this phenomenon as the 'internal brain drain', and as perhaps more important and dangerous to the LDCs than the external brain drain (visible geographical movement of highly qualified people) which has attracted so much more attention. It is on account of this internal brain drain as well as on account of the low efficiency of small and scattered R & D expenditures without adequate infrastructure and equipment (also discussed in the Sussex Manifesto), that one must be rather sceptical of the value of any targets of increasing the local R & D expenditures of LDCs from 0·2 per cent of their GNP to 0·5 per cent or any other figure, when such proposals are made in isolation.

It is only within the context of planned global change in the composition and direction of scientific and technological progress that such a target assumes a constructive meaning. And it is again because of the dominance of rich-country technology which not only dominates the R & D inputs and controls the R & D infrastructure, but also sets the tone and determines what is considered as 'progress' or 'modern' or 'efficient' even within the LDCs – however contrary to their true interests – that any such planned global change must include a restructuring of the R & D priorities within the richer countries. It is they who must re-define what constitutes 'progress' and where the 'frontiers of knowledge' lie. This they must do in such a way as to include more of the things which are useful to the LDCs (production on a smaller scale, simpler product design, tropical product improvement, protein foods for young children, etc.), and fewer of the things which are directly harmful to them (certain developments in synthetics, automation, machinery with extremely high repair and maintenance requirements, etc.). The target of the Pearson Report that the richer countries should shift $2\frac{1}{2}$ per cent of their R & D expenditures in this direction is an important, if modest, beginning.

For the purposes of our present discussion it should be noted that any such change in direction would be bound to give much higher priority to employment intensity, capital-saving and reduction of sophisticated skill requirements in operation, maintenance, etc. And let us not hear too much of the old canard that capital-intensity is good for LDCs because it economises in skills. All the evidence is to the contrary; and the landscape of the LDCs is strewn with the evidence of this fallacy in the form of under-utilized, broken down, idle, high-cost 'modern' capital equipment.

Hopefully in later years those after us will shake their heads incredulously at how we set about this business. We take technologists and other experts involved away from their familiar environment and drop them in another country (usually with insufficient briefing), leave them to find houses to live in and schools for their children, to find local counterparts, to find their ways in unfamiliar surroundings, and all too often whisk them back just when they become effective. If this reads like a parody, few with experience would deny that it contains elements of truth.

Surely, the first step in a global partnership must be to use the wonderful and dreadful machinery of science and technology where it is and where it can operate most effectively, and realize its potential blessing for world economic development. The sending of experts abroad and the building up of an indigenous scientific and technological capacity within the LDCs must take place simultaneously, and in alignment with a change of direction of progress within the dominant richer countries. The $2\frac{1}{2}$ per cent suggested by the Pearson Report is less than one-twentieth of what is now spent on military, space and atomic technology, less than what the richer countries will have added to their R & D expenditures between the June day in 1970 when this is written and the end of the same year.

And once again, as with trade and aid, the thinking within the LDCs will have to change as much as the thinking in the richer countries. Feasibility studies of projects will have to be based on spectra of technology and on pricing systems which reflect the real resources and needs of the LDCs. At present, any such movement is only too easily resisted as evidence of technological colonialism, on the grounds that the LDCs are permanently to be fobbed off with an inferior second-class technology. Tragically, exactly the opposite is true : the present dominance of a technology appropriate for the rich countries, a dominance obtaining within the LDCs no less than without, ensures a continued handicap for the LDCs. The present rates of population increase, the present capital-intensive trend of technology, and productive full employment are three things which simply cannot co-exist. Something has to give – and at present it is employment.

5. INTERNATIONAL LIQUIDITY

Here, of course, attention should be paid to the great step forward taken by the world community by the creation of the Special Drawing Rights. A little of that progress has rubbed off on development even at present, in that the LDCs, contrary to the original intentions, at least participate in the SDRs to the extent of their IMF quotas. Perhaps more important is the widespread conviction which has emerged that now the SDRs have been safely – and one hopes irrevocably – established, their potential for world development can be safely utilized without damage to their original and primary purpose. The technique for doing this is less important than the decision itself, although the opportunity to strengthen multilateral channels seems too good to miss – killing three birds with one stone!

The balance of payments objection to increased aid to the LDCs was never too convincing, except possibly as a question of redistributing the overall burden of aid among the richer countries. It could always be pointed out that as long as the LDCs did not use aid to increase their foreign exchange reserves – and with exceptions the main criticism of their policies was exactly the opposite – there was never a valid balance of payments argument against increases in overall aid. Now, with the creation of the SDRs we can go a step further. The richer countries, taken together, will not only not have a balance of payments deficit, but they will in fact have a positive balance of payments surplus. The case for linking this new progress in international relations with a step forward in development assistance seems very strong – but what better direction than to link this even more specifically with the objective of providing constructive employment for the young in the LDCs?

10 Unemployment in an African Setting: Lessons of the Employment Strategy Mission to Kenya*

Like earlier missions undertaken within the framework of the ILO World Employment Programme,[1] the ILO mission to Kenya soon discovered that Kenya did not have one employment problem but many, and that the nature and causes of these various employment problems could not be investigated without making a broader analysis of the structure of the economy at large and the trends in its development. Extreme differences in incomes, productivity, access to resources and government services created imbalances between the structure and location of the jobs in demand and the type and location of available work opportunities. The rapid growth of the total population, not to mention that of the urban population and of school outputs, has far exceeded the growth of wage earning employment. These internal imbalances are linked to extreme imbalances between the Kenyan economy and the world economy – in trade, technology, and the conditions governing private foreign investment. Many of the imbalances were inherited at the time of independence, others have grown up since. All of them underlie Kenya's employment problems.

Just as the causes of the problems are broad and fundamental, so is the strategy to deal with them. Thus, of necessity, the report of the Kenya mission takes into account a wide range of policy

* Reproduced by kind permission of Professor Richard Jolly (co-author) and the *International Labour Review* in which it appeared in Feb 1973.

measures with implications for virtually every sector and group in the economy. The underlying theme is, however, a coherent strategy for moving on from the post-independence policies of growth and Kenyanization formulated within the inherited economic structure to policies designed to diminish the imbalances through a complete restructuring of the economy. The resources for this restructuring would be found from a redistribution of the fruits of growth.

The emphasis is on growth as well as redistribution because of the low level of income per head in Kenya and the high proportion of the population living in the rural areas at near subsistence level. In view of these two facts neither growth nor income redistribution alone would be adequate. Both are needed and must be linked in a comprehensive strategy.

The employment problems of Kenya differ from those encountered in previous missions in a number of respects. Kenya's problems are, in fact, probably characteristic of African countries in general, though this would need to be ascertained on the basis of further experience, discussion and empirical research.

The most striking consideration is the overwhelmingly rural character of employment : the rural population accounts for some 90 per cent of the total population, and the urban population until recently maintained strong links with the countryside, as was borne out by a survey showing that about 20 per cent of all urban wage earnings were remitted to the rural areas, the proportion being even higher in the case of the lower wage incomes. This factor places the question of the disparity between urban wages and rural incomes in a somewhat special context, and means also that rural/urban terms of trade and the nature and sources of rural incomes must be viewed in a different light. In one sense, the preponderance of the rural sector lays the basis for a positive employment policy : small farms in Kenya show both larger labour inputs and higher output per unit of land – and this applies to food crops as well as cash crops. Thus, there is here and in a number of other areas a welcome harmony between more employment, greater equality and higher output. This provides a powerful reinforcement for the overall strategy of redistribution from growth.

However, one reason why the employment problem has become

(or has been felt to have become) so much more acute in recent years is that the traditionally strong links between the countryside and the urban population are beginning to weaken. Historically, the employment system evolved from the tendency towards a high labour turnover in urban employment due to the return to their villages of middle-aged and even younger workers after a period of urban employment, which created numerous vacancies for new entrants to the labour market. To counteract this tendency, a tradition of high urban wages was established – high relative to rural incomes – in order to induce the workers concerned to stay on in regular employment. This earlier policy of high urban wages has, as a result of changed circumstances, led to the 'distortion of factor prices', creating dualism and inequalities in the economic structure. The high wages have in fact served their purpose of reducing labour turnover only too well, in the absence of a corresponding rise in rural incomes; they have attracted young jobseekers far in excess of the quantity justified by the reduced number of job vacancies; and they have been both caused and supported by the prevalence of capital-intensive technologies in the modern urban sector. This in turn has resulted in the growth of an 'informal' urban sector, which represents society's way of reconciling the limited number of jobs in the modern urban sector with the increasing number of jobseekers and the inadequate rural incomes. Positive policies based on the existence and potential of this informal sector are proposed in the report of the Kenya mission, as is explained below.

In many other ways, also, recent history has placed its stamp upon the employment problem in Kenya. The question of productive employment for the mass of the African population is inextricably linked with the question of Kenyanization of the economy. As an overriding national objective, this must form part of any employment strategy. One approach to Kenyanization is to change the old racial structure – with Europeans on top, Asians in the middle and Africans at the bottom – simply by changing the people occupying the jobs in the various income strata, which is roughly what has happened since independence. However, this has simply perpetuated the problem of finding productive employment for the masses and has maintained existing inequalities where it has not actually intensified them or sown the seeds for increasing them in the future. A different approach to Kenyanization is to change the entire economic structure, by reducing the present stratification, so that the whole economy is more closely geared to the achievement of productive employment and the reduction of unemployment.

DIMENSIONS AND NATURE OF THE PROBLEM

Applying the conventional definition of 'unemployed' in the Kenyan context, i.e. taking into account persons lacking identifiable urban full-time employment – people working zero hours and having zero income – the mission estimated that the level of urban unemployment was between 11 and 12 per cent among men and considerably higher among women. In fact it was not possible on this basis to estimate the number of unemployed women in a satisfactory way; the usual methods of assessing labour force participation rates did not work, so that the mission felt compelled to use quite different methods. This was even more necessary as regards women in the rural areas, where the demarcation line between activities classifiable as 'economic' which stamp the person performing them as being in the 'labour force', and other 'non-economic' activities, performed by persons outside the labour force, is statistically arbitrary and, for purposes of indicating living standards, meaningless. Allowing for a higher level of urban unemployment among women than among men, the average urban unemployment rate may be said to be around 15 per cent. The situation is made all the more serious by the fact that this urban unemployment tends to hit hardest the younger people, who, on balance, are better educated than those currently employed. This creates a special problem in that it implies the frustration of the aspirations not only of the younger, better educated people, on whom the hopes for the development of the country must rest, but also of their parents and families who have invested in their school fees often desperately hard-earned capital. Taken together these two groups represent a powerful political force.

But though the urban unemployment rate is serious, it is only the tip of the iceberg. The 'working poor', i.e. those whose efforts do not earn them even the modest income needed to bring them above the threshold which marks the poverty level in a generally poor country, account for a much higher proportion of the urban population than the 15 per cent or so found to be directly unemployed. The mission did not define this group as 'underemployed' because in fact those involved are often working long hours in arduous activities. Again, this is particularly true of the women, when the artificial distinction between 'economic' and other activities is disregarded. Nor are the people in this category predominantly engaged in marginal or parasitical sham occupations. In fact, the mission placed great emphasis on the intrinsic value and vitality of a lot of activities in the 'informal sector', where many of the working poor are to be found. Without arriving at a precise estimate, the mission concluded on the evidence collected that those without sufficient productive employment accounted for at least 25 per cent of the urban population of working age, and probably for a higher proportion of the working age rural population.

TABLE 10.1 Proportion of Unemployed Persons and of the Working Poor in the Adult Population of Nairobi, by Sex and Household Status, 1970

	Males		Females	
	Heads of households	*All members of households*	*Heads of households*	*All members of households*
Unemployed*	4·9	10·0	10·8	22·8
Working poor	13·8	13·6	40·7	31·8
Unemployed* persons and working poor jointly	18·7	23·6	51·5	54·6

*Unemployed persons are those with zero incomes who are seeking work.
SOURCE: ILO: *Employment, Incomes and Equality* . . . , op. cit., p. 64

Though this article is not a summary of the mission's report, or of its recommendations – these can be found in the report itself[2] – it may be useful to pursue a little further the findings of the mission in respect of the informal or unenumerated sector just referred to. Mention of this sector often conjures up a picture of fictitious, marginal, parasitical or illegal activities – those of the beggar, the shoeshine boy, the thief, the prostitute. For the analytical economist the picture is one of 'underemployment' or 'disguised unemployment'; for the planner it is one of undesirable slum areas, of messy, uncontrolled and uncontrollable activities; for a newly independent country, it is one of reversion to primitive conditions, a denial of modernization and progress. The mission found that when applied to the informal sector in Kenya this picture was essentially unhelpful and misleading.[3]

The chief element of truth in this jaundiced view of the informal sector is that many of those active there are among the 'working poor'; they are unable to reach a minimum acceptable standard of living; but this is also true of many of the small farmers, or indeed of people working in the modern or formal sector (though here the incidence of poverty is less marked). The mission found that the informal sector, both urban and rural, represents a vital part of the Kenyan economy and that its existence reflects a necessary and, on the whole, beneficial adjustment to the constraints imposed by the prevailing economic situation. If a country like Kenya, which has to find jobs for a population increasing by almost $3\frac{1}{2}$ per cent a year (four to eight times as many proportionately as would have to be found in a developed country), with such a limited national income and with an even more limited capital formation potential (perhaps only one-twentieth proportionately of that of a developed country), tries to do so by using a technology broadly similar to that of the rich countries and requiring broadly similar amounts of capital per worker, the inevitable consequence is that the 'modern sector' thus created must exclude the bulk of the population. A number of adjustments can be made by reducing capital intensity even within the framework of conventional technology, or by changing the product mix in the direction of more labour-intensive products, particularly where there is a high proportion of rural employment, but these measures will not be sufficient to provide jobs for all the jobseeking population. The unemployed who cannot be maintained by the earnings of relatives or friends or who have no family farm to fall back upon, who cannot draw social security benefit or be assisted by the community in other ways, have to make a living by catering for the needs of their fellow citizens, who are frequently in a similar situation to themselves. This often means self-employment, using methods and resources within their grasp in the absence of a command of capital, access to credit, business know-how, etc.

The informal sector in Kenya, when looked at in this way, appears as a sector in which the adjustments to a prevailing situation have been made with a high degree of intelligence, entrepreneurship, ingenuity and appropriateness. The sector has served as a basis for the development of technological adaptations to actual circumstances which are often admirable. All this has been achieved in the face of frequent government neglect or even harassment due to the prevailing planner's belief in the supreme virtue of 'modern' – and thus high-cost – approaches and standards. The report of the mission recommends a major shift in government policies concerning the informal sector – a shift towards active encouragement and support. This would require a new look at health standards, housing standards, licensing policy, access of the sector to loans and technology, policies relating to industrial estates and rural industrialization, government contract policy and specifications, technological research decisions on products appropriate to the Kenyan economy, the development of subcontracting by larger-scale enterprises (specifically including foreign investors), etc. – all of these being relevant to any fundamental re-orientation of existing policies.

The above reflections also show why reports such as the one on Kenya have to take a comprehensive look at the economy as a whole. Simply to try now to extend the 'modern' standards of the formal sector to the informal sector – an attempt which would be hopeless in any case – by introducing everywhere the same 'modern' practices (minimum wages or other conditions) would be worse than mere neglect. What is needed are positive new policies for promoting the informal sector and linking it with the formal sector. This attitude ties in with the mission's belief that the informal urban sector in Nairobi, Mombasa and other Kenyan towns has come to stay and is certain to expand rapidly. It does not, as planners often assume, consist of temporary migrants who can be persuaded to return to the countryside, nor does the mission expect, or try to base itself on the assumption, that the rate of migration or urbanization in the future can or will be reduced by more than a small margin.[4]

There is also a very important rural and small-town informal non-agricultural sector which can be greatly strengthened. Although 90 per cent of Kenya's population still lives in rural areas, this in no way means that all of its income (other than the important urban remittances already mentioned) is derived from agricultural activities. The diversification of rural and small-town activities is, however, largely dependent on increasing agricultural prosperity. In any case, with Kenya's rapid rate of population growth and small urban population, even if the present rate of increase in the African population in the larger towns, amounting to between 8 and 10 per cent per annum, continues, the increase in the rural population will still account for most of the actual total population increase. That is why the mission's recommendations concerning the informal rural and urban sectors had to be formulated in the context of an intensification of labour use in agriculture. In Kenya the evidence suggested that smaller farmers were generally more efficient as well as more labour-intensive in the sense of producing more per acre and employing more persons per acre than larger farmers.

The agricultural strategy which the mission proposed has four main thrusts :

(a) the intensification of land use both for crop and livestock production with the major concentration of effort directed to the poorer families;

(b) a redistribution of land towards more land/labour-intensive farm units;

(c) the settlement of unused or under-utilized land in both high potential and semi-arid areas;

(d) the creation of non-agricultural employment opportunities through rural works and the development of the rural informal sector.

Under this strategy the recommendations of the mission centred on promotion of the cultivation of labour-intensive cash crops (coffee, tea, pyrethrum, rice, cotton, sugar, wheat, etc.), particularly by smaller farms. This presupposes the release of land for such cash crops by using less land for food crops, which in turn would have to be achieved by raising the productivity of food crop cultivation (still desperately important, in particular as regards high protein foods) through the rapid introduction of hybrid maize and related improved husbandry practices.

As regards the industrial sector, the mission paid particular attention to Kenya's relations with foreign investors, who account for the bulk of modern industrial employment and investment. Its recommendations in this connection, if accepted, would again call for considerabe shifts in policy : greater selectivity as to the types of investment to be encouraged; greater initiative on Kenya's part in formulating its own investment proposals and priorities through more active seeking out of investors and 'shopping around' among them, instead of just waiting for all the proposals to come from them; a sharply increased effort to enable Kenya to negotiate with foreign investors on more equal terms, on the basis of a better knowledge of the technological problems involved and available alternatives; and a new taxation structure which would be more effective in preventing the drain of capital out of Kenya. At the same time the mission recommended a reshuffling of the incentives or disincentives in the Kenyan economy for foreign investors, deriving from the tariff structure and price policies and from the exchange rate and fiscal policy. It found that Kenya's export policies also stood in need of considerable reexamination, and the report makes wide-ranging recommendations in this respect.

As already indicated, changes of policy were found to be necessary outside the agricultural and industrial sectors. Two vital areas are education and the labour market – linked because they have operated together as a way of channelling the lucky few into the better paid wage-earning jobs, thus aggravating the distortion in incentives already caused by the gross imbalances in the wage and salary structure. The mission suggested a chain of linked reforms, beginning with major changes in the wage structure and fundamental changes in the process of selection within the educational system and from the school system into jobs. These changes, if implemented, would help redirect the existing aspirations of students and their parents, and thus make possible long overdue shifts within the educational system, away from the white-collar, academic orientation towards a more flexible and diversified system comprising formal education, training and informal education, which would be better suited to the real needs of the country.

The need for a reform of the wage and salary structure is well known and will not be further elaborated on here. On the other hand, it would seem to be worth indicating briefly why a reform of the system of educational selection was seen as a crucial step towards the other reforms.

In Kenya, as in so many other countries, the school examination system has increasingly become the dominant device for deciding who will go on to secondary and higher education and who, in turn, will get the good jobs. Given the very rapid rate of educational expansion when compared with the rate of growth of well-paid jobs, the task of selection has year by year become more burdensome and the backwash effect on the earlier stages of education has grown ever more disastrous. Increasing numbers of children leave school labelled as rejects or failures, so that the psychological tension to which students are subjected at examination time is extremely severe; even those who succeed do so to an increasing extent by learning to qualify rather than by learning to understand or by developing the initiative and inner resourcefulness which would be useful to them in tackling any one of a thousand practical problems in their locality, their homes, or their farms. The pernicious effects of examinations are not confined to a few weeks a year – being the dominant influence, they interfere with and destroy the whole pattern of what is learnt throughout the year.

The mission felt that nothing less than a radical change in the entire examination system would be adequate. First, the extreme inequalities between districts and between good and bad schools would have to be tackled by introducing a basic quota under which a certain proportion of primary-school leavers from every school would be given secondary school places. (Detailed statistical analysis of past examination results showed that the examination as a selection device had virtually no predictive validity.) Second, a number of bonus quotas could be made available for the schools within each district whose overall examination results were well above average – thus providing school-focused incentives to spur teachers, parents and students to raise the quality of schools. Third, the examination itself would have to be changed, so as to improve its content and reliability and to supplement the 'book learning' parts with tests designed to assess grasp of local problems, as well as ability to deal with them.

REDISTRIBUTION FROM GROWTH

The basic decision of the mission to give priority in examining Kenya's employment situation to the problem of the low level – in fact the poverty level – of returns from work, which meant taking into account all those whose employment was not productive enough to earn them an income which was up to a modest minimum, had important repercussions on its whole approach to its task and on its recommendations. The full range of income distribution had to be considered and, at its lower end, the many different groups below the poverty line. This range is illustrated in the table overleaf, taken from the report.

For the 1970s and 1980s the mission proposed that Kenyan development strategy should focus on ensuring that all households achieved minimum income targets by specific dates. The targets proposed by the mission were, for rural households, 120 shs. a month, or £72 a year, by 1978 and £108 a year by 1985, and, for urban households, 200 shs. a month, or £120 a year, by 1978 and £150 a year by 1985.[5] A glance at table 10.2 will show the main categories of people at present below this poverty line. In addition there is the regional dimension : income disparities between different regions are very considerable in Kenya and the poverty problem tends to be concentrated in the areas outside Nairobi, Mombasa and the Central Province. There are also considerable variations in income levels even among the various districts and localities within the same province. Generally speaking poverty is especially severe in the semi-arid and arid areas – precisely those areas whose settlement will become increasingly imperative as the population continues to expand. The small holdings below the poverty line are concentrated in areas of high population pressure around Lake Victoria and elsewhere, and they also include a high proportion of farms managed by women in the absence of their husbands and other male family members in Nairobi. This situation in turn raises special problems of farm management, together with the question of who should benefit from extension services and have access to the cash income to be earned through the transition from food crop to cash crop production – all of which are very relevant for an employment strategy.

TABLE 10.2 Household Income Distribution by Economic Group and Income Size, 1968–70

Economic group	Annual income (K£)	Number of households* (thousands)
Owners of medium-sized to large non-agricultural enterprises in the formal sector of commerce, industry and services; *rentiers*; big farmers; self-employed professional people; holders of high-level jobs in the formal sector	1 000 and over	30
Intermediate-level employees in the formal sector; owners of medium-sized non-agricultural enterprises in the formal sector; less prosperous big farmers	600–1 000	50
Semi-skilled employees in the formal sector; prosperous smallholders; better-off owners of non-agricultural rural enterprises; a small proportion of owners of enterprises in the formal sector	200–600	220
Unskilled employees in the formal non-agricultural sector; a significant proportion of smallholders; most of the owners of non-agricultural rural enterprises	120–200	240
Employees in formal-sector agriculture; a small proportion of unskilled employees in the formal sector; better-off wage earners and self-employed persons in the informal urban sector; a small proportion of owners of non-agricuultural rural enterprises	60–120	330
Workers employed on small holdings and in rural non-agricultural enterprises; a significant proportion of employed and self-employed persons in the informal urban sector; a sizeable number of smallholders	20–60	1 140
Smallholders; pastoralists in semi-arid and arid zones; unemployed and landless persons in both rural and urban areas	20 and less	330
Total		2 340

*Very approximate.
SOURCE : ILO : *Employment, Incomes and Equality* . . . , op. cit., p. 74.

Essentially the report suggests a series of diverse but inter-related measures for ensuring more equal access to the opportunities provided by the expanding Kenyan economy for those now at a disadvantage in this respect and unable to obtain productive employment. This would require a reorientation of government expenditure towards the poorer regions and poorer elements of the population as well as the adoption of an overall economic policy which would shift employment and earning opportunities in the direction of these poorer groups. One device recommended by the mission for use in various contexts is the system of quotas; quotas for government expenditure in various regions (maximum quotas for Nairobi and minimum quotas for poorer regions); quotas for access to primary and secondary education, with special consideration for girls; quotas for entry into the civil service; regional quotas for access to health services, etc.; and quotas to enable the poorest farmers and women farmers to benefit from extension services.

The overall strategy of the report is described as being one of redistribution from growth. The Kenyan economy has been expanding regularly at the high rate of 7 to 8 per cent per annum in terms of aggregate production ever since independence. The mission did not make any specific quantitative analysis of the likely future growth rates but many of its recommendations would have the effect of raising the rate – for instance those aimed at raising the incomes of the lower income groups through more productive employment, at intensification of land use, at promotion of the informal sector, at easing balance-of-payments pressures through changed products, changed technology and revised economic policies, and at retention of a higher proportion of the profits of foreign enterprises. While measures to improve the position of the lower income groups might have the effect of reducing the growth rate at least temporarily, in the special circumstances of Kenya there is no reason why these measures should necessarily outweigh others tending to raise the growth rate.[6]

The model of redistribution from growth reproduced in the mission's report[7] is based on the assumption that the rate of growth of production will remain at 7 per cent per annum, that the real incomes of those in the top income bracket, i.e. the 1 per cent of the total population receiving 10 per cent of total income, can be stabilized for a number of years, and that the resources gained from this freeze of top incomes can be switched to a special labour-intensive investment package in favour of those in the bottom income bracket, i.e. the almost 40 per cent of the total population also receiving 10 per cent of total income. The content of this labour-intensive investment package can be derived from the recommendations of the report as a whole. This approach involves the additional assumption that, prior to redistribution, the benefits of economic growth at the rate of 7 per cent per annum would be equally spread over the poor and other sections of the population. There is little evidence as to whether or not this has been the case in the Kenyan economy as a whole,[8] but income distribution among the African population has almost inevitably become more unequal since independence, as a result of the Kenyanization of jobs (commanding incomes far above the average) and of land previously held by expatriates.

Through redistribution from growth, the incomes of the poorer 35 to 40 per cent of the population could be doubled within the relatively short span of a decade or less. The model demonstrates that the period required is not highly sensitive to the capital–output ratio of the special investment package. This doubling of the the incomes of the lower income groups could make a real impact on the proportion of the 'working poor' in the total population, especially if further refinement reoriented the measures towards improvement of the position of the neediest within the lower income groups, a notion which is central to the whole report.

If applied to all the aspects of development strategy, redistribution from growth would have a profound effect on the programme of each government department and in every area of the country. Full implementation would require a shift from central to local planning in order to permit adjustment in the allocation of government resources, as required, to meet the specific priority needs of each area for abolishing poverty.

The real issue is, of course, the political feasibility of the strategy proposed. Already the post-independence structures of incomes and land ownership, power and position, have become more firmly based, though the patterns of privilege and class are still affected by traditional family and other ties. Local interests are bound in important ways to interests abroad through the links of trade and private investment, particularly as regards the developed countries. This constellation of local and overseas interests, of which there are many but not all of which are concordant, makes it difficult to effect the change of strategy required. However, the objective of the Government, as stated in Sessional Paper No. 10 submitted to the National Assembly in 1965,[9] is clear : the benefits of growth must be equitably distributed. The question remains whether the changes required to achieve this objective can be set in motion before the interests inhibiting them strengthen to the point of obstructing all reform.

The rationale of redistribution from growth resides in the low levels of income in the country as a whole, together with the patterns of extreme inequality inherited from the colonial period. These characteristics Kenya shares with the majority of the African countries. That is the basic reason for supposing that the strategy proposed in the Kenya report, with approporiate modifications, may have relevance for other countries in Africa faced with similar problems of unemployment and poverty and gross imbalances in incomes and opportunities.

11 Income Distribution and Population Growth*

The question of income distribution, whether in relation to population growth or from some other angle, can be considered at various levels. There is the international or global distribution, essentially the problem of the 'gap' between the rich and poor countries; there is the question of income distribution within given developing countries which, in turn, has many different aspects : regional distribution, urban/rural distribution, income distribution within the rural or urban sector, distribution between economic sectors such as agriculture, industry, mining, etc.; distribution between the modern or 'formal' sector and the non-modern or 'informal' sector of the economy, etc. For each of these aspects can also be discussed and analysed either in relation to population growth in the country as a whole, or in the population or labour force attached to the particular sector under discussion. This paper concentrates on income distribution between rich and poor groups *within* developing countries; this is assumed to be the emphasis of the discussions at the meeting. But a few prior remarks on the international distribution of incomes may not be out of place.

INTERNATIONAL INCOME DISTRIBUTION

As a purely statistical statement, it can be said that the widening gap between rich and poor countries is entirely, or almost entirely, due to the more rapid growth of population in the poorer countries. If the 'gap' is defined as differences in *per capita* GNP

* Paper prepared for UN International Symposium on Population and Development, Cairo, 4–14 June 1974, preparatory to World Population Conference, 1974. I am indebted to my colleagues Robert Cassen and Nicholas Stamp for advice and assistance.

– admittedly not the only and perhaps not the most important measure of the gap – the data indicate that the aggregate GNPs of rich and poor countries are increasing at very similar rates, especially if we concentrate our attention on the Western countries as representing the 'rich' group. But while aggregate GNPs increase fairly uniformly, both at a little over 5 per cent,[1] for each of the two groups taken as a whole, there is the striking difference that in the rich group, over 75 per cent of the aggregate growth represents growth *per capita*, while only less than 25 per cent of the aggregate growth is absorbed in spreading the additional output over larger numbers. In sharp contrast, in the poorer developing countries about half of the total increase in aggregate GNP is absorbed by larger numbers, leaving only one half or so of the total increase available for improving the *per capita* supply of goods and services. Thus, while growth in *aggregate* production is more or less the same, the rate of growth in *per capita* production in the rich countries is about double what it is in the poor countries – and this difference is entirely due to the different rate of population growth.

This statement was described above as a 'statistical statement' – and this qualification must now be emphasized. We could also add the word 'static' to the description of this statement. We do not know whether with a different rate of population increase in the poorer countries, say one much lower and closer to the 0·6 or 0·7 per cent characteristic of the richer countries of Europe[2] than their current rate of $2\frac{1}{2}$ per cent or so, the aggregate increase in production would still be the same; nor even whether it would be lower or higher, if not the same. Hence, the above statement tells us nothing about the complex dynamic interrelationships between population growth and growth of production, and we must be careful not to draw unjustified conclusions from it. All the same, it is a prima facie important fact that differential population growth accounts for practically the entire growth in the relative gap between *per capita* incomes of rich and poor countries in the world today, even if it is a static and statistical statement.[3] The burden of proof to the contrary would seem to be on those who dispute the meaning of the statistical fact that differences in population growth are crucial.

There is still another relevant comparison between rich and

poor countries that we might make. This relates to income distribution within them, rather than the gap in *per capita* income between them. As a general statement it seems well established that income distribution in poorer countries tends to be less equal (more unequal) than in the richer countries. This is so whether we measure the distribution of incomes by some index based on the whole shape of the Lorenz curve, or whether we take more particular indicators such as the share of income going to the top of 10 or 20 per cent of the population, or the ratio of incomes of the top 20 per cent to the bottom 20 per cent. There is perhaps one exception, i.e. in very poor countries the *average* is so low that the poorest 10 or 20 per cent of the population may have – indeed *must* have, in order to survive – a higher ratio to the average than in richer countries. There are individual exceptions to the rule of greater inequality of income distribution in poorer countries : there are individual LDCs with a relatively equal income distribution, particularly in Asia,[4] and there are one or two richer countries (such as France or the Federal Republic of Germany) with a more unequal income distribution than some of the more equal LDCs.[5] It is also of interest for our purposes to note that those LDCs which have a more equal income distribution tend to be countries which (a) have a fairly high *per capita* income, bringing them into the 'intermediate' group closer to the richer countries; (b) tend to have a high growth rate of GNP; and (c) tend to have a falling birth rate, after significant recent reductions, and a comparatively slow rate of population growth both in relation to the average of LDCs and also in relation to what we would expect in the light of the broad relationship connecting *per capita* incomes on the one hand, and birth rates or rates of population growth on the other.

INCOME DISTRIBUTION WITHIN DEVELOPING COUNTRIES

(1) *Population Growth and Lack of Employment*
If we are concerned with income distribution, because we consider reduction of poverty as the real purpose of development, our attention is immediately riveted upon the question of *employment*. Poverty means a failure to attain a defined modest mini-

mum income and the standards of food, clothing, shelter, access to water, social services, etc., which go with this minimum income. The way to obtain these minimum incomes, by and large, is through productive employment.[6] Lack of productive employment is the major cause of poverty, i.e. of failure to obtain the stipulated minimum income. This is also the most useful definition of unemployment in the LDCs, where it does not, as is normally the case in the rich countries, take the form of measurable absence of a 'job'. Hence the question of income distribution largely overlaps with the question of more productive employment, or reduction of unemployment. It is from this angle that we can obtain a first rough picture of the relation of rapid population growth and income distribution/employment.

Taking for illustration a comparison between Kenya and the United Kingdom, Kenya has a rate of population growth – and therefore by and large of the adult labour force – of 3·3 per cent per annum,[7] compared with 0·4 per cent in the United Kingdom. Hence Kenya must find, per million population, eight times as many additional productive employment opportunities as the United Kingdom in order to cater for its growing population. But Kenya has available for this purpose only perhaps one-fifteenth of the total resources (GNP) for each million population as the UK. Thus, while eight times as many jobs have to be provided per million population, only one-fifteenth of the resources are available to do so. This means that for each job required only one-hundred and twentieth, or less than 1 per cent, is available as resources per job. If Kenya tried to provide the jobs required in such a way that the jobs would be of exactly the same kind as in the UK, only 1 per cent or so of the total number of additional needed jobs could be provided. The rest of the additional job seekers would have to remain 'unemployed', i.e. poor. In fact, of course, the distribution of jobs by sectors and types *is* different in Kenya and the resources required per job are, in fact, lower. All the same, our simple model shows that unless the technology, nature and distribution of jobs are very radically different, there is likely to be increasing unemployment among new job seekers, and increasing income inequality in Kenya, as a result of the more rapid population growth. In fact, the technology available is *not sufficiently* different to make up for the

120 : 1 discrepancy. Thus our simple model may serve as a first explanation of the rising unemployment, especially among young job seekers, and of the increased 'dualism' and new inequalities of income distribution in the LDCs.

It is a matter of semantics whether in the above example we say that the problem is due to the more rapid population increase in Kenya or to the absence of an appropriate technology. It is the relationship between these two forces which matters : the larger the rate of population increase, the more is a radically different technology needed to provide productive employment and prevent increases in poverty. With a given state of technology, rapid population increase clearly increases the danger of unemployment and rising poverty and inequalities.

Our simple model also helps us to understand another part of the population story. The richer countries of today were never faced, at a comparative stage in their development (say 80–150 years ago), with this kind of problem. Their rate of population increase was lower, because of higher death rates and lower birth rates, and also because of the possibility of emigration. Above all, however, in their days, the urban and industrial technology was much more labour-intensive; there was no superior 'more modern' labour-saving technology available for import from elsewhere, from countries with different requirements and resource endowments. Taken together, these factors meant that it was fairly easy for the presently developed countries to absorb the population increases in urban and industrial sectors; the number of people engaged in agriculture and in rural areas generally was first stabilized and then fell at a fairly early stage in development. This rapid urbanization and industrialization in the structure of employment was clearly related to the fall in birth rates. From all we know, falling birth rates are associated with urbanization and industrialization; the desire for smaller families is clearly more prevalent, and the effectiveness of family-planning programmes greater, among urban populations and especially those associated with modern industrial activities.[8] But in most of today's developing countries the number engaged in agriculture and living in rural areas will still have to increase for decades to come, while the percentage of the population engaged in modern industrial occupations is not rising as it did so

G

rapidly in the rich countries of today. Here again we see that the same configuration of more rapid population increase and a too capital-intensive technology creates both a dualistic and unequal economic structure with a limited high income sector, and a situation in which the fall in birth rates will be difficult and retarded in the absence of specific income and employment policies and perhaps family-planning policies.

(2) *The Traditional Model No Longer Applicable*
The traditional development model is no longer applicable for reasons implicit in what has been said already. According to this model,[9] the rural surplus population would be steadily absorbed in the industrial sector, while its existence will keep real wages in the industrial sector down so as to produce reasonable equality between rural and urban incomes (although possibly greater inequality as between capitalists and workers within the urban sector); with the prospect of a 'golden age' when the rural surplus population will be exhausted, both rural and urban incomes will rise together, and the income distribution will become more equal as a result of the strengthened position of labour, a weakening position of capitalists due to an abundance of capital, and the spreading of a 'welfare state' situation. Such a situation would also be clearly favourable to a reduction in birth rates; the increased standard of living would by all available evidence[10] reduce birth rates and the increased social security would make children unnecessary as a means to security for old age, while at the same time they would become unnecessary as earning assets as a result of higher incomes and they would turn into increasing economic liabilities as a result of parents' rising standards for their children and of the spreading 'welfare services', especially of education.

Paradoxically, this model applies to the rich countries of today much more than the developing countries for which it was designed. In the developing countries we face a different reality, based on the ratio of population increase to the nature of technology already described. Even though the towns may be increasing rapidly in absolute size and new elements of urban squalor and poverty with their own tendencies to high birth rates will spread, yet at the same time there will be an increase in rural population deprived of the capital resources necessary for effective rural development, and an increase in income inequality due to the privileged position of owners of capital and land and all those associated with the limited modern sector. The bulk of the population will not be placed in that position of increased material and social benefits, and the expectation of such benefits, which would create a situation in which the desire for smaller families takes hold and family programmes be come effective.

The traditional (Arthur Lewis) model is not so much wrong, but it omits to state that it will only come about as a result of development strategies which benefit the agricultural population through effective agricultural and rural development, increase the employment-absorption capacity of the economy, and which create 'welfare state' conditions of rising material and social benefits for the bulk of the population, which the model erroneously assumes to come about in the natural course of events.

(3) A 'Generation Gap' In Income Distribution

A somewhat neglected relationship between income distribution and population growth which deserves to be emphasized is the following. Where birth rates are high and population growth rapid, a high proportion of the population consists of children. Typically, in many countries, over 40 per cent of the population may be under fifteen years of age, compared with perhaps 20–25 per cent in the richer countries. This has been noted so far mainly because it results in a high dependency ratio, each producer having more dependents, thus lowering *per capita* incomes.[11] What it also means, however, is that there is one half of the population – children and very young people – which almost automatically lives at a much lower average standard of living. Where birth rates are high, the great majority of children are almost by definition members of large families. The *per capita* incomes of those living in large families are lower than those in small families, even if the birth rate is the same for different income groups. If the birth rate is higher for poorer income groups, as is almost invariably the case, the income gap between large families and small families is further widened.

It is a fairly safe assumption that if the average *per capita* income in a developing country is, say, US $200 per annum and the birth rate is correspondingly high, the average *per capita* income of children – heavily weighted towards large families – will be little more than half the national average, i.e. US $100. This aspect of the 'generation gap'[12] is particularly harmful from a developmental view point. The children with their full productive life before them need the 'human investment' provided by a minimum income *more* than the adults, rather than *less*. There is accumulating evidence that the poverty and attendant malnutrition of children result in mental as well as physical damage, thus reducing the effectiveness of future investments in education, equipment for producers, etc., in this way perpetuating the cycle of poverty and inequality.

Here is a clear demonstration of one of the many vicious circles at work : a high birth rate produces a high proportion of children and, through the generation gap, income inequalities which tend to perpetuate themselves; at the same time, income inequalities through their effect on the birth rate in general, and through the additional effect of differentially high birth rates among the poorer population, create new inequalities between the generations, laying a foundation for a new cycle of subsequent income inequalities. It is clear that deliberate government policies to shift income to families with children,[13] and/or to reduce the proportion of children in the population and the proportion of children within large families, are required to break these vicious circles.

(4) *A Model of Interrelationship Between Income Distribution and Population, with Policy Suggestions*

A model of interrelationship with population growth in which income distribution and the associated employment factor emerge in a crucial role is as follows. The desire for smaller families, as well as the capacity to translate this desire into action, are a function of a minimum level of income; and of those minimum levels of security and expectation of future progress and minimum levels of education, literacy, health, nutrition, etc., which are associated with such reasonable minimum levels of income. The bulk of the population, in poor countries, reaches such minimum levels only if the scarce resources of the country, and the scanty increments arising from their growth, are widely distributed to the great bulk of the population; in other words, only if incomes are either fairly equally distributed in the first place, or else are heavily redistributed in the direction of greater equality. An initial reasonably equal income distribution can be obtained from an appropriate economic structure with emphasis on small farming, small business, use of labour-intensve technologies, public services benefiting the masses of the population, rural development and a dispersed type of development widely spread over the different regions of the country, etc. A reasonably equal income distribution through redistribution can be obtained through appropriate incomes policies, tax policies and appropriate redirection of government expenditure. It is when such conditions are present that the bulk of the population will be willing and able to limit families, and the vicious circle of rapid population increase and poverty can be broken and converted into a cumulative process of improvement.

This theory has been most clearly described and supported by William Rich[14] who calls it the 'Development-Fertility Continuum'. This view seems consistent both with empirical data (although the possibility of testing it is limited by the general paucity of data relating to income distribution) and also generally with the results of simulation models (though again such models do not generally incorporate income distribution as a specific variable). We have already mentioned above that the developing countries with lower birth and death rates tend to be countries with relatively equal income distribution (such as Taiwan, Korea, Sri Lanka, Chile, Uruguay, Cuba, Barbados). In rich countries, of course, the necessary minimum level can be attained by the bulk of the population regardless of income distribution. This would seem to rule out income distribution *as such*, as an important factor in this situation. This also seems to be consistent with empirical evidence.

This view of the matter suggests a policy of moving the bulk of the population to the threshold level where smaller families are desired and practicable, i.e. a policy of reducing the incidence of poverty as quickly and widely as possible. As it happens, this is also increasingly proposed and accepted as the real purpose of development, and an objective which is not only politically preferable to an abstract objective such as maximizing the growth rate of GNP, but which will in effect (and perhaps paradoxically) also contribute more effectively to the growth of GNP. Perhaps the three pilot ILO employment missions in Latin America, Asia and Africa[15] undertaken by the ILO and financed by the UNDP may be cited as indicative of this new approach.

If we can now add to the other conclusive arguments in favour of such a policy an effect in reducing birth rates and thus releasing the upward cumulative movements flowing from such an effect on birth rates, the case for this reorientation of development policies would become even more overwhelming, and income distribution move into the centre of the development picture.

The most immediate impact of a reduction in poverty and the raising of the incomes of the bulk of the population towards a reasonable minimum (reasonable in relation to the resources of the country) would be likely to be on mortality rates rather than birth rates. A better income means better nutrition, better health, better education, etc., and a reduction in death rates is almost certain to be a result of such a syndrome of improvement. Superficially, it might be thought that the reduction in mortality would go against the trend of the preceding argument, since it would mean an increase rather than a decrease in the rate of population increase. But this view would be superficial for two reasons :

(1) An increase in population due to a fall in death rates has a quite different (more favourable) developmental impact than an increase in population growth due to rising birth rates. In the former case, the dependency ratio is improved (unless, of course, the reduction in mortality is very heavily concentrated on infantile mortality only). Premature death is an economic waste of resources, and its prevention (like the reduction in poverty) is in any case itself one of the fundamental development objectives.

(2) A second and more important reason is that the reduction in mortality rates is a factor which may be either necessary or at least important in helping to create a desire for fewer births. The desire for large families derives much of its force from the desire to have a number of children surviving for support in old age. If there is high mortality it can easily be seen that a desire to have two sons surviving into one's own

old age requires eight to ten births in the family; with reduced mortality this figure will come down to four or five. A model explaining the course of birth rates as partly a lagged conse- quence of the course of mortality rates has been developed and applied to Taiwan, Puerto Rico and Colombia with a great deal of explanatory validity.[16]

The time lag between falling death rates and falling birth rates will, of course, create a transitional period, during which popula- tion growth will be rapid. But the harmful effect of this would normally be offset by the economically beneficial effects of lower death rates in reducing the waste of loss of human investment in feeding, educating, training and equipping people who die before they have made their full productive contribution. What is bene- ficial for development is not just a low birth rate or a low rate of population increase, but a combination of low birth rates and low death rates. This has been achieved in the rich countries of today. In primitive communities, the rate of population in- crease may also be very low, but in their case as the result of an economically wasteful combination of high birth rates being off- set by high death rates. Hence, if the reduced mortality is a necessary first step towards achieving the more desirable low birth rate/low death rate type of equilibrium, it is a step in the right direction.[17] If more equal income distribution leads to lower mortality rates, as well as lower birth rates, this is not in any real sense an ambivalent or contradictory development.

This view of the development-fertility continuum is com- patible with various threshold constraints. The nature of the curve which links incomes and income security on the one hand, and birth rates on the other hand, may well not be a straight line. It may well be that in the LDCs, and particularly in the poorer ones, the level of income needed for an effective fall in birth rates is higher than can be achieved with present resources. In these cases it could again be superficially argued that if there is such a threshold effect, a policy of income distribution and employment creation should concentrate on the somewhat higher income groups close to the threshold level rather than on the poorest groups further distant from it. However, except as a very short-run policy, this *would* be short-sighted. Obviously, to raise incomes to the threshold level can only be a gradual and continuous process. Just as a reduction in mortality rates (apart from being desirable in itself) may be a necessary first step towards reducing birth rates, so to move the poorest population groups within closer striking distance from the threshold level, even if they cannot yet cross it, may be a necessary step in order to enable them to cross the threshold level at a later date (again apart from being a desirable policy on other grounds).

(5) *The Income Distribution/Birth Rate Syndrome*

Among the problems of quantification already mentioned is the limited range of data on income distribution and on the extent of poverty, resulting from the concentration until now on growth rates of GNP and other components of the classical growth model such as savings, investment, capital/output ratios, etc. It is to be hoped that this gap in our knowledge will be gradually filled, as attention becomes focused on more meaningful measures of development. There is however another difficulty in quantification and information gathering : this arises from the fact that the relationship between income distribution and birth rates is characterized by multiple and complex interlocking circular relationships with mutual cumulative feedbacks and difficulties of disentangling causes and effects. This is best expressed by saying that the dimensions of poverty form a syndrome, from which individual factors can only be disentangled at the risk of gross over-simplification. Poverty, as a result of inequality of income distribution, has a number of dimensions : lack of food, clothing, shelter, education, training opportunities; lack of access to social services, government services, information of all kinds; lack of hope and purpose in planning for the future; lack of willingness or ability to take the risks involved in new initiatives; lack of security. All these form major aspects of poverty and all these have direct feedback effects on birth rates : poor health and poor nutrition increase mortality rates and thus increase the birth rate required to achieve given survival rates; lack of literacy or access to government health services makes it more difficult to understand and obtain family planning services; risk aversion makes poor people that much more reluctant to change any of their traditional habits and patterns; improved access to social amenities such as electricity, educational facilities, entertainments, etc., is known to lower the birth rate.[18] Moreover, these various aspects of poverty are also mutually reinforcing amongst each other; lack of education and literacy worsens nutrition and health; lack of health worsens nutrition by making it more difficult to absorb calories, proteins and vitamins; poor housing or lack of access to piped water endangers health, etc. Thus, not only is there a reinforcing cumulative relationship between poverty and high birth rates, but there is also a similar reinforcing cumulative relationship among the various dimensions of poverty. This complex situation, while not conducive to the development of numerical and quantitative analysis and verification, does on the other hand establish a particularly strong case for action. If improvement in any of these factors is likely to lead to cumulative improvement in other factors and is likely through reduced birth rates to result in further reductions of poverty beginning a new cycle of improvement, it is obvious that the benefits of any initial improvement are much greater than a direct and static cost/ benefit analysis is likely to show. No doubt, much more sophisticated techniques of cost/benefit analysis, including all the indirect effects and feedbacks, can be notionally developed, but this does not resolve the underlying difficulty of finding the data for such a sophisticated analysis and defining the nature of the mutual relationships involved. It is for this reason that in the past simulation models and factors analysis, rather than cost/benefit analysis, have been applied. Another result is that as long as expenditures, whether by national governments or aid donors or international organizations, are based on the project approach and related types of cost/benefit analysis, investment will be biased against the kind of project which would break into the vicious circle between poverty and low birth rates. Heroic attempts have been made to calculate the cost/benefit ratio of family planning programmes and projects,[19] usually with very favourable results. But little attempt has been made from the other end, i.e. to include in the cost/benefit analysis projects designed to attack poverty, benefits arising from the relationship with lower birth rates.

H

TABLE 11.1　Growth of GNP and GNP *Per Capita* by Regions

		GNP % (*p.a.*)	GNP/Cap % (*p.a.*)
World (excludes China)	1960–65	5·5	3·4
	1965–70	5·4	3·3
	1960–70	5·6	3·5
Centrally planned economies	1960–65	5·9	4·8
	1965–70	7·1	6·0
	1960–70	6·7	5·6
Market economies	1960–65	5·2	2·9
	1965–70	4·8	2·6
	1960–70	5·1	2·9
Developed market economies	1960–65	5·3	4·0
	1965–70	4·6	3·6
	1960–70	5·1	4·0
Developing market economies	1960–65	5·0	2·3
	1965–70	5·8	3·1
	1960–70	5·2	2·5
Africa (excluding S. Africa)	1960–65	4·4	1·8
	1965–70	5·0	2·3
	1960–70	4·7	2·1
North America	1960–65	4·9	3·5
	1965–70	3·4	2·3
	1960–70	4·6	3·3
Caribbean and Latin America	1960–65	5·3	2·4
	1965–70	5·8	2·6
	1960–70	5·4	2·4
Asia, Middle East	1960–65	7·1	4·2
	1965–70	7·5	4·5
	1960–70	7·4	4·4
S.E. and E. Asia (excluding Japan)	1960–65	4·2	1·6
	1965–70	5·5	2·8
	1960–70	4·4	1·8
Europe	1960–65	5·0	3·8
	1965–70	4·8	4·0
	1960–70	4·7	3·8
Oceania	1960–65	5·1	2·9
	1965–70	5·3	3·2
	1960–70	5·1	2·9

SOURCE: UN Yearbook of National Accounts Statistics, 1971, Vol III (International Tables).

TABLE 11.2 Income Distribution Estimates

Percentage shares in total national income going to population groups of different incomes levels in 44 countries

	Poorest 20%	Poorest 60%	Middle 40–60%	Highest 5%	Highest 20%	Pop growth 1963–71
Argentina	7·00	30·40	13·10	29·40	52·00	1·5*
Bolivia	4·00	26·60	8·90	35·70	59·10	2·6*
Brazil	3·50	22·70	10·20	38·40	61·50	2·8*
Burma	10·00	36·00	13·00	28·21	48·50	?
Ceylon	4·45	27·47	13·81	18·38	52·31	2·2*
Chad	12·00	35·00	12·00	23·00	43·00	2·3*
Chile	5·40	27·00	12·00	22·60	52·30	1·4
Colombia	2·21	15·88	8·97	40·36	68·06	3·2*
Costa Rica	6·00	25·40	12·10	35·00	60·00	3·2
Dahomey	8·00	30·00	12·00	32·00	50·00	2·5*
Ecuador	6·30	42·60	26·10	21·50	41·80	3·4*
El Salvador	5·50	23·60	11·30	33·00	61·40	?
Gabon	2·00	15·00	7·00	47·00	71·00	?
Greece	9·00	34·10	12·30	23·00	49·50	?
India	8·00	36·00	16·00	8·00	42·00	2·2*
Iraq	2·00	16·00	8·00	34·00	68·00	3·2*
Israel	6·80	38·80	18·60	11·20	39·40	3·0*
Ivory Coast	8·00	30·00	12·00	29·00	55·00	2·4*
Jamaica	2·20	19·00	10·80	31·20	61·50	1·4
Japan	4·70	31·10	15·80	14·80	46·00	1·1
Kenya	7·00	21·00	7·00	22·20	64·00	3·1*
Lebanon	3·00	23·00	15·80	34·00	61·00	2·9*
Libya	0·11	1·78	1·28	46·40	89·50	3·7*
Malagasy	7·00	23·00	9·00	37·00	59·00	?
Mexico	3·66	21·75	11·25	28·52	58·04	3·2*
Morocco	7·10	22·20	7·70	20·60	65·40	?
Niger	12·00	35·00	12·00	23·00	42·00	2·7*
Nigeria	7·00	23·00	9·00	38·38	60·90	2·5*
Pakistan	6·50	33·00	15·50	20·00	45·00	2·1*
Panama	4·90	28·10	13·80	34·50	56·70	3·0*
Peru	4·04	17·10	8·30	48·30	67·60	3·1*
Philippines	4·30	24·70	12·00	27·50	55·80	3·0*
Rhodesia	4·00	20·00	8·00	60·00	65·00	?
Senegal	3·00	20·00	10·00	36·00	64·00	2·4*
Sierra Leone	3·80	19·20	9·10	33·80	64·10	1·6*
South Africa	1·94	16·27	10·16	39·38	57·36	3·1*
Sudan	5·60	29·30	14·30	17·10	48·10	2·8*
Surinam	10·70	37·00	14·74	15·40	42·40	?
Taiwan	4·50	29·00	14·80	24·10	52·00	?
Tanzania	9·75	29·25	9·85	42·90	61·00	2·6*
Trinidad and Tobago	3·60	18·52	9·16	26·60	57·00	1·4*
Tunisia	4·97	20·57	9·95	22·44	65·00	?
Venezuela	4·40	30·00	16·60	23·20	47·10	?
Zambia	6·27	26·95	11·10	37·50	57·10	2·9*
Averages	5·6	26	12	30	56	

SOURCES : I. Adelman and C. T. Morris, 'An Anatomy of Income Distribution Patterns in Developing Nations', in *Development Digest*, Vol IX, No. 4, Oct 1971.
UN Demographic Yearbook 1971.
* Signifies that figures cannot be regarded as reliable.

TABLE 11.3 Income Distribution in Ten Developed Market Economies

Country	Quintile Group					Topmost 5%	Pop. growth 1963–71
	1st	2nd	3rd	4th	5th		
UK (1964)	5·1	10·2	16·6	23·9	44·2	19·2	0·4
The Netherlands (1962)	4·0	10·0	16·0	21·6	48·4	23·6	1·2
Sweden (1963)	4·4	9·6	17·4	24·6	44·0	17·6	0·8
West Germany (1964)	5·3	10·1	13·7	18·0	52·9	33·7	0·8
Denmark (1963)	5·0	10·8	16·8	24·2	43·2	16·9	0·7
Norway (1963)	4·5	12·1	18·5	24·4	40·5	15·4	0·8
France (1962)	1·9	7·6	14·0	22·8	53·7	25·0	0·9
Finland (1962)	2·4	8·7	15·4	24·2	49·3	21·0	0·4
Australia (1966–7)	7·4	11·7	17·4	22·8	40·7	16·2	1·9
USA (1967)	5·0	12·4	17·8	21·3	43·5	17·8	1·1
Unweighted average	4·5	10·3	16·4	22·8	46·0	20·6	

SOURCES: 'Trends in Income Distribution; A Comparative Study', Economic and Scientific Research Foundation, New Delhi, 1971.
UN Demographic Yearbook 1971.

12 Science and Technology for the Development of Poorer Countries*

Until a few years ago nobody would have doubted that the tremendous development of the world's technological power, both of science (know-why) and of technology (know-how), presented great advantages for the late comers in the process of development of the poorer countries of today. Surely the more accumulated knowledge to draw from, the easier development must become?

So to a point, reality seemed to support this view unquestionably held by practically all economists. Germany and the US developed more rapidly than the UK, the pioneer country of the industrial revolution. But then Russia in turn, and even Argentine and Southern Brazil, looked like catching up rapidly, and so did a little later, Australia and Canada. Even the growth of the poorer countries of today, on an overall view, is quite fast by historical standards, with growth rates of GNP of 5 to 6 per cent. If this does not result in corresponding rises in per capita income, this is due to faster rates of population growth than the rich countries of today had to contend with at any time in their history, when they also had emigration outlets not open to the developing countries of today. Rapid population increase is a different problem, though for our present subject it may be relevant to reflect that the reduction in mortality rates is itself part

* This paper is mainly derived from the Sussex Manifesto 1970 (above p. 154 ff.). Material from this document is produced by kind permission of the other members of the group, (Charles Cooper, Christopher Freeman, Geoffrey Oldham, Oscar Gish, Stephen Hill, R. C. Desai) and the United Nations. Other parts of the paper are taken from a lecture in February 1973 at the Institut fur Weltwirtschaft at the University of Kiel.

of the impact of the rich countries' technology – in this case, health technology.

But there is now a spreading recognition that even growth rates of 5 per cent, 6 per cent or more of GNP do not represent real development – quite apart from the fact that so much of the growth is slowed up by population increase. It is now clear that rapid growth of output can, and does, go hand in hand with increased impoverishment of large sections of the population, a rapid rise in the number of people living below any acceptable poverty line, rise in underemployment, and a general failure in the development process to involve larger numbers of the population. Hence, I think we are bound to say that in the overall picture we do not see a satisfactory development of the poorer countries, and this in spite of the unprecedented accumulation of know-why and know-how. Why is this?

My thesis is that it is precisely *because* of the accumulation of science and technology, or rather because of the specific nature of this accumulation, that we witness such widespread failures of real development among the late comers, belying the unthinking optimism of earlier days.

This thesis can be best illustrated by pointing to two striking disproportions. The first disproportion can be seen in the fact that with a rate of population increase at least three times higher than in the rich countries, the developing countries of today – per million population – have to create three times as many new jobs; yet they have to do this with resources which are only perhaps one-twentieth or less than those of the rich countries. This means that resources per job required are only one-sixtieth or less. This in turn means that if the developing countries of today tried to create jobs of the same kind and with the same technology as the rich countries of today, only one-sixtieth of their new job-seekers, i.e. less than 2 per cent, would in fact be employed at 'modern' standards. The rest, over 98 per cent, would remain unemployed. In reality, of course, the situation is not quite as crass as that. Many more of the jobs will be in rural sectors and other occupations requiring less capital per job, and in many ways, the technology used even in similar jobs, will be less capital-intensive and hence require fewer resources. But all the same, our numerical exercise is sufficiently close to the way in which things are moving in the developing countries of today to be meaningful.

The other disproportion can be seen in the present distribution of the creation of new knowledge and technology as between rich and poor countries. Here we face the difficulty that the 'creation of new science and technology' is not directly measurable. However, as often in economics, e.g. in national income statistics, where we cannot measure the total output of something, we may be able to measure the total input or cost which goes into the production of the output. For example, in national income statistics we cannot really measure the output of civil servants or university professors, so we substitute the salaries paid to them. In this way we use input figures as a proxy for output figures. We do so without too much worry even though we know perfectly well that a good civil servant or university teacher may be worth to his country many more times more than his salary, while a bad civil servant or teacher may make a strong negative contribution.

In the creation of science and technology, we can also in principle and increasingly also in actuality, measure the inputs of countries of such a creation. These are the so-called R & D expenditures – research and development expenditures – which include basic and applied research, as well as pilot and prototype development, before investment takes over. To these expenditures should be added expenditures for the necessary infrastructure of scientific and technological services – laboratories with their equipment, research institutes, patent offices, scientific and technological laboratories, training institutions, etc. The rich countries of today, with less than one-third of the world's total population, account for pretty close to 99 per cent of total R & D expenditures. The same applies to the scientific and technological infrastructure expenditures. The poor countries, with more than twice the population, account for only 1 per cent. Expressed on a *per capita* basis, we have here a disproportion of over 200 : 1, an even more striking disproportion than the one of 60 : 1 applying to resources available per population required.

The point of the thesis here presented is that these two disparities are very closely connected; in fact, they are two sides of the same coin. Taken together, they share the falsity of the optimistic claim that there is a simple accumulation of science and technology which favours the newcomer in development. Ninety-nine per cent of the total creation of new science and technology being in the rich countries, this naturally represents a system of solving the problems of rich countries by methods which are suited to the circumstances and requirements of the rich countries. The vast preponderance of the new science and technology in the rich countries also ensures that the little that is done in the developing countries fails to reach the minimum scale at which it is effective, and that the scientists and technologists, as members of the scientific community, will accept the definitions of priority problems and suitable methods of those 99 per cent of their colleagues who live in the rich countries. They themselves will, in any case, have been trained in this image. The result is an international technology which, as shown by the first disparity, leads to a situation where growth is concentrated upon a small modern sector, while the resources of the poorer countries are insufficient to spread participation in growth over more than a minority of the population and thus convert growth into real development.

There is still another way of presenting this: the picture of a simple accumulation of knowledge, an increasing store on which the late comers can draw, is false. What we see is much more comparable to a flow than to simple accumulation. New science and new technology is created at one end, but displaces science and technology previously existing. Being located in the rich countries with their dynamic search for new knowledge and their vastly and increasingly different requirements, priorities and factor endowments, it is not surprising that the knowledge displaced or submerged at one end, may be more useful to the developing countries than the new knowledge added at the other end. Therefore it is by no means clear that from the point of view of the poorer countries of the world, there is in fact an accumulation of knowledge in the relevant science.

The brain drain is perhaps the clearest and most visible expression of the big social effect which the vast concentration on science and technology in the rich countries has on the poor countries. The tendency for scientists and technologists to migrate from the poorer countries is not only due to the attraction of higher salaries, but also to the intercultural advantages to a scientist or technologist to have contact with a much wider scientific community and to be properly supported by an ample infrastructure of equipment, laboratory and publication facilities, assistance, etc. The brain drain from rich to poor countries is clearly contrary to the global priorities which require more, rather than less, emphasis on the problems of the majority of mankind living in the poorer countries, and of more, rather than less, balanced distribution of R & D work between the two groups of countries. It is also directly harmful to the *developing* countries, in so far as they are losing their scarce intellectual élite and all the costs of training and education embodied in them.

However, we must make a qualification to this last statement. Although the brain drain – I would prefer to call it the *external* brain drain – is so visible and measurable because it involves movement of people across national boundaries, and yet in practice, the more important brain drain may be, what I would call, the *internal* brain drain. By this I mean the tendency already noted above that the scientists and technologists of the poorer countries will in fact behave as members of the scientific community with its centre of gravity in the rich countries rather than as citizens of their own countries. If you want a Nobel Prize or recognition from your peers, or even your articles published in the leading journals, you must work on the 'frontiers of science'. But it is the rich countries which decide where the 'frontiers of science' are. Parenthetically we may add that in addition to the external and internal brain drain, there is what I call the fundamental brain drain. This is the failure of human brains to develop to their full potential as a result of malnutrition of young children in the crucial period of nine months after birth until three years after birth (when most of the human brain should be developed). Brain development being development of protein synthesis, it depends crucially upon nutrition, and the vast majority of children in the poor countries – and they in turn are the vast majority of all children born in the world today – do not receive sufficient calorie-protein in the right combination to guarantee full brain development. This combination of brain drains – external, internal, and fundamental – represents a tremendous development obstacle, much more so than the limits of the neo-classical models :

saving, investment, foreign exchange, etc.* Certainly, they must make us extremely doubtful about the alleged advantages to the late comer.

Apart from the brain drain, another unfavourable social effect upon the developing countries which we can fairly clearly identify is the considerable scientific and technological effort devoted to the development of synthetic substitutes replacing natural materials on which the developed countries depend for their export proceeds. It is not so much that such research and development takes place, but that it is not balanced by corresponding efforts towards the improvement of natural products or of other local products of developing countries. By and large, it is true that our technological power has increased to a degree where we can best consider the R & D machinery as an established industry in which outputs depend more or less predictably on inputs. Just as we know that in the case of a shoe factory, if you feed in leather and tanning materials, equipment and labour, etc., at one end, shoes will pass out at the other end; so in the case of the R & D industry we can assume that if you feed in certain problems at one end, the solution of these problems will pass out at the other end. If it seems to those not in a position to make these decisions right and profitable to feed into the R & D machinery the problem of synthetic coffee, synthetic cocoa, or synthetic tea, which is indistinguishable from the natural product or even superior to it, we need have no doubt that such synthetic substitutes will pass out in due course. But we need hardly underline what this will do to the economies of countries such as Kenya which relies on coffee, or Ghana which relies on cocoa, or Ceylon which relies on tea. The point is that the decisions of what problems are being fed into the R & D machinery are being made in the rich countries in the light of their priorities and requirements.

GAP BETWEEN POTENTIALS AND REALIZATION

What are the main elements which have been responsible for the

* One is reminded here of the point so brilliantly emphasized by Leibenstein that the allocative efficiency so much worried about by the prevailing schools of thought among economists, is much less important than what he calls 'X-efficiency'.

limited impact of science and technology in the developing countries? They are :

(a) The weakness of scientific institutions in the less developed countries;

(b) The 'weight' and orientation of advanced country science and technology and its impact on the developing countries;

(c) The problems of access by the developing countries to world science and technology;

(d) The obstacles to the application of new technologies arising from underdevelopment itself.

There is, however, an additional factor which must be kept in mind. This is the very lop-sided nature of the present international division of labour in science and technology. We can give some rough quantitative guides to the international distribution of R & D efforts.

Table 12.1 indicates that 98 per cent of the R & D expenditure outside the socialist countries is made in the developed market economies. It is possible that the developing countries have a somewhat larger share of world Scientific and Technological Services (STS) expenditure, since the proportionate expenditure on non-R & D STS is probably higher in the developing than in the developed countries. It is also possible that the proportion of world R & D manpower in the developing countries is greater than the proportion of expenditure, since R & D expenditures per scientist (including the salaries paid) are typically a good deal lower than in the developed countries. Finally, the R & D expenditures of centrally planned economies, which are not available to us, should be included to complete the global concept. But, we do not believe that these caveats would lead to much modification of the picture given in the table.

TABLE 12.1   Distribution of R & D Expenditures in the World
(Excluding Centrally Planned Economies)

Country group	United States	Other developed market economies	Developing countries
Percentage of world expenditure	70	28	2

SOURCE : Calculation based on OECD data for the developed market economies; on UNESCO and Pan American Union (PAU) data for developing economies.

The international division of labour in R & D is profoundly influenced by the national political and economic objectives of the advanced countries. Table 12.2 shows the distribution of R & D expenditures in the developed market economies by major objectives.

TABLE 12.2   Percentage Distribution of R & D Expenditure in OECD Countries by Major Objectives, 1964

Atomic	Space	Defence	Sub-total	Economic	Fundamental and welfare research	Specific problems of developing countries
7	15	29	51	26	22	1

SOURCE : OECD data in *The Overall Level and Structure of R & D Efforts in OECD Member Countries* (Paris, 1967).

Although the developed market economies make certain expenditures on R & D related to specific problems of the developing countries, these expenditures, on available evidence (from the OECD International Statistic Yearbook for R & D), are very small, amounting to less than 1 per cent of gross expenditure on research and development in all cases.

The extreme lop-sidedness of world R & D expenditure and of science and technology efforts, as well as its orientation towards certain major objectives of the advanced countries, do indeed have some beneficial 'fall-out' effects upon the developing countries. But, in the main, they are responsible for the operation of the following specific factors accounting for the gaps between realization and potentials.

1. THE WEAKNESS OF SCIENTIFIC INSTITUTIONS IN THE DEVELOPING COUNTRIES

The global analysis of the international distribution of R & D expenditure shows that, in aggregate, the developing countries make very small allocations to these activities.

At the same time, there is a strong suspicion that the minimal expenditure of the developing countries is also less productive than the concentrated R & D activities of the advanced countries. They are less productive from the scientific point of view in the sense that the output of significant results seems to be small in relation to input of resources; they are less productive economically because the scientific work in question is often of little economic or social relevance to the country's own problems and also because the rate at which results are applied is low. Even the presently meagre effort of the developing countries in R & D yields less than optimal benefits to the countries concerned.

Low productivity is partly a consequence of problems in organization of science in the developing countries. University research is frequently 'squeezed out' by heavy teaching and consulting loads; applied work in government institutes suffers from lack of finance, red tape and lack of co-ordination between government departments or even within them. Even where there is an apparent concentration of scientific resources, say in agriculture, this hides a reality in which the total research activity consists of a large number of small projects bearing little relation to one another.

The weakness of scientific institutions in the developing countries extends to survey, testing and data-gathering activities. It is also reflected in the general shortage of scientifically and technically qualified people engaged in production activities. Finally, one immediate reason for the limited application of scientific results is generally presumed to be the weakness of the extension and service types of institutions in the developing countries.

These observations suggest that when qualitative factors are taken into account, the effective use of science and technology resources is even more lop-sided than the international resource distribution would suggest, and that the industrialized countries have a vast preponderance. But the matter does not rest there. The sheer weight of advanced country science, as well as its superior quality, has crucial effects in the developing countries.

2. THE WEIGHT AND ORIENTATION OF ADVANCED COUNTRY SCIENCE AND TECHNOLOGY AND ITS IMPACT ON THE DEVELOPING COUNTRIES

There are three main ways in which science and technology in the advanced countries affect the developing countries. We shall examine them under the headings : (1) the 'internal brain drain';

(2) the 'external brain drain' and (3) the composition of the stock of knowledge and its economic consequences.

The scientific institutions in the developing countries are weak and so particularly are policymaking and planning institutions dealing with R & D and STS. In addition, as we shall state later, there is very little demand or perception of the need for science and technology in the society as a whole. In consequence, the local influences on the orientation of science and technology in the developing countries are weak.

In these circumstances, the weight and orientation of world scientific effort has a preponderant influence on the way science develops and is oriented in the developing countries. Many observers have noted how scientific and technological activities in the developing countries tend to form an 'enclave'.

Moreover, it is clear that, even in the fundamental sciences, the orientation of science in the advanced countries is strongly influenced by the major national objectives to which the scientific efforts of the advanced countries are intimately linked; objectives like defence, space exploration, the development of atomic power and so on. (See Table 12.2.) By implication, the orientation of science in the less developed countries is often influenced and determined by objectives which are external to the countries themselves and which have little enough to do with the requirements of development. Sometimes the aid activities of the advanced countries in relation to science in the less developed countries have reinforced these contradictory tendencies.

The result is a phenomenon which we shall refer to as the 'internal brain drain', whereby a substantial part of the scientific work going on in the developing countries, in addition to being under-financed and poorly organized, is irrelevant to the environment in which it is being done.

3. THE 'EXTERNAL BRAIN DRAIN'

A more immediately noticeable consequence of the intensive development of scientific and technical activities in the advanced countries is the rapid growth in demand for scientific workers it generates : the 'external brain drain' is no doubt encouraged in considerable measure by this growth in demand. The 'external brain drain' must also be associated, however, with the incapacity of scientific institutions in the developing countries to absorb and use scientific workers.

The large-scale migration of highly qualified personnel from developing to developed countries is of recent origin. However, the volume of that movement (net) may already be approaching 40,000 per year and, as such, is larger than the movement of technical assistance personnel from developed to developing countries. Under prevailing conditions, this 'brain drain' is likely to increase over the next decade. The United States Department of Labour has estimated that 380,000 professionals (as well as about 600,000 middle-level workers) would enter that country between 1965 and 1975. A substantial proportion of those people will come from developing countries, and, in addition, further tens of thousands will be emigrating to other developed countries.

The output from the third level education is increasing in the developing countries at roughly two to three times the rate of aggregate economic growth; in some countries the difference is substantially greater. Unless some way is found of bringing the employment possibilities for trained people into line with their increasing numbers, this means educated unemployment and/or international migration.

The picture that comes out of the analysis so far is of a relatively very small scientific and technical capability in the developing countries, which is undermined by organizational weakness and also by the varied responses of scientific workers in the developing countries to the mass of attraction that advanced country science constitutes. The environmental conditions in the developing countries receive scant attention. A consequence is that whilst the stock of world scientific and technical knowledge is certainly increasing at an accelerating rate, its precise composition is such that there are large gaps in scientific and technological knowledge that would be particularly relevant to the developing countries. The work of the Advisory Committee for the Application of Science and Technology to Development has been concentrated to some considerable extent on identifying these gaps. The list of priority areas where the Committee specifies that new knowledge is urgently required is in one sense a demonstration of the important technical problems which have been left neglected and unsolved by the present concentration and orientation of scientific effort to the political and economic objectives of the advanced countries. Perhaps one of the contrasts is found in the relatively vast knowledge we have of technical development in agriculture in temperate as opposed to tropical regions.

In addition, the stock of scientific and technological knowledge is proportionately less and less directly suitable for use by the developing countries. This is particularly true where the knowledge in question is about the application of scientific principles. First, the new technology is not 'appropriate' for the developing countries in that it emphasizes production methods which are suitable for capital-rich, and unskilled-labour-short countries, i.e. the richer countries of today. The developing countries by contrast are short of capital and skills, but relatively rich in labour. This discrepancy between the resource-mix for which modern technology is increasingly designed, and the actual resource-mix in the developing countries places them at an increasing disadvantage. Secondly, the available technology emphasizes production on a large scale whereas the initial markets of developing countries (even including their realistic export markets) are usually small in economic terms. Thirdly, product design of plant, equipment and consumer goods emphasizes the needs of the richer industrialized countries. Finally, a very great deal of world scientific and technological effort is concentrated in industries which simply do not exist in the developing countries, and which will not exist there for many years to come.

But the problem is not only that the needs of the richer countries are dominant, but that the products of scientific and technological progress which result from this concentration are often such that they exert harmful 'backwash' effects on the economics of the developing countries. Apart from the 'brain drain', the development of synthetics replacing the natural raw materials produced in the developing countries is an important case in point.

Probably about $1,000 million per annum are being devoted to R & D on synthetic materials (plastics, fibres and rubbers) in the chemical industries of the advanced countries. This is almost equivalent to the entire expenditure on research of all kinds in the developing countries and is, of course, very largely devoted to new materials of primary interest to the advanced economies.

When the advantages and benefits of further development of synthetic substitutes are considered, the harmful effect on the producers and exporters of the natural primary commodities thus displaced is not normally taken into account. The results are all too apparent : the shares of such natural commodities as rubber, cotton, tin, vegetable oils, in total world consumption and trade have declined rapidly, partly as the result of research and development devoted to the economy in the use of such materials and/or the development of synthetic substitutes for them. Work on the development and improvement of natural primary commodities of special interest to the developing countries does not receive the emphasis it deserves.

4. THE PROBLEMS OF ACCESS BY THE DEVELOPING COUNTRIES TO WORLD SCIENCE AND TECHNOLOGY

A further problem is that the developing countries have highly imperfect access to the body of world scientific knowledge and also to world technologies.

Easy access to sources of information, and effective 'coupling' with these sources, are essential to the efficient functioning of the science and technology system in any country. This 'coupling' function has to be done across national and cultural boundaries which present exceptionally acute problems. Thus, studies of information flows in the R & D process generally concluded that information derived from formal literature search and from formal information systems account for relatively small proportions of total information inputs. The informal communication network is of critical importance, including direct personal contact, telephone calls and correspondence. This is one of the critical advantages of the industralized countries in the workings of their science and technology systems, and it poses special problems for the developing countries, which have to establish these informal links with the scientific community in the advanced countries.

Access to world technology on the other hand raises special problems. Much of the technology in question is in private ownership, that is, it is patented or at least secret. In general, the companies owning the technology 'release' it to the developing countries only if they are able to make direct investments there. The companies show a marked preference for direct investment as a means of exploiting the technological advantages in the developing countries, rather than entering into agreements with independent firms in the developing countries themselves. The main reason for this seems to lie in the lack of capital and skills in potential counterpart companies and also in the risks of inefficient operation of the new techniques by independent enterprises in the developing countries. The net results are that the flow of proprietary technologies to the developing countries are dependent on their capacity to bring in foreign investment (which is limited) and that the development and competition of domestic industry is hampered by lack of access to new techniques.

Even when technology is non-proprietary, there are problems of access for the developing countries. They have to obtain technology in an embodied form, that is, by importing capital goods and/or building up capital goods industries of their own. In these tasks, they are hampered by lack of domestic savings and lack of foreign exchange. The latter is, in part, the result of world science and technology effort which, as we mentioned before, has tended to reduce the earnings of the developing countries from the exports of primary products. On the other hand, the volume and costs of importing capital goods have been going up, partly reflecting the increasing sophistication of embodied technology. The capital goods which the developing countries import are not only more expensive *vis-à-vis* their exports, but, in most instances, malsuited to their resource endowments.

5. UNDERDEVELOPMENT AS A BASIC OBSTACLE TO THE APPLICATION OF SCIENCE AND TECHNOLOGY

Whilst these various factors are important in explaining why it has been so difficult to exploit science and technology for the benefit of the developing countries and why the growth of science and technology has had adverse consequences for them, they are really only proximate causes. The real causes lie deeper, in the nature of underdevelopment itself. In brief, many of the structural and organizational characteristics of the developing economies are antithetical to the application of science and technology and, by the same token, prevent the development of what might be termed a 'realized demand' for scientific and technical knowledge. It underlies both the limited transfer of technology into local industries in the developing countries and also the weak development of local scientific institutions and their marked susceptibility to orient their activities in line with external influences. This is a particular aspect of the 'vicious circle of underdevelopment': the resolution of many of the problems of the developing economies requires the application of science and technology to production, yet the conditions of underdevelopment itself tend to limit the possibilities for their application.

Hence, whilst science and technology are certainly necessary inputs for development, their application in the developing countries nearly always requires certain important structural and developmental changes as concomitants.

REMEDIES

What then is the nature of the action required? One of the goals must clearly be to increase the national power to create science and technology by the developing countries themselves, and direct it to their own problems and resources. As already explained at present only 1 per cent of the world's R & D expenditures are within the developing countries and the great bulk of these are wasted from our point of view. With three or four exceptions – India, Brazil, Mexico, Israel – the national capacity of developing countries is negligible or non-existent. At present, developing countries as a whole spend perhaps at little as 0·1 per cent of their GNPs on this vital factor in development as compared with $2\frac{1}{2}$–3 per cent in the rich countries. The United Nations has set a target of 0·5 per cent of GNP to be spent by developing countries on R & D alone, and a similar proportion on the scientific and technological infrastructure. This is probably the maximum rate of expansion possible in view of the built-in limits of training and supply of skilled personnel and the building up of institutions. Perhaps even more important is to make certain that these resources are more effectively used to solve the developing countries' own problems than is the case at present. This will often require regional collaboration by the neighbouring countries; it is not realistic for small and poor countries to try to develop a reasonably full range of such activities.

While such an expansion would still leave the developing countries by 1980 with only a very small share of global R & D work, it could at least be sufficient to carry the creation of science and technology in developing countries beyond the threshold below which ineffectiveness and brain drain are almost inevitable results. More specifically, it should give developing countries the minimum bargaining strength to enable them to select more purposefully and effectively the technology which they have to import from abroad, and to negotiate on more equal terms with those who carry the new technology; exporters of capital goods, foreign investors, aid donors, patent and licence holders, etc.

This last point is crucial. It is sometimes said that poor countries should not waste their resources in developing national capacities since they can import from abroad all the technology which they need. In the first place, this is not true because the technology which they specifically need may often simply not exist. But more importantly, the statement is inconsistent: a country which has no national capacity cannot know what technology is available to be imported, what the most suitable technology for itself is, where the best sources for such technology are, and what the best forms are in which such technology should be embodied – let alone bargain effectively about the terms on which such imports take place. It is often said that Japan is an example of a country which relied on imported technology, but research shows that Japan had an infinitely higher capacity to substitute, select and adapt, even copy and negotiate, than most of the developing countries of today. Thus, logically, the strengthening of the national capacity of developing countries must have priority.

In this endeavour however they will need the aid of the rich countries of today for a long time to come. Much of the aid presently being given results in the transfer of capital-intensive technology inappropriate to the circumstances of the aided countries and incapable of exercising the broad catalystic effect which would involve widening circles in the development process. This is particularly the case where the aid is given in the form of imported capital equipment for agreed projects, and is tied to the capital goods industries of the donor country. It would be far better if more aid were given directly for the development of national scientific and technological capacity inside developing countries to develop the use of local materials and local labour for types of product representing their genuine development priorities. Such aid could consist of equipment for laboratories, in sending technological assistance experts, in providing libraries and continuing contacts with visiting scientists and technologists, links with research institutes of the rich countries, etc.

The United Nations has suggested a target which in effect would amount to one-seventh of the total aid now flowing to be given in this form. This would not seem to be an excessive proportion.

But all this would still leave a big gap compared with the minimum that is required. To fill the gap it would be necessary for the rich countries deliberately to use at least a small part of their tremendous technological power inside their own countries for purposes of specific benefit to developing countries. To be sure, a little is already being done in this direction. There are institutes of tropical medicine, of tropical agriculture, tropical health, etc.; here and there, a little scattered work is being done on labour-intensive or small scale technologies inspired by the needs of poorer countries. But all this amounts to less than 1 per cent of the total R & D expenditures of the rich countries. The United Nations has suggested that this percentage be raised to 5 per cent. Such a target would of course be meaningless unless we specify for what purposes this should be earmarked. It is not enough to say : 'Spend 5 per cent of your R & D expenditure on things which benefit developing countries,' for this is too vague and rich countries would claim that practically everything they spend is potentially useful for developing countries. For this reason, the priority areas to which such earmarked R & D resources should be directed would have to be specified; the empty boxes will have to be filled. This was perhaps the most important indirect benefit from thinking about higher targets – the need to be specific. As a result the United Nations has specified thirty-one priority areas ranging from such things as spreading the Green Revolution of high-yielding varieties to such crops as millet, sorghum and cassava, to new fishing methods to fill the protein gap for young children, to new hydrographic surveys, control of live-stock diseases and development of cheap construction materials and roofing materials suitable for tropical housing. Just as the increased effort by the developing countries requires collaboration among them, so will an increased allocation of rich countries' R & D resources be the more effective if they do this through concerted action and international collaboration. Fortunately, the OECD in Paris has taken up some of these priority objectives and is trying to achieve some joint and concerted action by the OECD countries. This is a most encouraging sign and one would hope that the OECD initiative will find a ready response and will be successful.

Ideally, one would hope for some leadership in the United Nations in this field, with the United Nations Development Programme as the main agent. For this purpose a considerable share in the resources of the UNDP would have to be set aside for this purpose and the total resources of the UNDP would have to be expanded. Unfortunately, at the present time the system of 'country programming' adopted by the UNDP seems to preclude any such major role. In an unwise decision it has even been decided to limit global projects to only 1 per cent of the total resources, although there are already forces at work to modify this decision. Certainly much larger resources than that would be required for any form of reasonable international initiative. Perhaps the creation of a special fund or a special agency for this purpose will, in the end, prove inevitable. If we are right in pinpointing the question of science and technology as the area where the breakthrough in development is most likely and where the productivity of resources is likely to be very high, such a step could be well justified.

A shift of 5 per cent in total R & D resources over a period of ten years is not a major upheaval. Bigger shifts than this have been accepted with the rise and fall of military programmes, space programmes, and atomic programmes. We would all be served if political *détente* should make it possible to achieve the 5 per cent shift by running down the military programmes. Nor can it be said that such shifts would be difficult to achieve through changes in monetary allocations alone, because of supply bottlenecks in the required personnel. Quite on the contrary, all the signs are that the scientists and technologists of the rich countries, particularly the younger ones, would be only too glad to work on such problems as the control of bilharzia or development of drought-resisting plants for the arid areas of developing countries rather than the development of weapons or much of the other work for which they are now deployed.

13 Multinational Corporations and Technology Transfer: Some Problems and Suggestions*

We are here concerned with one aspect only of the foreign company – its role as an exporter of technology, not with an assessment of its total impact. The foreign company exports technology to other countries, including developing countries, either in embodied or disembodied (separate) form. Embodied export of technology is involved if the foreign company sets up a subsidiary (wholly or jointly owned) or supplies materials, equipment, etc., embodying its own technology. In this case, the embodied transfer of technology consists both in the standard of management and production technique employed by the foreign company in production, and the spread effects by training and force of example. Disembodied forms include licensing, transfer of patented or non-patented knowledge, and management contracts, consultants' services, etc. The embodied technology of the foreign company includes, also importantly, techniques of marketing and marketing channels. Embodied and disembodied forms of transfer of technology can be, and often are, combined. Transfer of embodied technology is certainly more

* Paper presented to OECD Conference on 'The Transfer of Technology', Istanbul, 5–9 Oct 1970. In preparing this paper, I have drawn upon the presentation by Mr E. P. Hawthorne in his paper on 'The Transfer of Technology' as well as on research by Mr Javed Ansari, graduate student at the University of Sussex. I have also benefited from discussions on private overseas investment at a recent conference in Cambridge on employment generation in developing countries, organized by the Cambridge Overseas Studies Committee.

important in the overall activities of the foreign company, but because this part is invisible, it is often underrated.

As an investor or supplier of equipment etc., the multinational corporation shares in the general problems of the foreign investor or seller of technology, but with some additional problems special to it. In practice, it is often difficult and not particularly useful to draw too fine a distinction between these two types of agents of technological transfer. In view of its importance much of what follows has been written with the multinational company specially in mind; this has the advantage of giving some concreteness to the present discussion. The activities and motivations of banks, oil companies, plantations, mining companies, the foreign company going into tariff-protected manufacturing and assembly producing, or farming out parts for production in developing countries etc., are all different, and generalizations can be misleading.

In the most general terms, the foreign company like other investors or traders, will be attracted by the prospects either of additional profits, or of additional growth in terms of strengthening the position of the foreign company against actual or potential rivals, or of safeguarding its present profits against threatened encroachment. In more specific terms, and with more specific reference to the type of technology transferred to developing countries, the foreign company will wish to spread the high overhead burden of its own past and present R & D expenditures over a larger volume of production (or secure additional returns on its R & D expenditures in the form of royalties), secure outlets for the products which are the results of its own technology (equipment, materials, end products, know-how), and thus secure funds for additional investment in new technology, enabling the foreign company to maintain its technological leadership. This whole process would then be leading to a new chain of further investments or other ways of securing a pay-off or renewed technological leadership, creating a continuing ongoing process. The host country may be more concerned with local reinvestment of profits, although the resulting market domination may also be unpopular.

It appears that the foreign company will not normally expect from its involvement in developing countries any major direct contribution to its research, product development or process development. Rather the contribution will be indirect, via increased funds and profits. This will be specially so in the case of smaller and clearly underdeveloped countries. Any feedback technology effect that can be secured even in those circumstances (perhaps from studying the potential use of a local raw material or from adopting some simpler and cheaper product or process) would, of course, be welcome to the foreign company – but it would be incidental rather than essential. Essentially, the developing country would be considered in terms of the additional market which it offers (either in terms of expansion or in terms of defence of an existing market against tariff barriers, or against international or domestic rivals) and the additional profits which can be secured. This does not mean that the foreign company may not in fact make a genuine contribution to the technological development of the host country – by the training it offers, by the spread effects of the investment and additional production, by the use of the taxes which it pays, by the sheer force of technological example and demonstration, etc. But essentially the foreign company will tend to treat the host country as a source of production and profit, while keeping the processes of research and development, of management policy and of output decisions centralized elsewhere, usually at its headquarters. It is also relevant that the foreign company will largely be concerned with larger-scale units of production where R & D work is normally concentrated. One can see that here are areas of potential conflict as well as potential mutually beneficial bargaining. Essentially, it is for the Government and the other groups concerned in the host country, rather than for the foreign company, to secure benefits in the form of technological advance from the activities of the foreign country.

This will not be true in anything like the same degree of the investments and other activities of the foreign company in more developed countries. R & D especially the D part of it will be more or less evenly spread over the various countries in which the foreign company operates, joint ventures will be entered into, cross licensing arrangements will be frequent, cross-exports will be developed, etc. Even here, the more fundamental type of research may be concentrated in the home country of the foreign company perhaps attracting personnel from other host countries by a brain-drain operation, with top policy management also brought from 'home'. So even here situations of potential conflict exist – the foreign company may still be felt as a '*défi*'!

The intermediate middle-income countries with which we are particularly concerned – sometimes counted as 'developing' and sometimes as 'developed', but fortunately all rapidly developing in the real sense – will be in an intermediate position in this respect also. They can make legitimate claims for a great deal more than to provide the geographical space for technological super-firms operating in colonial-type 'enclaves', and generally they are also in a better position than the poor countries to strike advantageous bargains with the foreign company to secure these more ambitious ends. At the same time, they in turn must be able to offer the foreign company solid reasons in terms of profit and security of production to secure their desired technology, rather than in terms of technological feedback or new product or process development. In what follows, these are the countries which we shall have in mind.

The foreign company being specially vulnerable as a result of its size and international structure, will above all look for safety and stability. It knows that risks are unavoidable but it will still wish to minimize such risks in so far as they can be predicted. A stable government; predictable policies; absence of sudden convulsions, bolts from the blue or arbitrary action; the prospect of a long-term orderly expansion of the market; peaceful labour relations, management quality, supporting institutions which bear a family resemblance to the foreign companies' own familiar landmarks in their home locations – all these are intrinsically more important to the foreign company than *ad hoc* baits through tax rebates, a temporary high tariff, or the offer of local monopolies. This does not mean that tax rebates, tariff protection, exclusive deals, etc., are not important as effective inducements to a foreign company. But they are more so as symptoms or indicators of government policy and of genuine acceptability than for their own sake, or in compensation for lack of confidence or absence of long-term risk.

The foreign company will, of course, be guided by a combination of the natural advantages, long-term prospects and special inducements or baits. In this sense, the motivation of the foreign company is always multidimensional; any deal is a 'package deal'. Special short-term inducements can compensate for less certain long-term prospects or vice versa. The nature of the involvement is important here. Direct investment is a long-term involvement; trade, management contracts, licensing much less so. The foreign company which wants to become part of the permanent economic landscape of the host country will be more swayed by long-term advantages. The firm which intends to get out soon again will be more influenced by special initial inducements. It will also be more ready to take advantage of a weak or ignorant bargainer, since it may expect to be out again before the rude awakening. Provided that reasonable arrangements for later disinvestment are made from the start, the foreign company may be quite ready to work on the basis of reasonable short-term and medium-term conditions.

It has been mentioned already that, in many ways, the foreign company is like any other investor or taxpayer. Administrative efficiency in day-to-day dealings with government departments, including local authorities, the facilities for getting proper information and reasonable answers to reasonable questions, to have its current daily problems dealt with reasonably promptly and with fairness – these matter to the foreign company as much as to all of us. Governments and others in the host countries often fail to realize this : too often government policies and pronouncements designed to attract the foreign company are in practice offset by local irritation, delays, lack of proper facilities or even information (sometimes the opposite is also true). An example for this may be quoted from Turkey where generous concessions to US investors made in 1957 were largely nullified by difficulties ensuing at the level of local authorities.[1] Rhetorics and broad policies are overrated, while administrative routine is underrated. The foreign company being typically hardboiled and experienced will not easily be attracted unless administrative practices are in line with acceptable policies. It is not easy to estimate the volume of potentially useful foreign countries' investment which may have been frustrated because of complicated forms or administrative requirements, or sheer inability to cope with a complicated licensing procedure, etc., but one suspects that it must be quite high. On the other hand, the foreign company should be, and normally is, prepared to supply all necessary and relevant information required by the Government to judge the desirability of the proposal and formulate its own position.

The foreign company however, as distinct from other investors, expects to derive special advantages from its international character. Among these are the privilege of centralized policy decisions for the foreign company as a whole. Compatibly with reasonable decentralization of management within the framework of the foreign company policy the foreign company will often have a marked preference for placing its own top management personnel. The opportunity inherent in the structure of the foreign company of shifting profits and resources between its various units to take advantage of tax differentials, foreign exchange restrictions, differential treatment of foreign exchange transfers labelled as 'profits', 'export proceeds' or 'import requirements' or 'royalties 'or what have you, may also be an important element in the operation of the foreign company. All these categories can be largely arbitrary substitutes in the internal accounting and transfer pricing of the foreign company. Centralized decision making tends to be facilitated by the development and speeding of data collection and particularly by the development of new electronic methods. The foreign company will be very reluctant to involve itself on any long-term and highly committed basis where it feels that the host government or host partner has no understanding for these special interests and policies of the foreign company. While fiscal and other units of the host governments should be able to prevent abuses arising from internal transfer pricing, etc., the host country will have to face the fact that a foreign company will wish to make decisions in the interests of the foreign company as a whole, and not necessarily in the interest of the branch or partner in the developing or intermediate country. This will have to be weighed against the other benefits which the foreign company brings with it. The alternative would be to be satisfied with the more limited, and possibly more expensive, contribution of the foreign company in the form of, say, a management contract of limited duration.

The foreign company having established its reputation for technological leadership and high quality of product and efficient management, will treat this reputation as perhaps its most precious asset. This is often not fully understood and appreciated by host government and host partners. The foreign company will not abandon full management control, will not license, enter joint ventures, accept minority shares, rely on local managers, train local personnel, rely on local suppliers, etc., if they feel that their present and future standards and leadership would be endangered by such arrangements. If forced to do so in spite of their misgivings or resistance they will exact a corresponding price. It follows that countries or partners which can inspire confidence in the quality of local management, personnel, skills, supporting institutions, or public services will be in a much more favourable bargaining position *vis-à-vis* the foreign company. In this respect also, the intermediate countries should be in a relatively and increasingly favourable position. It may also be much more economical for a host government to attract the involvement of foreign companies by, shall we say, having a proper office of standards and quality control services to offer, or by having management training facilities to supply acceptable labour relations managers or local sales managers, rather than by costly tax concessions or promises of liberal profit margins freely transferable. The foreign company is often aware that liberal concessions while needed to attract them, will always entail the dangers of resentment, unpopularity and future trouble.

The general proposition may be ventured that the foreign company will prefer a clear-cut situation to a hazy situation. This general rule has many applications. Thus, the foreign company will either prefer a situation clearly limiting its responsibilities or else assume full responsibility itself, rather than share managerial responsibilities with a local group which it does not know and which it does not fully trust. Or again, the foreign company will either wish to make a quick and good profit and then get out and unload its commitments, or else to become a part of the landscape of the host country building up its local network of suppliers, where it feels that reliable sources of supply exist or can be developed. What the foreign company will not like is to be pressed to use local components or supplies when it does not feel certain that dependable local quality supplies can be secured, or to be expected to take local roots and become part of the landscape of the host country, while yet at the same time being warily watched and made to feel that it is only tolerated until local people (or the local government) are ready to take over.

The interest of the foreign company in a clear-cut, dependable and familiar situation also implies that (contrary to popular myth) the foreign company does not like negotiating situations in which 'the other side' (local government and/or local business groups concerned) is clearly unable to understand or pursue its own interest. From the point of view of the foreign company this means that in the short run the foreign company could 'get away with murder', but that there would be bound to be a rude awakening later, with resentment and risk to the smooth operation of the foreign company. Much preferable to the foreign company is a situation where the arrangement is properly negotiated between equals and represents a balance of mutual interests. Where the other side is in the possession of the necessity cost/ benefit data or feasibility studies, where it has proper technical and commercial understanding or advice, where the potential business manager or licensee is experienced and competent, the resulting bargain is that much more likely to be stable. This implies also a reciprocal willingness of the foreign company to give reasonable information although there are natural limits to divulging data prior to an agreement. The possession of an indigenous R & D capacity – previously discussed – is an important element in creating a reasonable bargaining position on the host side. So is the absence of pressure of tied aid terms, expert credits, etc., which limit choice.

The preference of the foreign company for familiar situations often poses difficult problems for the host country. For instance, both the desire to cash in on R & D outlays and technological know-how and the desire to operate with a familiar technology will lead the foreign company to prefer a capital-intensive operation to the employment of large numbers of local workers. Machines are familiar and dependable; they operate more or less the same in Ankara, Athens, Belgrade, Madrid, Lisbon as in Chicago, Birmingham, Düsseldorf or Lille. Local labour is different, tricky, difficult to handle in developing countries with different traditions and structures from the industrial societies from which the foreign company's spring. Hence the foreign company will not mind paying good wages. Wages will still be low by the standards of the home countries of the foreign company; they will still be a small part of the total cost of a capital-intensive operation; they will be a good political investment for the foreign company; they will prevent labour trouble which could interfere with the smooth running of the machinery. But the foreigin company will be much less willing to adjust its technology to the local situation, and run a labour-intensive operation. It sometimes – although by no means generally – is also true that capital-intensive technology may reduce the need for certain types of skill which may not be available in the developing country, and may save the foreign company investment in training. Unfortunately the host country may be better served by employment-intensive technology, specially where production for the local market is involved. Local training would also be more desirable than skill-saving technology. High wages may be a doubtful blessing if they set impossibly high wage standards for local employers and put them out of business, or lead them to lose their best workers, or force them into premature mechanization on their part. The answer often is that the foreign company provides the employment indirectly. For instance a fertilizer factory may not itself employ many people, but greater availability of fertilizers (combined with water and other inputs) may make it possible to increase rural employment by introducing double cropping. Or the indirect employment may be provided by the Government organizing labour-intensive public works or infrastructure development financed out of the increased tax revenue directly or indirectly derived from the activities of the foreign company. Where the foreign company produces for export, as in oil or copper, the foreign exchange earnings can be used to import capital goods, thus breaking the major bottleneck preventing the employment of more labour. However, it takes a competent Government to reconcile the preference of the foreign company for its familiar technology with the needs of the host country which may be for more jobs for its people. The technology of the foreign company is, of course, research intensive and on occasions this may be capital-saving rather than capital intensive. The intermediate countries with which we are here concerned may not present these problems in the same intensity but they will not be absent or irrelevant. There is a good deal of empirical evidence for the higher capital-intensity of production in foreign company linked units. In part this may, of course, precisely be the transfer of a more modern superior technology. The foreign company may also be forced or tempted into more capital-intensive techniques than it would otherwise use by excessive labour legislation, by fear of inflation and other domestic factors on the side of the host country.

A special concern of the foreign company within the context of its general interest in the stability of the host country, will be the state of its balance of payments. In the last resort, the foreign company depends on payment and conversion into freely usable world currencies, of amortization on its invested capital, of interest and profits, dividends, payments for components and material, royalties, licence and management fees, etc. The foreign company is also aware that here there may be a potential conflict with the host country which may wish to protect its balance of payment by restricting or discouraging transfer. The higher the foreign company evaluates the risks, the more it may wish to limit its risk, e.g. by operating with locally raised capital rather than bring in capital, or make its profit by trade rather than by investment. Or else high risks might lead it to demand high profits thus accentuating the very risks to be guarded against. But all this may only sharpen the potential conflict with the host country; the last thing which the local Government wants to see is local capital pre-empted for the operations of the foreign company and then exported in the form of highly geared profits (paying only a moderate interest locally). Here again, it is important that both sides should be aware of their potentially conflicting interest and be reasonably balanced in bargaining skill and bargaining strength in order to arrive at acceptable stable compromise arrangements. As already pointed out the opposite condition creates the danger of a vicious circle where high risks and tough terms reinforce each other.

The foreign company in general has an interest in dealing with countries and operating in environments where advantage can be taken of the potential benefits of the transferred technology. This will give the host country the resources to pay the profits or royalties, etc., which the foreign company expects and become an expanding market for its products. It will also ensure the acceptability of the foreign company as having been a 'good bargain' and hence protect its operation. Other things being equal, therefore, the foreign company will operate with greater confidence in countries which have the R & D capacity to build upon the results of the transferred technology and provide the related skills and production facilities. In this respect, the intermediate countries should be in a favoured position compared with the underdeveloped countries. This general interest of the foreign countries (which coincides with the national interest of the host country) has, of course, a natural limitation. The foreign company will not be interested in buiding up in the host country R & D or technological capacity which directly duplicates and displaces its own, thus cutting off the flow of royalties or profits from sales of equipment, etc., too soon. Indispensability is an important protection for the foreign company. The interests and motives of the foreign company in this field are complex, mixed and finely balanced.

A foreign company will be specially attracted to situations where a labour force – at various levels – of high educational and skill standards is available at relatively low wage rates (by the standards of the home base of the foreign country). Alternatively the foreign company may have confidence that it can train workers to high standards of productivity by use of its own experience and key personnel : in that case, lower wages *per se* will be an attraction. If these attractions are absent, they can still be replaced by the prospect of gaining or preserving a market made profitable by high and dependable tariff protection, or made attractive by the prospect of rapid expansion. In this latter connection, obviously the prospect of sharing in the market expansion provided by economic integration with neighbouring countries may be a special attraction, as is shown by the attraction of the EEC, EFTA, or even the Central American Common Market for US investment, including the multination companies. In this sense, host countries have the means of attracting the foreign companies (and strengthening their bargaining position with them) in their own hands : collaboration with other countries in wider free trade or preferential trading areas. The small markets for manufactured products have been one of the major barriers to the economical application of foreign company technology. The fact that foreign private investment tends to concentrate in the 'developed' part of the world, reflects in part the much higher degree of economic integration that exists there. The European Economic Community has been a very important factor which has influenced the inflow of foreign (i.e. United States) investment into Europe. Greece, Turkey, Portugal, Spain and Yugoslavia benefit to different extents from European economic integration. An increase in the level of integration among the (relatively) underdeveloped part of Europe would be desirable from the point of view of attracting foreign investment.

Where this is possible without loss of managerial efficiency and/or policy control, the existence of local intermediaries or partners will be considered a useful asset by the foreign company specially if it helps to give the foreign company a better national image or better national contacts. Local intermediaries or partners are particularly looked for in such matters as raising local finance, forming joint ventures, relations with governments, labour relations, local sale policy and development of local markets. The identification of suitable local partners who can be trusted with joint venture management or as licensees, etc., is difficult for foreign companies, particularly smaller ones and those investing for the first time in a given developing country. This will involve reliable and often confidential information. Local development finance corporations of which there are now over 150 (25–30 of them private), local banks or local insurance companies can be of valuable help to the foreign company in finding a suitable local partner.

Foreign companies seek local collaboration for a wide range of reasons. Local intermediaries are necessary to cope with officialdom, obtain licenses[2] and sympathetic interpretation of regulations. The foreign firm might enter into agreement with public local authorities for just such reasons : in developing economies 'easy access to Government authority is itself an important factor of production'.[3] Mediation with local financiers is another incentive for collaboration particularly for firms primarily interested in the sale of know-how and licenses and for firms who wish to keep their own financial commitments to a minimum. For developing economies when partnerships take place there seems to be a definite functional specialization in which the foreign company deals mainly with matters relating to technology, management, foreign supplies and finance, while the local partner plays the role of mediator and deals directly with the local market, as well as handling sales, labour-relations[4] and publicity. If the foreign enterprise wants to minimize its own risk capital collaboration will be sought in order to raise local capital. Reluctance to commit foreign exchange funds and limitations on imports favour the use of collaboration as sales outlets for the foreign company. Sometimes sales is the most important part of a joint venture. For example the Pharmaceutical Enquiry Committee of India pointed out that 'huge royalties on finished products (were paid), which were imported in bulk and only repacked in this country'.[5]

As part of its motive of market protection or market development, the foreign company will be keen to secure rights as exclusive suppliers in connection with any joint ventures, licensing agreements, etc., entered into. For instance, Attal Co. Agreement with Cyanamide in India appointed the latter as the sole purchaser for Attal in the USA. If the foreign company has a high degree of vertical integration it may secure for itself a market by selling requisite materials to its partner. This may clash with local interests in obtaining lower prices through competition, or simply to diversify contacts and technologies. Such conflicts are capable of reasonable compromise and reconciliation, but this again presupposes mature and balanced negotiating positions. It is also important that the economy of the host country should give the right signals to the foreign company : an overvalued foreign exchange rate, for instance, is an obstacle to the development of local sources of supply in that it makes it profitable to the foreign company to import. The same applies to deficiencies in the necessary credit, banking or infrastructure facilities for local suppliers. In such cases, a genuine conflict can only be said to exist after the host government has done what it can reasonably be expected to do to remove obstacles and distortions at its end.

This note would not be complete without noting that foreign companies increasingly are becoming aware of their responsibility, in their own long-term self-interest, to make their contribution to the long-term development of their host economies. Their resources enable them to do so over a broad front : the development of indigenous technological capacity and entrepreneurship, encouragement to smaller industries and rural development, improvement of education and training facilities, development of neglected regions, classes, age groups, etc. One feels that where governments are able and willing to enlist this sense of responsibility, the response might be surprisingly favourable.

Although foreign companies, especially the larger multinational firms, prefer wholly owned subsidiaries in the interest of centralized management and decision making, cases of fruitful joint ventures are numerous. In Turkey, for example, the Eregli Iron and Steel Works has been established by a co-operation of Turkish enterprise, American companies[6] and the Chamber of Commerce and Industry of Ankara. The plant is based on a highly modern semi-automatic system. One hundred American specialists have trained the local worker on the basis of the on-the-job training method. Hershlag ('Turkey – the challenge of growth') states that the Eregli plant 'tends to lead in efficiency . . . the (public sector) Karabuk plant even though under-utilization of capacity and excessive overheads adversely affect its financial performance.' The total capacity of Eregli is to expand to 470,000 tons by 1970. Profitability is also high. Profits were 12 per cent (of investment) in 1968.

Another joint US/Turkish venture is the tyre factory of US Royal Lastik Turk AS at Adapazari. Established in 1962 it started production in 1969. It has a total investment of TL 136 million with gross sales of TL 132 million and profits of 10 per cent of investment. Only the top staff is American; all the rest are local and technical training has been given to most workers by the foreign company.

Joint ventures are also quite common in Latin America. However joint ventures tend to work better among foreign companies operating in developed countries, as the contracting partners are of equal bargaining strength and possess more or less similar technical and managerial potential. When foreign companies set up joint ventures in developing countries the scope for misunderstanding, mistrust and suspicion is greater as the junior partner is not usually in a position to assess the deal that the foreign company offers it. In case studies it can be shown that domestic companies have sought a way out by negotiating and contracting with two or three companies from different countries who are each other's competitors.

An example of joint ventures relating to Taiwan and Japan may be drawn from Baranson ('The Technological Gap between Rich and Poor Countries'). Taiwan's automative industry is relatively small. It produces a wide range of goods. It is relatively a high cost industry. There is protection and a good deal of import substitution. Procurement of quality parts at reasonable cost is a major problem of Taiwan. This has been due to duplication of production facilities, and underutilization of capacity. This fragmentation (of production) influences the nature and quality of acquired technology and increases the problems of transference.

The industry has been developed in technical co-operation with Japanese firms. Since the introduction of joint ventures costs have gone down and the quality of production has improved (Nissan, Honda, Toyota and Toyo Kogyo all have affiliates in Taiwan). The Japanese have helped Taiwan to launch export ventures in the automative field. One Japanese firm has a plant which manufactures car radios for export to Europe and America. Relatively low wages are one of the chief attractions to the Japanese. There is a particular interest in products that are low-volume items in Japan, as they tie up equipment in Japanese plants and require disproportionately higher amounts of labour. Japanese firms are highly responsive to their own government's directives. These favour investment in Taiwan for production which is to be exported to Europe and the USA. Such export ventures have proved to be highly successful.

If a foreign owner of know-how is unwilling to invest directly in the developing country, or alternatively if the government does not wish him to undertake production directly, licensing agreements can provide a vehicle for the transfer of the technical knowledge. A licensing agreement is a contract by which the owner of a production process grants a company the right to utilize the process (with or without patent rights) in exchange for financial compensation. (If the compensation takes the form of a share of ownership of the new productive operation, we are in the field of joint ventures, which are discussed in the next section.)

Licensing agreements are by themselves no guarantee against the monopolistic features of the patent system, since the conditions written into the agreement can be just as restrictive as those inherent in the holding of a patent. In this case, however, the conditions are more visible, and thus more subject to regulation by the developing country's government. As an extreme measure, the developing country's government can resort to compulsory licensing, especially if the patent has not been worked by the foreign patentee himself for a certain period of time. The critical problem, however, is not in the legal aspects of the patent, but in the transfer of know-how. Even though the patented knowledge may be forced open to any national who might be able to utilize it in new production, such knowledge is only a small part of the total knowledge required. The real bottleneck lies not in the technical specifications of the patented process, but in the much broader know-how required for the successful application of the process. When such broad know-how does not exist (as in the normal case in a developing country), the willing co-operation of the patentee is an indispensable element of an effective transfer of technology; this co-operation must be paid for.

Payments by developing countries for the importation of technology are, common sense tells us, far greater than the receipts (if any) of developing countries from exporting technology. The concept of a 'technological balance of payments' has been elaborated relatively recently, and gives one a preliminary but interesting tool for estimating the financial magnitudes involved. It has been estimated that in 1965 total technological payments by developing countries were in the neighbourhood of $100 million, and that by 1980 they would rise to about $400 million yearly. Although these figures do not seem very large by comparison to research and development expenditures in advanced countries, they constitute a very high proportion of total research and development expenditures in developing countries. In the case of Japan during the 1950s, technological payments abroad have been about one-fourth of total research and development expenditures; and most developing countries are certainly dependent on imported technology to a much greater extent than Japan, probably from fifty per cent of total R & D expenditures upwards.

Still, as noted earlier, these payments ought not to be considered a measure of the technological dependence of developing countries, but rather a measure of the extent to which this dependence is alleviated. The cost to the developing country will depend not on any feature inevitable in licensing agreements, but on the actual terms and conditions which the licensee is willing or forced to accept. Of particular legitimate concern to governments of developing countries are the amount of financial compensation to the foreign owner of technology and the various possible restrictive features of licensing agreements, features which diminish the benefit of the technology transfer. Undue financial sacrifices may appear not only in the form of excessive direct fees, but also in excessive prices paid for materials or components bought from the patentee, unduly high management fees, and so forth. It will be seen that the financial terms of the agreement are not easily controlled. Proper control would call for consideration of the terms of a licensing agreement as a whole, not only of the royalty item in them. It is also unquestioned that full control calls for considerable administrative resources which may be beyond the administrative resources available for this purpose in many developing countries. Restrictive features of licensing agreements may take the most varied forms. Some of the most frequent ones are : stipulating that the licensee shall purchase his materials and/or equipment exclusively from the patentee or from sources approved by the patentee; submitting prices and marketing policies as well as the quality of products to the control of the patentee; giving the patentee a say in day-to-day management policy; limiting sales to the domestic market or to specified foreign markets only; limiting the level of production, and so on. Again, it is theoretically within the power of governments of developing countries to control such unduly restrictive features of patent licensing. They could do this either as part of general legislation directed against restrictive business practices (such as exist in most developed countries), or else by specific screening and control of the terms of individual license agreements. In actual fact developing countries may lack either the general legislative basis or the specific administrative resources required for such control.

The only safe generalization that can be made with regard to licensing agreements is that they are typically 'two-party' deals; the scheme of the agreement varies not only from industry to industry and from country to country, but also from individual case to individual case. Payment, terms, limitations of licensing agreements depend on the importance of the technology in question, on the production and marketing programme for the project, on the prevailing financial and legal practices of the industry and of the country, and above all, on the corporate policy and bargaining power of the companies and of the local government concerned. The following case is typical in its complexity. At the end of 1963 National Distillers and Chemicals of the United States licensed Toyo Soda Manufacturers of Japan to use the former's high pressure polyethylene process for ten years and on an exclusive basis. In exchange, National Distillers received a combination of fees and royalties : a fixed licensing fee of $600,000, an engineering fee of $250,000, a research 'contribution' of $1,250,000 (spread over five years), and finally a sliding scale of royalties on sales. Some firms, instead, and particularly the smaller firms in the developed countries are willing to enter into licensing agreements in exchange for a fixed fee or for equity participation in the project (see the next section); these firms therefore tend to specialize in the production and marketing of technical knowledge, and are the ones likely to have evolved a standard form of agreement as a basic modus operandi, to serve as a skeleton for the specific contract.

LICENSING AGREEMENTS[7]

Licensing an independent company to use patents and trademarks of the foreign company is becoming an increasingly important source of technological transfer. Patents and know-how are considerably more often licensed than are trademarks. In one study 20 per cent of all licences issued were for patents, trademark and know-how and another 49 per cent for patents only.[8]

Data on the geographic distribution of 55 US foreign companies are summarized in the table overleaf.

Geographic Distribution of Licenses

Area	As percentage of total
British Commonwealth*	47
Continent	30
Japan	8
Latin America	11
All other	4

SOURCE : Behrman, Loc. est., p. 123.

* Excluding Canada.

About 85 per cent of all licenses are given to firms in the developed countries.

Licensing of independent companies is more important than licensing of affiliates. According to returns from 207 US licensors during 1957 and 1959, they held 4114 foreign licensing agreements of which two-thirds were with independent companies. However the subsidiaries and affiliates that were licensed account for 80 per cent of all affiliates of US foreign companies. The reasons for licensing a subsidiary are usually financial or legal. If exchange restrictions favour remission of royalties paid for desirable know-how or patents as compared to remission of dividends or there is a tax advantage, the foreign company might choose to license or sell patents to its subsidiary.

The possibility of a profitable return on royalties is the major inducement for licensing. Non-royalty income in the form of dividends may also be sought. Returns may be in the form of cross licensing agreements. Trade restrictions and restriction on currency remittance in developed and underdeveloped countries might also provide an important reason for licensing.

The distribution of annual royalty returns by 54 US firms is as follows :

Annual Royalty Returns of US Firms

Royalty	No. of firms
None (programme too new)	5
$1,000–$5,000	2
$5,000–$25,000	13
$25,000–$50,000	4
$50,000–$100,000	2
$100,000–$500,000	21
$500,000–$1 million	–
$1 million	7
Total	54

The variation is very wide and quite clearly other considerations besides direct profitability are likely to be important to the foreign company issuing licences. For nearly 80 per cent of US companies' income from foreign licensing accounted for less than 2 per cent of total income. There is a tendency to take standard royalty rates prevailing in the country due to the uncertainties in the cost and the existence of considerations other than price in the contract. The general practice is to impose a percentage royalty (from one per cent to 10 per cent) on the sales of the licensee.

Policies of European governments have tended to view with favour the remission of royalties on licences as compared to remission of profits. This has induced US foreign companies to increase the issue to their European partners. Some countries such as Japan and Colombia, however, do restrict royalty payments.

Import controls have encouraged licensing as compared to exports to foreign countries. Licences may become relatively useless, however, if import policy does not permit the import of necessary equipment to make the licence worthwhile.

The areas of conflict between the parent and the recipient firm with respect to TT involve questions regarding pricing, ownership and long run technological development. These factors are usually affected by the competition among parent firms, the relative bargaining power of the contracting partners and the policy of the host governments. It is commonly the view of the developing economies that the price of technology is too high. They prefer licensing to foreign control. Foreign companies usually prefer direct investment to licensing in LDCs. Among other reasons the desire to maintain the quality of the product is cited as a reason for this preference. Foreign companies have sought to affect compromises between these two views.

For example, Ciba, a Swiss manufacturer of chemicals and pharmaceuticals prefer direct investment but are prepared to set up joint ventures, and licence techniques resulting from screening and testing. Pilkington Bros. – a British concern – has also used licensing for partners and collaborators in Europe and Asia.

An example of the method through which licensing works as between a foreign company and an independent venture of a developing country may be cited. Attal Products Ltd, of India, in the early 1950s approached Cyanamide of the USA to collaborate in the setting up of a new dye industry in India. Cyanamide bought 10 per cent of the shares of this enterprise. Production began in 1952. By 1958 the industry became profitable and in 1957, two loans have been obtained from the Government. The major contribution of Cyanamide is through its licensing agreement. It furnished Attal with technical data and information and helped purchase and install initial machinery. It provided production specifications and necessary technical staff. It trains technicians at cost to Attal. Cyanamide receives $2\frac{1}{2}$ per cent of the net sales value of each of the products sold during the first ten years. Cyanamide permits the use of its name in advertising. Attal also has an agreement with Ciba to obtain manufacturing rights to chemical products and pharmaceuticals. It also collaborates with ICI India. The personnel employed by Attal are almost wholly Indian who have been trained. Management is mainly in the hands of the Indian investors.

The process of modernization in Japan, which began in the latter part of the nineteenth century, was accompanied by a deliberate and vigorous governmental policy to foster the acquisition of foreign science and technology, mainly by hiring foreign experts and sending students abroad. Between 1860 and 1914 Japan received about 1400 foreign experts, 900 of whom were invited by the Government, and during the same period about 600 students were sent abroad. After the initial 'big push', the acquisition of foreign technology was gradually turned over to the private sector. At the end of the Second World War, a middle course was followed, apparently with considerable success : the importation of technology was left to the individual firms which might be interested, but the specifics of the licensing agreement were subject to approval by both the Ministry of International Trade and Industry (MITI) and the Bank of Japan, thus giving the economic authorities of the country a weapon to regulate the sectoral allocation of imported know-how, and to keep in check undesirable features of the agreements. Under this system total expenditure on licences during 1950–65 amounted to over $1,000 million, with a peak in the number of contracts reached in 1963. A detailed analysis of the agreements approved during 1950–61 yields the following conclusions :

(a) Nature of contracts
28 per cent of all contracts provided only for patent rights; 15 per cent . . . only for know-how; 39 per cent . . . provided both for know-how and patent rights.
(b) Limitations on export markets
53 per cent of all contracts contained an export limitation clause.
(c) Terms of compensation
39 per cent of all contracts contained provision for an initial payment, 25 per cent for a minimum payment, 84 per cent for royalty payments, and 24 per cent for the supply of blueprints.
(d) Kinds of technology introduced
56 per cent of all contracts related to manufacturing processes and 17 per cent to the acquisition of equipment, 4 per cent . . . were 'control' technologies and 21 per cent . . . were for comprehensive technologies.
(e) Country of origin of agreement
Technologies were imported from 19 countries, of which the United States accounted for 65 per cent of the total number of agreements . . .

In relation to underdeveloped countries, the intermediate countries are in a better position to find the foreign companies willing to license, issue patents, agree to joint ventures, etc., in so far as the foreign company can have more confidence in finding skilled and satisfactory licensees, patentees, management partners. On the other hand, the foreign company may be less willing to invole itself in the intermediate countries (still comparing with really underdeveloped countries), in so far as the danger of the licensee, partner, etc., becoming a serious business rival and independent of the supplies, etc., of the foreign company is more pronounced. The opposite relationship would apply if the position of the foreign company *vis-à-vis* the intermediate countries is compared with that *vis-à-vis* fully developed countries. Even when only these two involved factors pulling in opposite directions and only these three types of potential partner countries (developed/intermediate/underdeveloped) are considered, the complexity of the situation is already becoming apparent. And this is still a highly over-simplified model of the real world.

In the light of much recent experience, the foreign company might be attracted rather than repelled by the provision of orderly and fair divestment (repatriation of investment) policies and arrangements in the host countries, provided these are non-arbitrary and preferably established in non-discriminatory fashion and known in advance. This includes the orderly transfer of control of the new technology involved to local units by a fixed and prearranged schedule. In this connection, the proposal of divestment companies made by A. O. Hirschman (for Latin America) deserves serious study.[9] The host countries will be keener to secure a succession of new pioneer operations in preference to a continuing expansion of existing operations – here again the idea of orderly divestment/reinvestment cycling can be helpful to all sides, and might well be further discussed and developed. Hirschman maintains that some form of planned divestment may be – quite plausibly – acceptable to the foreign company. He puts forward a scheme for an 'Inter-American Divestment Corporation' which should provide financial assistance to foreign companies which have had to divest. This is one of a number of ways to reduce the ever-present threat of nationalization and introduce an element of relative certainty in the situation. Divestment by foreign companies operating in centrally planned economies such as Yugoslavia has been more automatic and less painful. Private companies selected in Western Europe and the United States have been able to do business in East European countries through 'co-production agreements' by means of which capital goods, technology and skill are transferred with repayment schedules on a medium or long term basis.

Hirschman's proposal in brief is the establishment of an Inter-American Divestment Company which should have funds allocated to it from the foreign companies. The company should buy up stock of foreign companies or foreign investors it wishes to divest, hold this stock and sell it at opportune moments to the Government of the LDC and local investors.

Hirschman opines that since foreign companies are agents of

TT : therefore divestment of foreign investment might lead to a slowing of technical advancement : the local firm is usually not in a position to maintain as rapid a rate of technical development as a foreign company is. Hirschman writes 'An independent expert commission could be created with the task of appraising whether in any individual case the contribution of a foreign firm to the implanting of technological research and innovation warrants a slowing down of the divestment schedule . . . A developing country may spell out for foreign investors several distinct lines of objectives among which divestment may be only one and the foreign investor could elect the particular mix that corresponds most closely to his taste and capabilities.'[10]

MANAGEMENT CONTRACTS AND SALES

Data on the extent of such arrangements has been prepared by the US Patent, Trademark and Copyright Foundation of George Washington University. 33 out of 66 US foreign companies provided managerial services to their partners and their subsidiaries as part of a capital contribution or under a licence agreement. 29 companies sold managerial (and other technical) services, but only to those foreign enterprises which were licensees under patent or know-how agreements, or were partners. It is maintained that the total return on the scale of management services is low relative to the return on licensing. Six firms covered in this study sold managerial services to non-licensees overseas. The 1957 Census of the US Department of Commerce showed that management fees from subsidiaries of the US foreign companies was low. Subsidiaries working in the development regions (mainly Latin America) were usually treated preferentially. However fees for management services from non-licensees were high.

Further technical assistance agreements are also made between foreign companies and their subsidiaries in foreign countries or with independent foreign firms. Payment is usually on a royalty basis. Sometimes fixed sums are also stipulated by the foreign company. In some cases know-how is built into a foreign plant constructed by the foreign company but payment is extended over a longer period and may or may not take the form of royalties on net sales.

Technical assistance contracts usually accompany patent or trademark agreements. To use the patent, special knowledge might be required – and if the seller refuses to disclose all necessary knowledge along with the patent, the technical assistance agreement becomes indispensable. Special techniques for example, might be necessary to maintain the quality of a product or to produce efficiently. Technical assistance may take the form of a guarantee on the part of the foreign companies to inform the foreign firms of all developments in this product line. 'When such agreements have been made they tend to become long run relationships and constitute a type of inter-company integration even among firms not financially related.' (Behrman, loc. cit.)

Technical assistance programmes include product specifications and layouts, formulae 'trade secrets', selling techniques and the training of technical personnel.

In developing economies such agreements – both technical and managerial – are indispensable if foreign participation, to any extent whatsoever, is desired. Usually such agreements are part of the overall policy of a foreign company to invest in or collaborate with firms in developing economies. Management contracts – independent of other agreements and sorts of collaboration – are rare as far as private foreign investment in developing economies is concerned.

CONCLUSION

The discussion in this paper has been presented from the viewpoint of the private corporate foreign investor as an exporter of technology. It has been shown that the interests of the foreign corporation, themselves mixed and ambivalent partly coincide and partly conflict with the interests of the (technically advanced) home country on the one hand, and with the interests of the host country and local business community on the other. Obviously, only highly sophisticated models – rather than the simple approach of this paper – could hope to do full justice to the interactions of all these different subsystems (each of them also by no means homogeneous).

But if we are to single out two issues, arising from our discussion as crucial, we could define them as first the mitigation of dependence by the developing countries upon the technical knowledge of any single corporate private source, and second, the need for a dispersion of decision-making. The relation between the developing country and the private foreign company will never be comfortable, as long as the fact as well as the feeling of unilateral dependence exists. As long as the host country feels that the vital decisions which directly affect it are being made mysteriously, without its having the power to influence the decision-makers, the relation between developing country and foreign corporation will continue to be one of mistrust.

Dependence is, of course, also translated into high cost, not always apparent on the surface. Although the cost of obtaining technology by the route of transfer from companies is by no means the whole story, it is an important part of it. Both the forms and the magnitude of the cost should be clear and reasonable. International organizations, such as the OECD, the UN and BIRPI could have a useful role to play.

Notes

Chapter 1

1 In an essay entitled 'Economic Possibilities for our Grandchildren' (reprinted in *Essays in Persuasion*, London, 1931, pp. 358–73) Keynes quotes an inscription on the tombstone of a charwoman who has slaved hard all her life: 'Don't mourn for me, friends, don't weep for me never, For I'm going to do nothing for ever and ever!' Galbraith's *The Affluent Society* (Houghton Mifflin, Boston, 1958) is also much concerned with this theme.

2 J. M. Keynes, *General Theory of Employment, Interest and Money*, Macmillan, New York, 1936, p. 200.

3 The Japanese always gave trouble in this scheme, but this could be got over by describing them as 'Prussians of the East' or 'Puritans of the East'; and in any case, did they not live in a temperate climate?

4 Oxford, Fair Lawn, N.J., 1957.

5 Ibid., p. 8.

6 Ibid., p. 14.

7 Cambridge, New York, 1960.

8 The economist who has done most to construct models of this kind, where population appears as a big hurdle for slow rates of growth which would disappear if growth were to be accelerated, is Harvey Leibenstein, particularly in his book *Economic Backwardness and Economic Growth*, New York, 1957.

9 The theory of the big push in relation to overhead capital is perhaps most closely associated with the name of Prof. Paul Rosenstein-Rodan.

10 It will be remembered (see the first section of this chapter) that the difficulty of finding markets or purchasing power for additional output was precisely what worried Karl Marx, except that he attributed lack of purchasing power to changes which accompanied economic progress in its later stages.

11 S. G. Checkland, 'Theories of Economic and Social Evolution: the Rostow Challenge', *Scottish Journal of Political Economy*, Nov 1960, p. 174.

12 Ibid., p. 178.

13 Colin Clark, *The Economics of 1960*, London, 1942, and W. A. Lewis, 'World Production, Prices and Trade', *Manchester School of Economic and Social Studies*, 1952.

14 This was emphasized particularly by Albert O. Hirschman in his *Strategy of Economic Development,* Yale, New Haven, Conn., 1958.

15 See *International Financial News Survey,* 30 Sep 1960, p. 519.

Chapter 3

1 A more statistical factor might be mentioned. Some underdeveloped countries – Iran would be an illustration – exclude important parts of their exports and imports from their foreign trade statistics in so far as the transactions of foreign companies operating in the underdeveloped country are concerned. This is a tangible recognition of the fact that these pieces of foreign investments and their doings are not an integral part of the underdeveloped economy.

2 Often underdeveloped countries had the chance to use royalties or other income for foreign investment judiciously for the transformation of their internal economic structure – a chance more often missed than caught by the forelock!

3 See *Relative Prices of Exports and Imports of Under-developed Countries,* United Nations, Department of Economic Affairs, sales No. 1949 II, B.3.

4 According to data of the WPA research project, output per wage earner in a sample of fifty-four manufacturing industries increased by 57 per cent during the twenty years 1919–39; over the same period, agriculture increase only by 23 per cent, anthracite coal mining by 15 per cent, and bituminous coal mining by 35 per cent. In the various fields of mineral mining, however, progress was as fast as in manufacturing. According to data of the National Bureau of Economic Research, the rate of increase in output per worker was 1·8 per cent per annum in manufacturing industries (1899–1939) but only 1·6 per cent in agriculture (1890–1940) and in mining, excluding petroleum (1902–39). In petroleum production, however, it was faster than in manufacturing.

5 For details see the UN study, *Relative Prices of Exports and Imports of Under-developed Countries.*

6 *Economic Survey of Europe in 1948,* United Nations, Department of Economic Affairs, pp. 93–106, especially 97–9, sales No. 1949, II, E.1.

7 This ambivalence of changing terms of trade has also been stressed in a different context by Lloyd Metzler in his important article 'Tariffs, Terms of Trade and Distribution of National Income', *Journal of Political Economy,* Feb 1949.

8 In more recent years, especially since 1924, United States capital accumulation had of course become quite independent from the original stimulus supplied by immigration, and proceeded without any visible

check in spite of a heavy reduction in immigration. The argument
put forward here is meant as a historical explanation rather than an
analysis of the present sources of capital investment.

Chapter 4

1 I am thinking particularly of Prebisch and Myrdal who were – unknown to me – also beginning to think along similar lines at that
time.
2 Concealed by the way in which tariff schedules are published, i.e. as
percentages of total final value rather than as percentage of value
added by processing.
3 There is an analogy here to the Todaro model (M. P. Todaro, 'A
Model of Labor Migration and Urban Unemployment in Less
Developed Countries', *American Economic Review*, Mar 1969). In the
Todaro model unemployment brings into equilibrium the urban wage
rate and the rural living standards. In my suggested model, unemployment brings into equilibrium the available technology and the
factor endowment of developing countries.
4 See C. P. Kindleberger, 'Europe's Terms of Trade'. This issue was
also discussed at a conference in 1957 (see *Review of Economics and
Statistics*, Feb 1958).
5 See my contribution in *Review of Economics and Statistics*, loc. cit.

Chapter 5

1 For a discussion of these distinctions see Henry J. Bruton, *Principles
of Development Economics*, Prentice-Hall, 1965.
2 I am indebted for these estimates to my colleague Mr Charles Cooper.
These figures exclude the eastern countries on the side of the richer
countries, but they also exclude China on the part of the LDCs. With
both categories included, the actual figure for the LDCs might
possibly be higher, but at most 3 or 4 per cent instead of 2 per cent.
3 My colleague Oscar Gish informs me that he has used this same term
previously.
4 Surendra J. Patel, *The India We Want*, Bombay, 1966, p. 20.
5 The very use of this term, although it comes naturally, reflects this
one-way standard setting. Intrinsically, an improvement to handlooms or 'simple' agricultural tools should be considered as potentially
equal in sophistication to the development of the lunar module or
the supersonic Jumbo Jet – but the plain fact is that it is not the
case.
6 However, it may be noted that the total sum allocated for research
in the UK within the British technical assistance programme repre-

sents less than 0·01 per cent of the British national income, less
than 0·5 per cent of total British research and development expenditures, and only a little over 1 per cent of total British aid. One of the
obstacles of giving research a proper place in technical assistance lies
in the basis of country requests: many problems in this field are of
considerable collective interest to many underdeveloped countries,
but are not given national priority in its specific requests by any
particular country. To some extent each may rely on the other. The
Rockefeller Foundation did not wait for 'specific requests' when
developing the IR-8.

7   G. J. Stigler, 'The Division of Labour is Limited by the Extent of
the Market', *Journal of Political Economy*, June 1951.

8   These are terms used by Michael Shanks, 'When Companies Span the
Frontier', *The Times Business Review*, 20 Aug 1969. It may be noted
that Mr Shanks feels that the bargaining position of the British
Government *vis-à-vis* these large corporations has declined with the
stagnation of the British economy. If this is an 'unpalatable fact'
for Britain, how much more so for the underdeveloped countries with
their puny local markets?

9   M. P. Todaro, 'A Model of Labour Migration and Urban Unemployment in Less Developed Countries', *American Economic Review*, Mar
1969.

10 H. A. Turner, 'Can Wages be Planned?' Paper prepared for the
Conference on the Crisis in Planning, University of Sussex, July 1969,
p. 7.

11 Todaro, op. cit.

12 A. R. Jolly, 'Employment, Wage Levels and Incentives', from *Manpower Aspects of Educational Planning*, International Institute of
Education Planning, UNESCO. Reprinted in the Joint Reprint Series
of the School of African and Asian Studies and the Institute of
Development Studies, at the University of Sussex, No. 26. (Dr
Jolly gives interesting examples for the case of teachers in Uganda,
p. 240.)

13 Richard Symonds, *The British and their Successors*, Faber & Faber,
London, 1966, especially Chapter 11.

14 Jolly, op. cit., p. 241.

15 Incremental capital–output ratio.

Chapter 6

1   Robin Marris, 'Can we measure the need for development assistance?',
Economic Journal, Sep 1970; and Thomas Weisskopf, 'The impact
of foreign capital inflow on domestic savings in underdeveloped
countries', *Journal of International Economics*, Feb 1972.

2   Kaj Areskong, 'Foreign Capital Utilization and Economic Policies in

Developing Countries', *Review of Economics and Statistics*, May 1973, pp. 182–9.

3 William Tyler, 'Employment Generation and the Promotion of Manufactured Exports in Less Developed Countries: Some Suggestive Evidence'. (Papers prepared for the Kiel Conference, 'Problems of the International Division of Labour', July 1973.)

4 This point has been made and elaborated by the ILO employment missions to Colombia, Sri Lanka and Kenya.

5 See above, Chapter 5, p. 78. The figure of 25 per cent as a typical figure for the extent of unemployment, underemployment and extremely unproductive employment (disguised as unemployment) has emerged among other data from the three ILO employment missions to Colombia, Sri Lanka and Kenya. See also data in the OECD study by David Turnham.

6 Tyler, op. cit.

7 My own guess has been 7·5 per cent, but not of the total 'labour force' but of the total working population. The two estimates are very close when allowance is made for this difference.

8 See UNCTAD Document TD/B/429/add 2, 'The Recent Economic Exports of Developing Countries in Relation to the Goals and Objectives of the International Development Strategy'.

9 'A World Price Equilibrium Model', Agricultural Commodity Projections 1970–80. FAO Document CCP 71/2/0, Rome, 1971.

10 William Tyler, in a study of eight development countries that are major exporters of manufactured products, i.e. Brazil, Egypt, India, Mexico, the Philippines, South Korea, Taiwan and Yugoslavia.

11 Study by Professor Lydall on 'The Relationship between Foreign Trade and Employment', prepared for the ILO World Employment Programme. I am indebted to Professor Lydall for allowing me to see some of the preliminary results of his work.

12 Disregarding Commonwealth Preferences in the case of the UK.

13 1 : 1·95 for LDCs as against 1 : 1·76 for industrial countries.

14 Forty-five per cent cut versus 33 per cent cut for SITC sections 5–8; 42 per cent cut versus 28 per cent cut for all SITC sections 0–8.

15 This association has also been noted in the 8-volume study 'Export Expansion Possibilities through Tariff Preferences' prepared by the Export Promotion Division of US AID, New Delhi, for the Indian Ministry of Foreign Trade; see vol. 1, p. 33.

16 See, for instance, Tracy Murray, 'How Helpful is the Generalized System of Preferences to Developing Countries?', *Economic Journal*, June 1973.

17 Peter Tulloch, 'Agricultural Trade and the Enlarged European Community', ODI Review 6, London 1973.

18 Resolution 62 (III).

19 UNCTAD document TD/B/AC9(III)/CPR3, 7 Dec 1971.

Chapter 9

1   This would be questioned by some, either on more general grounds that aid is 'bad' for LDCs, or on more specific grounds such as by A. Qayum in 'Long-term Economic Criteria for Foreign Loans', *Economic Journal*, June 1966.

2   M. Todaro, 'A Model of Labour Migration and Urban Unemployment in Less Developed Countries', *American Economic Review*, Mar 1969, pp. 138–48.

3   *Towards Full Employment: A Programme for Columbia*, prepared by an inter-agency team organized by the International Labour Office. ILO, Geneva, 1970.

4   *Partners in Development*, Report by the Commission on International Development, Praeger, New York, Washington, London, 1969, p. 177.

5   World Plan of Action for the Application of Science and Technology to Development, UN document E/AC 52/L 68, 19 Oct 1969.

Chapter 10

1   For an outline of the World Employment Programme, which aims to make productive employment for large numbers of people a major goal of national and international policies for development, see David A. Morse, 'The World Employment Programme', in *International Labour Review*, June 1968, pp. 517–24. The report of the Kenya mission was published by the ILO at the end of 1972 under the title *Employment, Incomes and Equality: A Strategy for Increasing Productive Employment in Kenya*.

2   See *Employment, Incomes, and Equality* . . . , op. cit., pp. 9–30.

3   This is not to say that disguised unemployment, undesirable activities and other obstacles to progress do not exist there. But the mission felt that fastening on these aspects tended to obscure the real role and dominant activities of the informal sector and all too often led to the healthy and promising elements being jettisoned along with the noxious elements.

4   The mission did recommend policies which it expected would reduce somewhat the net flow of rural-urban migration, particularly the net growth of the larger towns.

5   At 1972 prices. At the time of writing, the Kenya £ was worth about 20 per cent more than the £ sterling.

6   A comparative analysis of the situation in different developing countries fails to show any connection between the growth rate of GNP and the degree of income inequality, a point made also by the President of the World Bank Group in his address to the 1972 meeting of the Board of Governors; see Robert S. McNamara, *Address to the Board of Governors*, 25 Sep 1972 (Washington, IBRD, 1972).

7 See *Employment, Incomes and Equality . . .* , op. cit., Technical Paper 6, pp. 365–70.

8 If this assumption is not correct and the poor sections do not participate in general progress, redistributive action would have to be that much greater. It is very likely that the position of the poorer groups in terms of access to public services – health clinics, water, roads, transport – has improved not only absolutely but also relatively.

9 Republic of Kenya, National Assembly: *African Socialism and its application to planning in Kenya*, Sessional Paper No. 10, 1965.

Chapter 11

1 In the case of market economies the figures are 5·1 per cent (developed) and 5·2 per cent (developing) for 1960–70. *UN Yearbook of National Accounts Statistics 1971*, vol. III, United Nations ST/STAT/SER 0/1/add 2. See Table 11.1.

2 *United Nations Demographic Yearbook 1971.*

3 The *absolute* gap will, of course, go on increasing even in the absence of differential population growth.

4 For example South Korea, Sri Lanka and India.

5 See Tables 11.2 and 11.3.

6 Allowing, of course, for elderly persons, orphaned children, invalids, and other groups for whom other means of providing the minimum income may be more appropriate.

7 See *Employment, Incomes and Equality: A Strategy for Increasing Productive Employment in Kenya*, International Labour Office, Geneva, 1972, p. 121.

8 This association is largely explicable in terms of higher incomes and better health and education facilities in the urban industrial centres. See Richard Nelson, *Structural Change in a Developing Economy: Columbia's Problems and Prospects*, Princeton University Press, p. 22.

9 Especially associated with the name of Arthur Lewis, 'Economic Development with Unlimited Labour Supplies', *The Manchester School*, 1954.

10 See for example W. Rich, 'Smaller Families through Social and Economic Progress', Overseas Development Council, 1973.

11 Although, as noted before, this particular effect may be partially offset by a tendency for young children in poor countries to be economic producers at an early age, especially in rural areas. This offset, however, involves in turn a lack of education and perpetuation of the poverty syndrome.

12 For further discussion of this see H. W. Singer, 'Children in the Strategy of Development', *Executive Briefing Paper No. 6*, UN Centre for Economic and Social Information and UN Children's Fund, United Nations, New York, 1972.

13 Without creating incentives for more children!

14 'Smaller Families through Social and Economic Progress', Overseas Development Council, Washington, 1973.
15 *Towards Full Employment: A Programme for Colombia*, ILO Geneva, 1970. *Matching Employment Opportunities and Expectations: A Programme of Action for Ceylon*, 2 vols, ILO, Geneva, 1971. *Employment, Incomes and Equality: A Strategy for Increasing Productive Employment in Kenya*, ILO, Geneva, 1972. The author acted as a consultant to the ILO in developing its World Employment Programme, and was the chief of the mission to Kenya. (See Chapter 10 above.)
16 R. Nelson *et al.*, *Structural Change in a Developing Economy: Colombia's Problems and Prospects*, Princeton Universitiy Press, 1971. Similar findings were made by T. P. Shultz, 'Explanation of Birth Rate Changes Over Space and Time: A Study of Taiwan', *Journal of Political Economy*, vol. 81, No. 2, Mar/Apr 1973.
17 It may be added that if the fall in death rates is a necessary condition for the fall in birth rates, then the sooner it happens the better for the smaller the population when 'equilibrium growth' is achieved.
18 In Puerto Rico and elsewhere, rural electrification has been observed to diminish the birth rate as village after village was reached. The same is certainly true of water supplies: as irrigation reaches villages and standards of living rise, the birth rate will tend to decline as a result of higher standards of living and new aspirations. Often of course, the effect of such individual factors as electricity, irrigation, etc., may be difficult to isolate.
19 See Stephen Enke, 'Economic Consequences of Rapid Population Growth', *Economic Journal*, vol. 18, No. 324, Dec 1971. For an abstract country called Developa, Enke estimates the benefit/cost ratio of reducing the gross reproduction rate by about 50 per cent in twenty-five years. Such a reduction he says should lead to economic benefits (in terms of income *per capita*) 50–150 times greater than the costs, over a thirty-five year period. Enke's calculations have, however, been criticized.

Chapter 13

1 Z. Y. Hershlag, 'Turkey – the challenge of growth'.
2 Sometimes stipulated by law.
3 M. Kidron, *Foreign Investments in India*, Oxford University Press, 1965.
4 If it has a high gearing ratio.
5 Kidron, op. cit.
6 Koppers Associations S.A. representing two other American firms.
7 This section draws upon H. W. Singer and S. Schiavo-Campo, *Perspectives of Economic Development*, Houghton Mifflin, Boston, 1970, pp. 122–6.

8   J. N. Behrman, 'Direct Private Foreign Investment', in R. Mikesell, US Private and Government Investment Abroad.
9   Albert O. Hirschman, 'How to Divest in Latin America and Why', Princeton Essays in International Finance, 1969.
10 Ibid., p. 22.

Index

African Development Bank, 119
Agency for International Development, 124
agriculture
  agricultural trade, 104, 105
  Kenya, 165
aid to developing countries, 20, 114
  -32, 140, 141, 150-3
  effect upon balance of payments, 127-9
  effect upon employment, 152
  food aid, 140, 153
Argentina, income distribution, 187
Asian Development Bank, 119

balance of payments, effect upon
  foreign aid, 127-9
Boeke, I., 82, 86
Bolivia, income distribution, 187
'brain drain', 72, 154, 192, 193, 198, 199
Brazil, 203
  income distribution, 187
Burma, income distribution, 187

Central American Common Market, 218
Ceylon, income distribution, 187
Chad, income distribution, 187
Chenery, Hollis B., 26
Chile, income distribution, 187
Clark, Colin, 16
Cobb-Douglas model, 25
Colombia, 150
  income distribution, 187
companies and corporations
  Attal Co., 220, 228
  Ciba, 227, 228

Cyanamide, 220, 228
Eregli Iron and Steel Works, 221
Honda, 222
ICI India, 228
licensing agreements, 222-31
management contracts, 231, 232
National Distillers, 225
Nissan, 222
Pilkingkton Bros., 227
Toyota, 222
Toyo Kogyo, 222
US Royal Lastik Turk AS, 221
Costa Rica, income distribution, 187

Dahomey, income distribution, 187
Domar, Evsey, 8

economic theories and models
  'backwash' theory, 12, 13
  'balanced growth' theory, 11, 12
  'big push' theory, 10, 11
  Cobb-Douglas model, 25
  Harrod-Domar model, 7, 8, 10, 25-8, 30-2, 37-9, 41, 42, 89
  Lewis Model, 85-7, 179
  Ricardo model, 85, 87
  Todaro model, 83, 150
Ecuador, income distribution, 187
education
  influence upon employment, 134
  Kenya, 166, 167
EFTA, 218
El Salvador, income distribution, 187
employment
  developing countries, 75-9, 82-9,

employment—*continued*
    92–101, 103, 133–57, 176, 190
  effect of trade upon, 92–101, 103
  influence of education, 134
  Kenya, 158–64, 176, 177
  multinational firms, 153, 216, 218
European Economic Community, 218, 219
  trade with developing countries, 103, 104

food, aid to developing countries, 140, 153
Ford Foundation, 74
foreign investment in developing countries, 44–7, 153, 154, 208–33

Gabon, income distribution, 187
Gini, Corrado, 55
GNP, 19–21, 25–8, 35, 36, 174, 186, 189, 190, 203
Greece, income distribution, 187

Harrod, R. F., 25
Harrod-Domar model, 7, 8, 10, 25–8, 30–2, 37–9, 41, 42, 89
Helleiner, G. K., 66
Hirschman, A. O., 137, 230, 231
Hone, Angus, 107, 110
House of Commons Select Committee on Overseas Development, 102, 111

Iliff, W. A. B., 17
ILO, 21, 150, 158, 182
income distribution, 171–85, 187, 188
India, 203
  foreign investment in, 220
  income distribution, 187
International Trade Centre, Geneva, 110
investment, foreign, in developing countries, 44–7, 153, 154, 208–33

Iraq, income distribution, 187
Israel, 203
  income distribution, 187
Ivory Coast, income distribution, 187

Jamaica, income distribution, 187
Japan, 148, 204
  co-operation with Taiwan, 222
  imported technology, 223, 224
  income distribution, 187
  licensing agreements, 225
  technical manpower, 228
Jevons, W. S., 24
Jolly, A. R., 84

Kennedy Round, 101–3, 107, 140
Kenya
  agriculture, 165
  education, 166, 167
  employment, 158–64, 176, 177
  foreign investment in, 166
  income distribution, 159, 160, 168–71, 187
  population, 158, 159, 163, 165, 176, 177
  wages, 160, 166
Keynes, John Maynard, 2–4, 6, 22–5, 82
Kindleberger, Charles, 63

Lary, Hal B., 148
Lebanon, income distribution, 187
Lewis, Arthur, 16
Lewis model, 85–7, 179
Libya, income distribution, 187
licensing agreements, 222–31

Malagasy, income distribution, 187
Malthus, T. R., 23, 24
management contracts, 231, 232
Marshall, Alfred, 13, 24
Marx, Karl, 2, 3
Mexico, 203
  income distribution, 187

Mills, John Stuart, 24
models and economic theories, *see* economic theories and models
Morocco, income distribution, 187
multinational companies and corporations, 208–33
  employees, 216, 218
  licensing agreements, 222–31
  management contracts, 231, 232
  wages, 216, 218
Myint, Hla, 67, 79, 87
Myrdal, Gunnar, 12, 26, 27, 35

Niger, income distribution, 187
Nigeria, income distribution, 187
Nurkse, R., 11

OECD, 206
Olano, Sr, 118

Pakistan, income distribution, 187
Panama, income distribution, 187
patents, 224, 225
Pearson Commission and Report, 140, 149–51, 156
Peru, income distribution, 187
Philippines, income distribution, 187
Pigou, A. C., 24
population
  developing countries, 135, 173–85, 187, 190
  Kenya, 158, 159, 163, 165, 176, 177
Prebisch, Paul, 13, 120

Rhodesia, income distribution, 187
Ricardo, David, 2, 3, 24
Ricardo model, 85, 87
Rich, William, 181
Rockefeller Foundation, 74
Rostow, Walt, 9

Schumpeter, Joseph Alois, 2, 3, 14
science and technology

'brain drain', 72, 154, 192, 193, 198, 199
developing countries', 58–66, 70–90, 154–6, 190–206
Seers, Dudley, 150
Senegal, income distribution, 187
Sierra Leone, income distribution, 187
Smith, Adam, 1, 2
Sombart, Werner, 5
South Africa, income distribution, 187
Special Drawing Rights, 112, 156, 157
Stamp, Maxwell, 128
Stigler, G. J., 75
Sudan, income distribution, 187
Sunkel, Oswaldo, 60
Surinam, income distribution, 187
synthetic materials, 194, 200, 201

Taiwan
  co-operation with Japan, 222
  income distribution, 187
Tanzania, income distribution, 187
theories and models of economics, *see* economic theories and models
Tinbergen, Jan, 26
Todaro model, 83, 150
trade
  British, 53, 54
  developing countries', 44–66, 91–113, 116–20, 141, 142, 146–9
  effect upon employment, 92–101, 103
  non-tariff barriers, 104
trademarks, 225
Trinidad and Tobago, income distribution, 187
Tropical Products Institute, 74
Tunisia, income distribution, 187
Turkey, US investment in, 212, 221
Turner, H. A., 78, 79
Tyler, William, 99

UNCTAD, 141, 147
UNDP, 182, 206
UNICEF, 32
United Kingdom
employment and population, 176
trade, 53, 54
United Nations Development Programme, 182, 206
United States
industrialisation, 55
investment in India, 220
investment in Turkey, 212, 221

Venezuela, income distribution, 187

wages
developing countries', 143, 144,
153
Kenya, 160, 166
multinational firms, 153, 216, 218
Wealth of Nations, The, 2
Weber, Max, 5
World Bank, 21, 152

Zambia, income distribution, 187